The Limits of Russian Democratisation

Russia's transition towards greater democracy and the rule of law seems danger-ously limited by Boris Yeltsin's 'superpresidential' constitution that makes the Chief Executive technically unimpeachable and allows him to take on emergency powers under which individual liberties can be severely curtailed. These powers are not just theoretical, but have actually been exercised on several occasions.

This book examines the nature of states of emergency and emergency powers and respective provisions in the Russian constitution and contemporary legislation. The author discusses the use of emergency powers in earlier Russian and Soviet history, and appraises the legal thought underpinning such powers. A wide-ranging analysis of the origination and use of emergency powers in Western and non-Western countries is provided, tracing the theories and practicalities of emergency orders throughout the world history. The author warns that the longer an emer-gency regime lasts, the less effective the measure has a tendency to become. States of emergency have a high risk of backfiring and of lending unintentional support to the terrorists and extra-state actors that such measures are aimed at in the first place. In addition, he finds that the 1993 Russian Constitution – adopted in the aftermath of the infamous violent dissolution of Russia's first democratically elected parliament – is actually a step backwards not only from the Russian law of 1991 but even from a Soviet act on emergency powers of the Gorbachev period. The negotiation of rights and powers under Russia's emergency legislation and national security law ties into the larger problem of constitutionalism in this still-developing democracy.

With original research and remarkable insight, *The Limits of Russian Democra-tisation* will be of interest to students and scholars examining contemporary Russia with her inherited and newly acquired contradictions, and those studying Russia's legal and political systems in the context of Russian and world history.

Alexander N. Domrin is a former Chief Specialist of Russian parliamentary com-mittee on foreign affairs and Moscow representative of the US Congressional Research Service. He earned his advanced academic degrees at the leading educa-tional institutions in Russia and America. He has taught at numerous universities in the USA and was a Fulbright Fellow at Harvard Law School. His publications include *The Constitutional Mechanism of a State of Emergency* (Moscow: Public Science Foundation, 1998) and reports to Russia's Council for Foreign and Defence Policy.

BASEES/Routledge series on Russian and East European studies
Series editor:
Richard Sakwa, Department of Politics and International Relations, University of Kent

Editorial Committee:
George Blazyca Centre for Contemporary European Studies, University of Paisley
Terry Cox, Department of Government, University of Strathclyde
Rosalind Marsh, Department of European Studies and Modern Languages, University of Bath
David Moon, Department of History, University of Strathclyde
Hilary Pilkington, Centre for Russian and East European Studies, University of Birmingham
Stephen White, Department of Politics, University of Glasgow

This series is published on behalf of BASEES (the British Association for Slavonic and East European Studies). The series comprises original, high-quality, research-level work by both new and established scholars on all aspects of Russian, Soviet, post-Soviet and East European Studies in humanities and social science subjects.

The Limits of Russian Democratisation

Emergency powers and states of emergency

Alexander N. Domrin

R Routledge
Taylor & Francis Group

LONDON AND NEW YORK

First published 2006
by Routledge
2 Park Square, Milton Park, Abingdon, Oxon OX14 4RN

Simultaneously published in the USA and Canada
by Routledge
711 Third Avenue, New York, NY 10017

Routledge is an imprint of the Taylor & Francis Group, an informa business

© 2006 Alexander N. Domrin

Typeset in Times by Wearset Ltd, Boldon, Tyne and Wear

British Library Cataloguing in Publication Data
A catalogue record for this book is available from the British Library

Library of Congress Cataloging in Publication Data
A catalog record for this book has been requested

ISBN - 978 0 4156 4972 8

To my parents,
Nadezhda Alexeevna and
Nikolay Alexandrovich Domrin

No republic will ever be perfect if she has not by law provided for every-thing, having a remedy for every emergency, and fixed rules for applying it.

Niccolo Machiavelli (1469–1527)

Men go away, but constitutions never fall.

Sir George Downing (*c.*1624–1684)

Contents

Preface

Chrezvychainaia situatsia, chrezvychainye polnomochia, chrezvychainoe polozhenie ... Since the end of the 1980s these Russian synonyms of an 'emergency situation', 'emergency powers', a 'state of emergency' have always been among the most frequent terms in Soviet and contemporary Russian legal and political lexicon. They are arguably as often used now as the words *glasnost'* (openness, transparency) or *pravovoe gosudarstvo* (Russian equivalent of *Rechtstaat* or 'law-governed state', 'state based on the rule of law') were used in the Gorbachev period of Soviet reforms. After several decades that had passed since the issue of about a dozen decrees and resolutions in 1917, 1919–1920, 1923 and 1926 (declaring the 'Soviet Republic a War Camp', initiating the 'Red Terror' against 'enemies of the Revolution', imposing a state of siege and martial law, introducing other emergency measures for the 'salvation of the Bolshevik revolution' and maintenance of 'revolutionary order' and 'military communism')[1] and the period of martial law during the Great Patriotic War (1941–1945), the term a 'state of emergency' came again to hold an increasingly prominent place in decisions by first USSR and now Russian government, as well as both executive and legislative branches of government of the Newly Independent States (NIS).

Addressing the second session of the USSR Congress of People's Deputies (CPD) in November 1989, Vadim Bakatin, then USSR Minister of the Interior, identified 30 'hot spots' on the territory of the Soviet Union, 'undermining stability of both economic and social development, creating tensions' in inter-ethnic relations, and 'creating real danger to the people's life'.[2] During the CPD fourth session in December 1990, 53 prominent USSR Congress deputies and Soviet officials (including Leningrad Party head Boris Gidaspov, Joint Chiefs of Staff Chairman Mikhail Moiseev, Patriarch of All Russia Aleksii II, and USSR Minister of Culture Nikolai Gubenko) called on President Gorbachev to declare a state of emergency and rule by decree in rebellious regions of the country. Gorbachev responded to the appeal saying that he indeed was considering a state of emergency or presidential rule in the most dangerous areas. According to the Russian Ministry of Security, approximately 1,500 terrorist acts were committed in Russia in 1991. Between 1990 and 1993, 160 terrorist acts were aimed only against members of legislatures and representatives of authorities; as a result, 21 persons were killed, and dozens wounded.[3] In 1988–1994, a war in only one 'hot spot', Nagorno-Karabakh in the Caucasus ('arguably the most intractable of all the conflicts that accompanied the collapse of the Soviet Union'[4]), reportedly claimed more than 15,000 lives and produced over 1.4 million refugees.[5]

In his new book, the Russian Federation Prosecutor-General Vladimir V. Ustinov, gave official statistics of 272 Russian citizens who were kidnapped and transported to Chechnya in 1995. By 1997–1998 (when Chechnya enjoyed a brief period of 'independence' granted to its leaders by Russian federal authorities), this figure had grown to 1,140 and 1,415 persons, respectively. Ransoms were demanded for each kidnapped person – in the range between US$10,000 and US$4 million.[6]

That would be an exaggeration to speak about a major improvement of the situation after Putin's accession to power in 2000. According to official statistics, in the last five years spendings on law enforcement agencies and national security from the federal budget have grown five-fold (taking into account inflation rates).[7] The 2005 draft budget of Russia prescribes an additional 26 per cent increase of spending for those purposes. In an exclusive TV interview in September 2004, Russian Minister of Finance Alexei Kudrin stated that since 2000 budget spendings on the Federal Security Service (FSB) had grown four times, Ministry of the Interior (MVD) – three times, border patrol service – two-and-a-half times.[8]

In the last 15 years a 'state of emergency' and emergency regimes have been introduced by the USSR and republican authorities approximately 30 times, thus gradually becoming an everyday reality in many regions of the former Soviet Union.[9] In ten years after disintegration of the Soviet Union, Russian estimates of deaths in conflicts on the territory of the Commonwealth of Independent States range from 100,000 to 600,000, with other damages being assessed at US$15 billion.[10]

The strength of a society based on the rule of law can be measured by its ability to cope with extraordinary situations. It is under these conditions that constitutional guarantees of individual rights are in the greatest tension with the state's need of self-preservation. In Justice Thurgood Marshall's words, 'history teaches that grave threats to liberty often come in times of urgency, when constitutional rights seem too extravagant to endure' (*Skinner v Railway Labor Executives* (1989)).[11] As a citizen of a country that had recently overcome the Communist regime, I possessed an understandable suspicion of any governmental infringement on individual liberties (often exercised for the sake of 'national security' and 'public safety' maintenance) and began my study of emergency powers and states of exception doubtful of their legitimacy in a country based on the Rule of Law.

Upon completing this study, my conclusions are somewhat different and not so straight-forward. There are times even in a democracy when extraordinary power must be used, notwithstanding many risks that must be run when a state of emergency is declared. World history, including the history of Britain, the U.S. and other democratic nations, contains dozens of examples when the governments faced with crisis were forced to acquire and exercise extraordinary powers or face extinction.[12] It is obvious that providing for regulation of governmental powers in emergencies is the best way to protect individual liberty and ensure the swiftest return to constitutional normalcy. Well-conceived and publicly debated legislative or constitutional provisions, adopted *long in advance* of actual emergence of grave dangers, but invoked and strictly regulating governmental conduct *during* times of crisis may, on the one hand, be far more palatable than doing nothing at all, and, on the other hand, prevent the society from gross abuse of governmental powers in the name of 'salvation of the country in the time of dire straits'.[13]

Constitutionalists, today, are necessarily comparativists. 'One tries to profit from the often difficult and painful, occasionally trial-and-error expertise of other countries trying to deal with political, social, and economic challenges similar to our own, and to see the lessons that those other countries may have to offer us'.[14] So although the monograph is not dedicated exclusively to the Russian material, the inevitable purpose of this study was to evaluate legal (first of all, constitutional) regulation of emergency powers and a 'state of exception' in the countries of the world *from the Russian perspective*, with a view to understanding the problems associated with interpreting and applying these legal and constitutional provisions to *past and, especially, present Russian circumstances*, and, finally, to learn *both positive and negative lessons* of respective foreign legislation and its practical implementation in the countries of the world which can be used for *further development* of contemporary Russian law in this sphere.

In the fall of 1986, the author was denied a permission of his supervisors (in the Institute of Soviet Legislation, Moscow) to select 'legal regulations of a state of emergency in foreign countries' as a topic of a dissertation. Then Deputy Director of the Institute characterised the topic as 'interesting and peculiar in principle, but irrelevant and not compelling for the Soviet law'. An 'applied' character of the Institute of Soviet Legislation, attached to the USSR Ministry of Justice, didn't encourage research that couldn't be used for drafting new Soviet statutes and legal regulations.[15]

Hardly a surprise, adoption in 1990 of the first USSR Act '*On the Legal Regime of a State of Emergency*' and its use suggested at the time inadequate familiarity with what Nicole Questiaux calls the 'theory of exceptional circumstances',[16] as well as with foreign legislation on emergency powers and states of emergency and especially with the experience of its implementation. No books specially dedicated to the legal mechanism of a state of emergency were published in Russia between 1908[17] and 1998[18] except one, a predominantly propagandist pamphlet denouncing emergency legislation in West Germany.[19]

Yet, foreign and Russian imperial experience in the sphere of regulation of emergency powers and states of emergency is vast and so is relevant legislation. Both of them – Russian legislation and experience – are often overlooked by Western scholars.[20] That's especially regrettable, because Russian academic interest in studies of this area of history, law and public policy has been experiencing a true renaissance lately.[21] I truly hope that this book would fill the gap to some extent, as it goes into the historical perspective of the theme, analyses origins and elements of the institution, critically examines respective constitutional experience of Russia, USSR and some other countries of the world.

The work is divided into four chapters, with an introduction and conclusion.

The introduction is dedicated to national emergencies as a world phenomenon of the twentieth century and their role in contemporary constitutional process in Russia and other counties of the world.

Origins of the concept of 'emergency' or 'constitutional dictatorship', legal, philosophical, and historical roots of 'emergency powers' and their evolution are studied in the first chapter. Definition of the constitutional mechanism of a state of emergency is given in the second part of the chapter.

Comparative study of emergency provisions in constitutional law of the countries of the world is undertaken in the second chapter.[22] Elements of the constitutional mechanism of a state of emergency were the main object of the analysis here. International norms and standards dealing with states of emergency, especially the 'derogation clause', are also highlighted in this chapter.

Chapters 3 and 4 are dedicated exclusively to the analysis of the legal regulation of emergency powers in the Russian law throughout its history: from the first emergency act of 1881 ('*Ordinance on Measures for the Preservation of the State Order and Public Tranquillity*'), and *Basic State Laws of the Russian Empire* of 1906 to the USSR and Russian statutes in this sphere (adopted in 1990–1991, and in 2001–2002) and practice of their implementation. Chapter 4 also contains a case study of the longest state of emergency on the territory of the Newly Independent States – in North Ossetia/Alania and Ingushetia (1992–1995), and an emergency regime in Russia in September–October 1993, its legal and political reasons, circumstances and consequences. Particular emphasis was placed upon the inherent deficiencies and dangers within the Russian legal system that, in turn, threaten the abuse and infringement of the people's constitutional rights and freedoms. The analysis in the last two chapters is based primarily on the Russian sources.

Conclusions, observations, and some concrete recommendations aimed at further development of Russian legislation in the sphere of regulation of emergency powers and states of emergency are formulated in the concluding section of the work.

The author wishes to express his deep gratitude to the late Professor Boris I. Kluev of the Moscow State Institute of International Relations and to Professor of Law and Philosophy William B. Ewald, III, of the University of Pennsylvania Law School for their guidance and comments on early versions of the study; friends and colleagues at the Russian Parliamentary Library, the Library of Congress and U.S. Congressional Research Service for their help in collecting materials for this book. Last, but not least, I would like to express my thankfulness to my wife Elena and daughter Lena for their love, understanding and confidence.

Introduction

States of emergency as a legal mechanism which implies certain derogations from human rights standards is a well-known institution recognised in
almost all legal systems. No country in the world, whatever its socio-
political system or level of economic development, is safe from periodically
emerging critical situations, tensions, contingencies, crises, conflicts, disturbances, unrest, natural disasters and calamities, technological and ecological catastrophes. It is evident from the history of humankind that
whenever the existence of an individual or a society is endangered by some
sort of a threat, there is an immediate reaction to guard against it, and in
this process the individual or a society assumes measures which are special,
uncommon, and extraordinary. Legal and political systems of whatever
nature usually provide for effective equipment to deal with abnormal phe-
nomena that came to be branded as 'emergencies'. By all means, the legal
mechanism of a state of emergency has deserved the reputation of 'one of
the most important institutions of the Constitutional Law'.[1]

Socio-economic evolution of the group of countries, usually described
as 'developing', is often (if not usually) accompanied by a deepening of the
internal contradictions of the transitional period. Besides their attempts to
end crises through socio-political measures and manoeuvring, the leader-
ships of these countries are often compelled to resort to restrictive legislative and administrative mechanisms and outright suppression of
inevitable socio-economic, religious, communal and ethnic conflicts. In
such cases national emergencies often become a 'reserve system of repression'[2] and the institution of emergency powers (or of a state of emergency)
takes the place of a normal state of affairs. It should be specially stated in
this context that not always at all, a state of emergency in this group of
countries might have *legal* (and moreover *constitutional*) character and be
regulated by exclusively *legal* norms and provisions.

As a constitutional institution, national emergencies are an important
element of legal systems of democratic, industrially developed countries.
Back in 1948, Clinton L. Rossiter observed in his famous book *Constitutional Dictatorship: Crisis Government in the Modern Democracies*: 'No
democracy ever went through a period of thoroughgoing constitutional

dictatorship without some permanent and often unfavourable alteration in its governmental scheme ... A constitution which fails to provide for whatever emergency action may become necessary to defend the state is simply defective'.[3] Needless to say that a state of emergency has become an indispensable component of national security systems of 'developed democracies'. Besides general reasons typical for all other countries (such as war, external aggression, natural disasters), this is due above all to the need to react to periodical aggravation of social class antagonisms, regionalist and secessionist movements, or industrial conflicts. In Great Britain, for example, Emergency Powers Act of 1920 (with changes of 1964) was used 12 times in 1921–1974 exclusively to combat strikes and other forms of labour unrest.[4]

The before-mentioned factors have predetermined extensive recourse to a state of exception, which has become organic for many political regimes, inseparable from them. A distinguished Nigerian constitutionalist observes that 'in many parts of the underdeveloped world, notably Latin America, Middle East and Asia' national emergencies 'have tended to become the normal order of things, thus replacing' the usual system of government with 'emergency administration as the normal system of rule'.[5] A scholar of regimes of exception in Spanish America agrees that 'intolerance, inquisitorial suppression of opposition, constitutional dictatorship, and militarism became everyday ingredients of Latin American politics', and adds that by the end of the nineteenth century, 'no Spanish American nation lacked legal foundation for constitutional dictatorship' (defined by him as 'the constitution of tyranny') as well as a 'history of revolts, civil war, and military participation in politics'. The quoted conclusion has more than just a historical importance, for the 'political solutions' of Latin America in the nineteenth century 'molded twentieth-century patterns of civil-military relations and political tyranny from Mexico to the Strait of Magellan'.[6]

Frequent use of emergency powers, including excessive introductions of a state of exception is often an indication of unsatisfactory status of a *normal* government of the country and its state mechanism. After President Franklin D. Roosevelt declared 39 emergencies within six pre-War years, Congressman Bruce Barton (1937–1941) protested: 'Any national administration is entitled to one or two emergencies in a term of six years. But an emergency every six weeks means plain bad management.'[7] Indeed, the excessive recourse to states of emergency in peacetime, 'betokens the weakness, or at least inefficiency of a political system rather than its strength'.[8]

Although a state of emergency is an exceptional measure and is supposed to be limited in time, actually it often lasts for years and even decades.

Israel, Sultanate of Brunei, and Zimbabwe have been living under a state of emergency since 1948, 1962, and 1965, respectively. A state of siege and a state of war imposed in Syria and Jordan in 1963 and 1967 were lifted only in 1990 and 1991. In the last 30 years, a state of emergency was repeatedly declared in Sri Lanka. First it was in effect from 1971 through 1977; between 1977 and 1983 it was declared five times; once imposed in 1983 it was in effect (with a short break) through 1991. Martial rule was in effect in Pakistan between 1971 and 1977; in the Philippines – between 1972 and 1978; in Bangladesh – between 1975–1979, and then in 1981, 1982–1986, 1987–1988 and 1990. Morocco lived under a state of emergency between 1965 and 1970; Sierra-Leone – between 1970 and 1978. In 1963–1977, a state of emergency was imposed four times in Malaysia: twice in the whole Kingdom, and twice on the territory of several regions. In the 1980s, a state of emergency was imposed in more than 30 provinces of Peru. Declared in some regions of Cameroon at the end of the 1950s and in the whole country in 1969, a state of emergency had been in effect until the beginning of the 1990s. More than 35 laws, orders and decrees used to extend the state of emergency every four to six months in that country. Once imposed in December of 1976 in 13 of Turkey's provinces, by September of 1980 a state of emergency had covered all provinces of the country, and at the end of the 1980s was still in effect in nine of them. This list might have no end.

It is indicative that national emergencies have become a permanent factor in the domestic policy of both authoritarian (or semi-authoritarian) and liberal (or even democratic) regimes.

People of Chile, for instance, lived under a state of emergency for 15 years (September 1973 through August 1988). Once imposed in 1973, it was temporarily lifted between August 1983 and March 1984. A nation-wide state of siege was additionally declared after an unsuccessful life attempt on Chilean president, General Pinochet in September 1986.

Authors of the 1978 report of the Inter-American Commission on Human Rights admitted that it was not possible to determine exactly how long Paraguay had been under a state of emergency since the regime of exception seemed to date back to 1929, with a brief six-month interruption in 1947. A state of siege was in force almost continuously for as long as 33 years (May 1954 through April 1987, although confined since 1978 to Asuncion and the Central Department), after General Stroessner came to power in a coup. It was occasionally suspended for 24-hour periods on election day.

The Martial Law (*chieh yen fa*) promulgated by 'generalissimo' Chiang Kai-shek in Taiwan on 19 May 1948 was lifted with an adoption of National Security Law 39 years later – in July 1987, although not com-pletely: some legal restrictions introduced in the period of 'National Mobilisation for Suppression of the Communist Rebellion' are still in effect. Over nearly four decades, the scope of military trial jurisdiction in Taiwan had gradually been reduced: from 104 charges that could be ini-tially lodged against an (even civilian) individual who was to be tried before a military court to nine serious crimes in 1976.[9]

Even the most superficial pretexts can sometimes be used for an introduction of a state of exception, as it happened in the Philippines. National constitution of the country allowed the president to suspend the privilege of the writ of *habeas corpus* or declare martial law in 'case of invasion, insurrection, or rebellion, or imminent danger thereof, when the public safety requires it' (art.7, sec.10(2)). Interpretation of what constitutes any of those 'cases' and what exactly can be required by the 'public safety' of the Philippines is at the discretion of the chief executive. On 21 August 1971, President Marcos invoked the constitutional provision and suspended the writ of *habeas corpus* following the explosion of a grenade in Manila during an election rally. The explosion was officially pronounced as 'the existence of a state of rebellion'.[10] The suspension of the writ was ended on 11 January 1972, but not for long. Eight months later, on 21 September 1972, martial law was declared in the whole country and was in effect until 17 January 1981. But even after that the writ of *habeas corpus* has remained suspended in Mindanao nearly all the time. Martial law was in full force when: a new national constitution was prepared, approved and subsequently amended (in both cases in referenda of 10 January 1973 and 16 October 1976) in the absence of the legislature; the judiciary reorganised (in 1972) in order to remove undesirable judges; and presidency of Marcos extended (in yet another popular referendum of 27–28 July 1973) beyond eight consecutive years.[11] Five years after the end of martial law, public disillusionment with Marcos's authoritarian 'reforms' led him to resign, flee the country and (three years later) die in exile.

Constitutional history of Bolivia of the last half century reads as a chronology of coups, military juntas, and states of emergency. In ten years only (between 1956 and 1965), one might count 12 impositions of a state of siege, including those aimed at dealing with 'hunger riots' (23 September 1956), a 'revolt' in the oil mining area of Santa Cruz (on 14 May 1958), 'student riots' (21 October 1961), and 'rioting' in La Paz by striking workers and a seizure by tin miners of hostages and a mine (17 May 1965). Some other were caused by various 'threats': of a 'plot to overthrow the government' (21 February 1961), and then of 'Communist' (7 June 1961) or 'revolutionary' (29 September 1962) 'plots'. Three times, a state of siege was declared as a 'general' one (or having a nationwide character): following 'unrest' in Santa Cruz oil mining area (29 October 1957), army actions against an anti-government strike in La Paz (21 October 1958), and an 'armed revolt of tin miners', in which several persons were killed (20 September 1965).[12]

Another Latin American country, Colombia, has been governed for most of its history since the 1940s under a state of siege. It was declared in April of 1948 and lasted eight months. In November of 1949 it was declared again and wasn't completely lifted until January of 1962, for nearly 14 years! Once imposed in May of 1965 under a pretext to suppress student demonstrations against the U.S. invasion of the Dominican

Republic, a state of siege was in effect for more than three years and was lifted in December of 1968, only to be reintroduced ten months later, in October of 1969. 'For the next two decades, except for periods of varying length totalling less than three years, the country was under a state of siege.'[13]

As far as more democratic and liberal (or relatively liberal) regimes are concerned, Canada, India and Egypt are probably the best examples here.

As incredible as it sounds, for more than 20 years, and for about 40 per cent of the time between 1914 and 1970, the people of Canada were 'governed under emergency legislation' – the War Measures Act: 1914–1919, 1939–1945, 1945–1947, 1947–1951, 1951–1954, October 1970–April 1972 (with a short break in December 1970).[14]

Since declaration of India's independence of the British colonial rule (on 15 August 1947), a national emergency has been introduced three times in the largest democracy in the world, as India is often called. First, it was caused by China's aggression (in India's North-Eastern Frontier Agency, NEFA) and imposed by President Sarvepalli Radhakrishnan on 26 October 1962. The emergency proclamation was still in effect, when the beginning of the 1965 Indian-Pakistani military conflict made the Government of India to issue another proclamation. The conflict ended with signing the Tashkent Declaration on 10 January 1966, but the proclamation was repealed only two years later, on 10 January 1968. The second national emergency was caused by another war with Pakistan and proclaimed by President V.V. Giri on 3 December 1971. The war lasted for two weeks only and led to a complete defeat of the Pakistani army, but, as in the first case, emergency was not lifted again. The proclamation was still in force, when on 25 June 1975, President F.A. Ahmed introduced another emergency, this time under a pretext of dealing with an 'internal disturbance'. Two last proclamations were repealed on 21 and 27 March 1977. Besides 'national' emergencies, so called President's Rule has been introduced more than one hundred times in practically all states of India.[15]

A national emergency that was declared in Egypt in 1967 is still in force in that country. It was temporarily lifted on 15 May 1980 only to be reimposed on 6 October 1981 following the assassination of President Anwar Sadat.

In a truly paradoxical situation, a Nation can for decades live under a declared state of emergency, and isn't aware of it. It came as a shock to many members of U.S. Congress in 1971 to learn that the United States had been in a state of national emergency since 9 March 1933, when President Roosevelt proclaimed an emergency to cope with the banking crisis (Pub. L. No.1, 42 Stat. 1 (1933)). In addition to the banking crisis emergency proclamation, three other declarations of national emergency remained in force until the 1970s: issued by President Truman on 16 December 1950 in response to China's entry into the Korean War (Proclamation No. 2914, 15 Fed. Reg. 9029 (1950)), by President Nixon on

23 March 1970 to deal with the Post Office strike (Proclamation No. 3972, 3 C.F.R. 473 (1970)), and on 15 August 1971 when balance-of-payments problems led Nixon to impose a 10 per cent surcharge on dutiable imports (Proclamation No. 4074, 3 C.F.R. 60 (1971)).[16]

The fact that the Korean war had stopped about ten years earlier did not prevent President Kennedy from using Truman's emergency proclamation to provide the legal justification for the embargo against Cuba in 1962. The U.S. Senate Special Committee on the Termination of the National Emergency stated in 1973: 'A majority of the people of the United States have lived all of their lives under emergency rule. For 40 years, freedoms and governmental procedures guaranteed by the Constitution have, in varying degrees, been abridged by laws brought into force by states of national emergency.'[17]

Similarly, on 10 March 2001, Polish newspaper *Rzeczpospolita* reported that the infamous 1981 martial law decree was still in force. The martial law decree, issued by the then State Council, was confirmed by a law of 25 January 1982 on special legal regulations during martial law. Article 2 of the law stated that the decree would remain in force until the adoption of an appropriate law on a state of war. By 2001, Polish lawmakers had failed to adopt such law, even though the president submitted a so-called 'crisis package' to the parliament, including a draft bill on the introduction of a state of war. The newspaper reminded its readers of General Wojciech Jaruzelski address to the nation on 13 January 1981, announcing the introduction of martial law in Poland, and his words: 'Our Fatherland has found itself on the verge of a disaster ... It is necessary to tie the hands of adventurers before they draw the Fatherland into an abyss of fratricidal fight.' It turns out that if the government wanted to 'tie some adventurers' right now, it could do that under the same decree Jaruzelski utilised, the newspaper sarcastically added.[18]

All in all, according to an estimation of the Amnesty International, as of 1 January 1985, a state of emergency (in one form or another) was maintained in more than 35 countries of the world.[19] In the last 15 years it has been introduced even more often. A more recent report on human rights and states of emergency prepared by Leandro Despouy, Special Rapporteur of the UN Sub-Commission on Prevention of Discrimination and Protection of Minorities, listed 80 (!) states that had, since 1 January 1985 'taken measures which constituted the proclamation, extension, maintenance or termination of emergency regimes in various forms'.[20]

It's important to note that the Special Rapporteur used a formula 'emergency regimes' rather than a 'state of emergency'. Not all of those regimes were technically *legal* or, moreover, *constitutional*. Some governments took such drastic measures as suspension of certain civil rights and freedoms (that could be legally undertaken only in virtue of a formal and official declaration or prolongation of a 'state of emergency' with an immediate notification to the United Nations) without a formal introduction of a state of emergency in any of its numerous forms. Indeed, as of 31 March 1992, only 22 out of those 80 states had made formal notifications to the U.N. Secretary-General under Article 4(3) of the International Covenant on Civil and Political Rights.[21] In some other instances (like declarations of a 'state of emergency' in Moscow and 'some areas' of the USSR during the failed August 1991 'putsch', or in Moscow again in October 1993) that was done in violation of respective legal acts (of the USSR and the Russian Federation). In such cases, the introduced states of emergency could be defined only as emergencies *de facto*, rather than *de jure*.[22]

Arguably, not all of those 'emergency regimes' listed by Leandro Despouy would agree with his interpretation of their character (as *emergency* regimes). Still, as it was noted by Allan Rosas, Professor of State Law and International Law of Abo Akademi University (Sweden), the figure given by Despouy 'for a period of only seven and a half years illustrates the gravity of the problem of public emergencies'.[23]

Needless to say that deteriorating social, economic, political (and in some cases ethnic and religious) contradictions heavily affect many so-called post-Communist 'transitional regimes', including Russia.

'Paradoxically, despite all those slogans and programs of reforms, progress, and social concord, antagonisms have been drastically aggravating. Collision – that's the essence of all attempts, endeavours, and actions today', writes a modern Russian legal scholar.[24] Lack of solid legal traditions, a relatively low level of legal and political culture,[25] underdeveloped institutions of civil society[26] and neglect of socio-economic problems in post-Communist societies add to social tensions. Richard Sakwa's observation that 'the whole epoch of Soviet power can be considered a period of "extraordinary politics" '[27] is even more correct so as far as post-Communist politics in Russia are concerned (especially in the Yeltsin's period).

The average Russian expresses distrust of seven out of ten key institutions of Russian society, with political parties as the least trusted (7 per cent)[28] and the courts and the army as the most trusted institutions in the country (40 per cent and 62 per cent, respectively).[29] Only 14 per cent of Russians (every seventh one of us) consider Russia a democratic state, with 54 per cent saying that 'overall' it is not. Sixty per cent do not believe that their votes are capable of changing anything.[30] Although as few as 6.9 per cent of the 1,500 Russians polled by the Russian Public Opinion and Market independent research centre (ROMIR) believe that a situation in which political leaders make arbitrary decisions as they see fit would be best for Russia, and although as few as 2.8 per cent believe that military rule would be very good for Russia, only 9.1 per cent of Russians believe that democracy is 'the best form of rule despite certain problems it poses' (an additional 38.7 per cent 'to some degree' share this view).[31]

An analytical report *Attitude of Population to Federal Laws and Bodies of State Power* prepared at the Institute of Legislation and Comparative

Law under the Russian Government indicates that 70 to 80 per cent of Russians think that 'laws overall do not work': 28.2 per cent of civil servants recognise that they have to ignore or violate federal laws in their work; 70 per cent of the population believe that they have to undertake illegal actions in order to guarantee their legitimate rights more often now than before the beginning of legal reforms in the country; 56 per cent of the population (and 58.9 per cent of civil servants) consider the government and other federal bodies of the executive branch the most corrupt. Since the end of 1989, people's trust in the federal legislature has shrunk from 88 per cent (for the USSR Supreme Soviet) to 4.3 per cent (for the State Duma). Only 3.7 to 3.9 per cent of Russians (4.8 to 5.1 per cent of civil servants; 7 to 8.7 per cent of Russian elite) agree that Yeltsin's decade was a 'necessary stage in development' of the Russian society.[32] As many as 95.1 per cent of the population (and 94.4 per cent of civil servants) voted for a 'decisive restoration of order in the country'.

Although as many as 89 per cent of the 1,600 Russians polled by the All-Russia Centre for Public Opinion Studies (VTs IOM), 'strongly support or more or less support' guarantees of democratic rights and freedoms of every citizen, an increasingly growing per centage of Russians (from 71 per cent in February 1998, to 81 per cent in April 2000) believe that order (*poryadok*) is the 'most important issue for the country at the moment', 'even if it is necessary to break some democratic principles and limit people's personal freedoms to establish it'. According to another opinion poll (conducted by *Monitoring.ru*), 68 per cent of the Russians favour such a restrictive institution as *propiska* (versus 23 per cent who say that it should be abolished) and believe that citizens of the Russian Federation should have to register at their place of residence via the *propiska* system.[33]

War of *kompromat* between TV channels controlled by rivalling oligarchs, profiteering,[34] overcommercialisation, de-intellectualisation and a general degradation of 'liberal' mass media in Russia,[35] have led to quite expectable consequences – the second-oldest profession has nearly lost its function as a means of expressing independent public opinion and, in the words of Oleg Poptsov, a veteran of the *glasnost* campaign and the president of *TV-Tsentr* (under jurisdiction of the Moscow city government), 'has now moved closer to the first oldest [profession] than ever before'.[36] As a result, although there is not much support for introducing any kind of political censorship, over 60 per cent of respondents (across all categories) in a May 2001 opinion poll are prepared to approve some sort of a preliminary checking or censorship of press reports and publications, in order to ensure 'objectivity of information and a balanced evaluation of current events'. An even more significant majority of Russians (three-quarters of respondents, regardless of their age or education levels) are in favour of censorship aimed at safeguarding public morals.[37]

According to a poll conducted by VTsIOM in June 2001, about three-quarters of Russians (72 per cent), including Alexander Solzhenitsyn, a symbol of moral resistance to the Communist tyranny of the past, federal Minister of Justice Yuri Chaika, and many other leading figures of Russian society and culture, openly and vigorously support restoration of the death penalty for certain crimes, whereas only 19 per cent want it abolished. Responding to the demands of the society, on 15 February 2002, the State Duma resolved 266–83 to urge President Putin to reconsider the moratorium on the death penalty in Russia. This demand gained new momentum after the tragedy in Beslan in September of 2004.

To a large extent, the secret of Vladimir Putin's popularity in Russia can be explained by the fact that after a decade of Yeltsin's 'shock without therapy' the society itself voted for *poryadok*, as the permissible coercive imposition of stability in the country. In September of 2004, 82 per cent of Russians spoke out in a survey in favour of increased police document checks, 92 per cent favoured travel restrictions, and 65 per cent approved greater control over the press.[39]

Putin inherited a crushed, looted, and humiliated country struggling to survive the 'liquidation regime' of radical 'reformers'. Deindustrialisation, depopulation and general degradation of Russia in the 1990s are well-documented.

According to official statistics, between 1990 and 1998, the country lost 54 per cent of its industrial output (by 2002, it was reduced to 38 per cent). The 'reforms' had a more devastating impact on machine-production industry that lost 63 per cent of its output in 1990–1998,[40] and an even bigger impact on light and food industries that lost 81 and 53 per cent of their output in 1990–2000.[41] For comparison, as a result of the Great Patriotic War (1941–1945), when about 27 million citizens were killed by Nazis or died, about a half of the European part of the USSR was occupied, and more than 1,700 cities and 70,000 villages were destroyed in warfare, the reduction of industrial production was equal to about 30 per cent.

Russia's population has been shrinking by up to half a per cent a year – making Russia less populated now than Pakistan. Its increase in mortality rates (60 per cent since 1990) has been 'unprecedented in any country during peacetime since the Middle Ages'.[42] After 12 years of anti-human 'reforms' Russia ranks 134th among all states in terms of male life expectancy and 100th in terms of female life expectancy. By 1997, death rate among Russian males had equalled that of war-ravaged Liberia, and dropped lower than in Egypt, Indonesia or Paraguay. Men in 'democratic' Russia have a smaller chance of surviving to age 60 than under the tsar a century ago. In estimation of Nicholas Eberstadt, in the vein of similar demographic catastrophes under Pol Pot in Cambodia in the 1970s or Ethiopian famine in the 1980s, 'excessive mortality' in Russia reached two million people in 1992–1998. For comparison, the country lost 1.7 million citizens during the civil war of 1918–1921.[43] In the last ten years, the number of orphans in Russia has doubled and officially reached 700,000.[44] This list may have no end. If these trends are not reversed, by 2050 Russia's population could go as low as 100 million people or less.[45]

According to a report of the Institute of Economics of the Russian Academy of Sciences, in just first two years of market 'reforms' (by December 1993), an income gap between 10 per cent of the richest and poorest people in Russia increased nearly twice: from 5.4-fold to 10.4-fold.[46] Since then, the gap has grown even wider and led to erosion of the middle class, a backbone of stability in any society. Even though according to the data of the All-Russian Centre for People's Living Standards the middle class has reportedly doubled over the past five years of Putin's administration, in absolute terms it still constitutes not more than 13 million or eight to nine per cent of Russia's population.[47]

In just two years (1991–1993), a number of Russian scientists shrank by 1.23 million or nearly 40 per cent. The share of mineral resources in Russia's export grew from 55 per cent in 1986 to more than 80 per cent in 1994; at the same time, the share of machinery and technological equipment was cut by a third: from 15 per cent to 10 per cent. By 1995, Russian spending on space exploration had equalled that of Pakistan or Israel.[48] In the estimation of Russian scholars, between 1991 and 1996, a combined loss to Russia as a result of the drain of her material and cultural assets to the West (approximately 70 per cent of them to the United States) reached US$800 billion.[49]

An unprecedented social catastrophe in Russia, which the UN Development Program characterises as 'a human crisis of monumental proportions',[50] and which has been largely ignored by the Western community, makes any discussion about 'stability' in post-Communist Russia simply irrelevant and artificial.

Even after Putin's obvious success in his consolidation of power versus predatory oligarchic elite and survivors of Yeltsin's kleptocratic regime, the situation in the country is far from being 'normal'. Since Putin's appointment in 1999 as a new Russian Prime Minister (and Yeltsin's successor), the death toll from terrorist acts has exceeded 1,230 people, including victims of bombings of apartment buildings in Buynaksk (64), Moscow (230) and Volgodonsk (18) in 1999, bombings of a Victory Day parade in Kaspiysk (45) and of a government building in Grozny (70) in 2002, of a hospital in Mozdok (50) and Essentuki suburb trains (48) in 2003, and victims of a hostage-rescue operation in a Moscow theatre (128) in November 2002. The first half a year of Putin's second presidency term witnessed assassination of a pro-Moscow Chechen leader Akhmat

Kadyrov during celebration of Victory Day (9 May 2004); murderous terrorist raids in Ingushetia and Grozny, capital of Chechnya, in June and August (death toll in both cases claimed at least 120 people); a banking crisis in July; major political unrest over changes in pension benefits system over the summer; the twin bombings of two passenger airliners that killed 90 people in August; a suicide bomber that instantly killed ten and injured 51 Moscovites on August 30; and finally, a barbaric act unprecedented in world history of hostage-taking of more than 1,200 kids (the youngest of them was just one year and 8 months old), their parents and teachers in the secondary school in Beslan in North Ossetia during a ceremony to mark the first day of the new school year, with at least 328 victims,[51] all form a pattern of events that challenge the notion that the federal government has things firmly under its control. The domestic situation in Russia today is anything but 'normal', thus provoking emergency politics of Vladimir Putin in the aftermath of the Beslan tragedy (appointment of governors, reform of electroral system, etc.) Titles of recent publications 'Under Martial Law' (with a subtitle 'Political Leaders Must Take Tough Measures to Restore Order in Russia') and 'State of Siege' by Russian and American authors of radically opposing views sound like a motto of the day.[52]

At the turn of the twentieth century, a prominent Russian lawyer, Vladimir Gessen, characterised the legal institution of a 'state of exception' as 'one of the most painful questions of contemporary reality'.[53] One hundred years later, this observation is still relevant for the Russian Federation and most republics of the former Soviet Union.

1 Legal origins and evolution of the 'emergency powers' concept

Constitutional mechanism of a state of emergency

I

As legal (and pre-legal) institutions, emergency powers and a state of emergency (in their different forms) have deep roots and origins. 'Prerogative', 'legal' or 'constitutional dictatorship', the concept of 'necessity' (*raison d'etat*, *Staatsraison*) have always been in the sphere of attention of classic writers of Western law, philosophy, and history. 'From Machiavelli to Hegel, security and survival of the state and more especially of the good state, of the constitutional, civilised political order had challenged the ingenuity of the best minds'.[1] One particular aspect of a state of emergency – the issue of the protection of human rights in emergency situations – reflects the general problem of the relationship between the individual and interests of the community to which he belongs and has existed from the moment people started living in organised societies.

Origins of the concept of 'emergency' reach back to the Greek city-states and the Roman republic. 'Great calamities deserve great means', was proclaimed by a Roman speaker, philosopher and politician Marcus Tullius Cicero (106–43 BC) in his unfinished dialogue *On Laws* (*De legibus*; begun approximately in 52 BC). In the same dialogue Cicero formulated his famous maxim: 'Social necessity is the supreme law' (*Salus populi* (or *Salus rei publicae*) *suprema lex esto*) (III, 4, 8)[2] that laid down the basis of the concept of necessity. As the Romans used to say, 'when arms clash, laws are silent' (*inter arma silent leges*). In Cicero's view, there are no other more important social relations than the one given to all of us by a social order.[3] When the prosperity of the state (as of a joint treasure of the people) is threatened, with the people's consent a wise statesman 'as a dictator should establish order'. Doing this the statesman acts not pursuing his selfish goals, but in common interests as a saviour of the republic.[4]

As a constitutional institution, emergency powers (called by Carl J. Friedrich 'some species of constitutional dictatorship')[5] started with Greek and Roman Law. Dictatorship, as a legal and political phenomenon of ancient Rome, when in time of crisis an eminent citizen was temporarily granted absolute power to defend the republic from a foreign invasion or internal strife, inspired Machiavelli and Rousseau. Both of them analysed this institution in their works and made complimentary remarks to it.

No writer has ever spoken more openly and frankly than Niccolo Machiavelli (1469–1527), 'the first modern analyst of power',[6] about the political necessities of violence.[7] Yet it would be appropriate to note that Machiavelli is unfairly remembered as something he was not. Partly because of his pragmatic view of the relationship between ethics and politics – the leader of the state 'must stick to the good so long as he can, but, being compelled by necessity, he must be ready to take the way of the evil' – Machiavelli has been widely misinterpreted. The adjective 'Machiavellian' has become a pejorative used to describe a politician who manipulates others in an opportunistic and deceptive way.

The Prince (1505) was written with the author's focus on *monarchies* (and as a futile effort to get a job from Lorenzo de'Medici, the 'prince' of the city-state of Florence, where Machiavelli lived).[8] It overshadowed his major work *Discourses on the First Ten Books of Titus Livius* (1513–1521) where the author was mainly concerned with '*republics*', defined as states controlled by a politically active citizenry. In fact, the basic idea of *Discourses* is the superiority of the democratic republic and the ultimate reliance of even the most despotic regimes on the mass consent of the people. In *Discourses* Machiavelli emphasised that for a republic to survive, it needed to foster a spirit of patriotism and civic virtue among its citizens. He argued that a republic would be strengthened by the conflicts generated through open political participation and debate.

Even though many pages of *Discourses* were dedicated to dictatorship, the term 'dictatorship' itself was used exclusively as a constitutional institution of ancient Rome, not as a synonym to 'tyranny', or 'totalitarianism' in their modern understanding. (There was nothing 'tyrannical', as we understand this term now, in Greek 'tyrants' either). Machiavelli reminded us that 'the Dictator could do nothing to alter the form of the government, such as to diminish the powers of the Senate or the people, or to abrogate existing institutions and create new ones'. And continued: 'It is the magistracies and powers that are created by illegitimate means which harm a republic, and not those that are appointed in the regular way, as was the case in Rome, where in the long course of time no Dictator ever failed to prove beneficial to the republic'.[9] In this very context, the next Machiavelli's maxim should be understood: 'Those republics which in time of danger cannot resort to a dictatorship, or some similar authority, will generally be ruined when grave occasions occur' (I, 34).[10]

Central contention of Thomas Hobbes of Malmesbury (1588–1679), English political philosopher and author of *Leviathan, or The Matter, Forme, & Power of a Common-wealth Ecclesiasticall and Civill* (1651), which is sometimes called probably the most important single work in the history of political philosophy, is that without an effective state power people will lapse into a state of war.[11] In his words, 'the office of the

Sovereign, be it a Monarch, or an Assembly, consisteth in the end, for which he was trusted with the Soveraign power, namely the procuration of *the safety of the people*; to which he is obliged by the Law of Nature, and to render an account thereof to God, the Author of that Law, and to none but him'. In his declaration of the Sovereign's accountability to God only (as 'the Author' of natural law), and respectively unaccountability to any written statute, Hobbes went even further and made the following statement: 'By *Safety* here, is not meant a bare Preservation, but also all other Contentments of life, which every man by lawfull Industry, without danger, or hurt to the Common-wealth, shall acquire to himself'. (Part Two. Of Common-wealth. Chapter XXX. Of the Office of the Soveraign Representative) (*italics added – A.D.*).

English philosopher, physician, economist and legal thinker of the Restoration period, founder of British empiricism, and one of the main 'intellectual forces' behind the U.S. Constitution John Locke (1632–1704), argued in one of his basic works *An Essay Concerning the True Original, Extent and End of Civil Government*, also known as *Second Treatise on Civil Government* (1690), that personal liberty was the very object of the government and the sole justification for political power. Limitations on governmental powers are central to Locke's theory, whereas personal safety and security are the purpose of the law, the very opposite of 'extemporary arbitrary decrees', and could be secured, in his opinion, only by 'promulgated and established laws', applied by 'known authorised judges', in order that 'both the people may know their duty, and be safe and secure within the limits of the law; and the rulers too kept within their bounds, and not be tempted, by the power they have in their hands, to employ it to such purposes, and by such measures, as they would not have known, and own not willingly' (Chapter XI. Of the Extent of the Legislative Power. Sections 136–137).

But even this thinker, certainly deserving a reputation of a 'champion of the supremacy of legislature' and a 'leading philosopher of freedom', insisted in the same work that it is the executive ('the Crown') that should possess a number of discretionary powers ('the prerogative') to deal with 'accidents and necessities that may concern the public'. (Chapter XIV. Of Prerogative. Section 160). In his opinion, such circumstances were not limited by a necessity to wage a war or resist domestic violence only; discretionary powers could be employed for '*public good*' and '*benefit of the community*' (section 161) in a very wide sense. '*Salus populi suprema lex* is certainly so just and fundamental a rule, – Locke assured, – that he who sincerely follows it cannot dangerously err' (Chapter XIII. Of the Subordination of the Powers of the Commonwealth. Section 158). It's quite symbolic that the same Cicero's maxim *Salus populi suprema lex esto* was used by Locke as an epigraph to the whole work of *Second Treatise on Civil Government*. In general, Locke defined three branches of government: legislative, executive, and 'federative'. The last consisted of '*the power of war* and peace, leagues and alliances, and all the transactions, with all persons and communities without the commonwealth' (Chapter XII. Of the Legislative, Executive, and Federative Power of the Commonwealth. Section 146) *(italics added – A.D.)*. The 'federative' power, which can be probably called 'war and foreign powers' today, in Locke's opinion, was 'much less capable to be directed by antecedent, standing, positive laws, than the executive' (section 147), and in fact 'the executive and federative power of every community ... are hardly to be separated'. Separating them, Locke warned, would invite 'disorder and ruin' (section 148).[12]

In the main book of his life *The Spirit of Laws* (work on it lasted for about 20 years – between 1728 and 1748), systematising philosophical, historical, legal and economic views of the author, Charles Louis Montesquieu (1689–1755) concluded: 'In countries where liberty is most esteemed, there are laws by which a single person is deprived of it, in order to preserve it for the whole community ... Own I must, notwithstanding that the practice of the freest nation that ever existed, induces me to think that there are cases in which a veil should be drawn for a while over liberty *(pour un moment un voile sur la liberte)*, as it was customary to veil the statues of the Gods'. (Book XII. Of the Laws That Form Political Liberty in Relation to the Subject. Chapter 19. In What Manner the Use of Liberty Is Suspended in a Republic).[13]

Political philosophy of Jean-Jacques Rousseau (1712–1778) is based on two primary principles. The first of them is that *politics and morality should not be separated*. When a state fails to act in a moral fashion, it ceases to function in the proper manner and ceases to exert genuine authority over the individual. The second important principle is *freedom*, which *the state is created to preserve*. The goal of government, in Rousseau's view, should be to secure freedom, equality, and justice for all within the state. Respectively, as he wrote in *The Social Contract* (1762): 'It is obvious that the People's first concern must to see that the State shall nor perish'. (Book IV. Chapter 6. Of the Dictatorship).[14] In the same work, Rousseau made one important clarification that 'the suspension of legal authority does not imply its abolition'; and an even more important warning: 'Only the gravest dangers can justify any fundamental change in public order, and the sacrosanct nature of the laws never should be interfered with save when the safety of the State is in question' (IV, 6).

Even so, decisive supporter of the idea of parliamentarism, and one of the foremost 19th-century spokesmen for liberalism as John Stuart Mill (1806–1873), admitted in his book *Considerations on Representative Government* (1861) that 'in well-balanced governments, in which the supreme power is divided, and each sharer is protected against the usurpations of the others in the only manner possible – namely, by being armed for defence with weapons as strong as the others can wield for attack – the government can only be carried on by forbearance on all sides to exercise those extreme powers, unless provoked by conduct equally extreme on the part of some other sharer of power'. 'And in this case, – Mill articulated, – we may truly say that only by the regard paid to maxims of constitutional morality is the constitution kept in existence' (Chapter 12. Ought Pledges to be Required from Members of Parliament?). J.S. Mill recognised the right of the executive to dissolve the parliament, as well as the right of the legislature to resist 'breach of trust' of the 'chief magistrate' in case of his 'attempt to subvert the Constitution, and usurp sovereign power'. 'Where such peril exists, no first magistrate is admissible whom the Parliament cannot, by a single vote, reduce to a private station'. Finally J.S. Mill concluded: 'There ought not to be any possibility of that deadlock in politics which would ensue on a quarrel breaking out between a President and an Assembly, neither of whom, during an interval which might amount to years, would have any legal means of ridding itself of the other' (Chapter 14. Of the Executive in a Representative Government).[15]

A model similar to the one expressed by the cited authors, especially by Locke and Mill, was defended by the famous eighteenth century jurist Sir William Blackstone. In his *Commentaries on the Laws of England* he described the king's prerogative as 'those rights and capacities which the king enjoys alone'. Some of the prerogatives he considered *direct* – those that are 'rooted in and spring from the king's political person', including the power to make war. By vesting in the king the sole prerogative to make war, individuals entering society gave up the private right to make war: 'It would, indeed, be extremely improper, that any number of subjects should have the power of binding the supreme magistrate, and putting him against his will in a state of war'.[16] It can be assumed from the context of the *Commentaries* that, in Blackstone's opinion, 'individuals entering society', that he mentioned, also include parliamentarians ('individuals elected to the Legislature').

Under classic absolutism, there was no the very reason to regulate emergencies through legal means, because a separation between normal and special powers hadn't been developed yet, 'normal' laws were already sufficiently arbitrary and severe, so even 'normal state of affairs' was to a large extent 'exceptional'.

To justify the absolutist state doctrine, emerging in most European countries in the thirteenth to fifteenth centuries, medieval 'legists' used maxims of a famous Roman jurist Domitius Ulpian (?–228): 'What is deserved by the Principle, has the power of law' (*quod principi placuit, legis habet vigorem*); the Principle himself 'is not bound by law' – he is 'superior than law' (*princeps legibus solutus est, supra leges constitutus*).

German King of the twelfth century Friedrich Barbarossa (1156–1190) is the alleged author of this colourful expression: 'To do whatever you like without a fear of punishment – that is what it means to be the Principle' (*omnia impune facere, hoc est regem esse*). And Louis XIV (1643–1714), author of the legendary phrase 'the State is Me' (*l'Etat, c'est moi*), wrote in his *Memoirs*: 'All power, all force is concentrated in the hands of the King, and there cannot be any other power in the Kingdom, except one established by Him.'[17]

In Baruch Spinosa's (1632–1677) *The Theological-Political Treatise* (*Tractatus Theologico-politicus*; published anonymously in 1670), one can encounter a phrase that could belong to his contemporary, same Louis XIV: 'The King is the State Itself' (*Rex est ipsa civitas*). In evaluation of Boris Chicherin, a prominent Russian legal scholar of the nineteenth century, this formula was not 'an insane glorification of absolutism, but rather an expression of an established political view, having its origins in [contemporary – *A.D.*] practice and philosophical thought'.[18]

The accent from rights to *duties* of the Monarch was shifted by an apologist of 'enlightened absolutism' Friedrich II of Prussia (1712–1786), who proclaimed a new principle: 'King is the first *servant* of the state' (*italics added – A.D*). D.M. Petrushevsky, the most influential Russian analyst of early English constitutional acts, wrote about a 'living consciousness of the Monarch's responsibility to the God for the people, trusted to Him by the Supreme Will'.[19] Emphasising the divine origin of the Royal Power, great Russian philosopher and legal thinker Ivan Aleksandrovich Ilyin (1883–1954), concluded: 'This is the very essence of monarchic law-consciousness that tsar is *a sacred person intimately related to God* and that this relation is the source of his emergency *powers*, as well as … of his exclusive *duties*, and his exclusive *responsibility*.'[20]

As we see, under classic absolutism, the Crown concentrated both executive and legislative powers in its hands, and did not require 'emergency powers' because prerogatives of the Crown were not really limited by any legal rules. The term 'absolute' itself gave countenance to the idea that the king had a large and indefinite reserve of power which he could on occasion use for the benefit of the state.

Evolution of 'emergency powers', as a legal institution, in European countries (first of all, in England) is inseparable from the development of the Rule of Law. As a public law institution, a 'state of emergency' began taking shape during these countries' transition from absolutist to constitutional monarchy.

British transition to the Rule of Law is probably the best illustration of this thesis.

The development of the Rule of Law in England is intimately linked to the rise of Parliament in the fourteenth to fifteenth centuries and its growing feud with the monarchy over the latter's pretension to absolute power. The real test took place in the seventeenth century, under the Stuart dynasty, both for Parliament and the judges. Absolutism reigned in Europe and it was quite natural for that time to claim, like an English jurist Dr John Cowell did, that the King was above the law and indeed above Parliament.[21] Another typical statement belonged to an English Judge Sir Robert Berkley: 'Law by itself is an old and trusted servant of kings which use it to rule the people. I've never heard or read about *Lex* as

Rex, but a widely spread and correct view is that *Rex* is *Lex*, because the former is *Lex loquens*, living, speaking and acting Law'.[22] In *Bates's Case* of 1606 (2 S.T. at 389), Judge C.B. Fleming used the famous Cicero's maxim and gave an unlimited definition to the 'absolute power of the king ... which is applied to the general benefit of the people and is *salus populi*'. In another case Judge J. Crawley again placed the Crown above the (parliamentary) law: 'In the king are two kinds of prerogative: *regale et legale*' (*R v Hampden, The Case of Ship-Money*, 1637 (3 S.T. at 1083)).

The Petition of Grievances presented to the king by the Commons in 1610 illustrates the many abuses that gave rise to complaints, including the royal proclamations, illegal taxes and special tribunals interfering with the common law. This seems to be the first document in which appears the expression 'Rule of Law', the concept in which the great British constitutionalist of the nineteenth century, Albert Venn Dicey, saw one of the basic principles of the English Constitution.[23] Said the *Petition*: 'Amongst many other points of happiness and freedom which your Majesty's subjects ... have enjoyed under ... Kings and Queens of the Realm, there is none which they have accounted more dear and precious than this, to be guided and *governed by certain rule of law* ... and not by any uncertain or arbitrary form of government ...'[24] (*italics added – A.D.*).

The first court decision on the Royal Prerogative in England – *R v Hampden*, also known as the *Ship-Money Case*, was made in 1637. Not by coincidence, it happened nine years after adoption of the *Petition of Rights* and 12 years before the Glorious (or 'Bourgeois', in Marxist lexicon) Revolution (and execution of King Charles I).

To take a step aside, it would be appropriate to note that there is an obvious parallel and a striking resemblance here with the Soviet Law, when the first-ever parliamentary statute regulating a 'legal regime of a state of emergency' was adopted in April 1990, or 73 years after Bolshevik Revolution in Russia and 20 months before disintegration of the USSR.

General antagonism between the Crown and the Parliament in the first part of the seventeenth century ('legislative supremacy involves not only the right to change the law but also that no one else should have that right'[25]) had a number of particular contradictions. A prominent English jurist, Professor of Oxford University William Anson, thus identified one of them: 'There should be a person or an institution capable of making immediate actions in sudden emergencies'.[26] *R v Hampden* (1637) became the precedent that initialised the process of legal solution of this contradiction, still topical in many countries of the world three-and-a-half centuries later.

The occasion for the court deliberations was the refusal to pay a special tax (in a form of the so-called 'ship money') by John Hampden (1594–1643).[27]

It is necessary to remind the reader that in the seventeenth century, the control of the Crown and Council over fiscal matters was far less extensive than in some other spheres of life. 'Even Henry VIII knew that he could not disregard the authority of Parliament in this department of government. But though the crown and Council did not dare to impose any general tax upon the nation, they managed, indirectly, to assume considerable powers over the raising of money.'[28] Ship-money was one of such 'indirect' taxes, levied even from inland towns in a national emergency (in time of 'danger to the Kingdom') to build, arm and furnish ships. Ship money had its origins in the eleventh century, in the Anglo-Saxon period of British history. Reimposition of the tax was proposed by Thomas Wentworth, a former leader of the parliamentary opposition who later defected to the Royal side, got a title of Earl Strafford, and was executed in 1640.[29] The idea was very smart, because a reimposition of a tax that had existed *before* creation of the Parliament could become a precedent of an actual introduction of a *new* tax, without Parliament's consent, but at the same time without formal violation of the Petition of Rights (granting the Parliament the 'power of the purse'). Moreover, the King could avoid this unpleasant (for him) necessity to convene the Parliament at all.

Annual levy of ships and ship-money first in the maritime towns and counties in 1634 – according to their estimated population and wealth – and then, in 1635, in the kingdom at large, as well as an 'emergency situation' caused by a 'revolt' in autonomous Scotland in 1637–1638 (after an attempt of Charles I to put it under a more rigid control) gave a reason to English nobility to suspect that the *temporary* tax can easily become a *permanent* one. Indeed, Lord Strafford advised Charles I 'to avoid a war for several years, so that his subordinates got used to the new tax, and he would become more powerful than all previous kings'.[30] For this very reason, although Hampden's share in the tax for citizens of Buckinghamphire was quite symbolic (20 shillings), he omitted to pay his share of the quota, and in November of 1637 was proceeded against in the Court of Exchequer.

In *Hampden's Case* a constitutional issue was raised, and the 'government made Hampden's a test case'.[31]

Hampden's counsel, Holborne, acknowledged that 'the Crown has the same power as private individual of taking all measures which are absolutely and immediately necessary for the purpose of dealing with an invasion or other emergency'. (Since then, this principle has been known as 'Holborne's argument'[32]). He also admitted that sometimes the 'existence of danger' would justify taking the subject's goods (confiscation of property) without his consent, but argued in his client's defence that such confiscation can be appropriate only in 'actual' as opposed to 'apprehended' or 'threatened' emergency'. If a ship has been damaged in a storm and is in a grave danger, the captain has a right to throw away the passengers' baggage, Holborne said. But if he sees that the storm is going away, the sun is coming out, and throws away the baggage, I doubt that the jury would find a reason to justify his actions.[33] Another counsel, Oliver St.

John, in his speech tried to place the Crown into the 'constitutional field', when he – quite poetically – suggested: 'His Majesty is the fountain of justice; and though all justice which is done within the realm flows from this fountain, yet it must run in certain and known channels.'[34]

The Crown conceded that the subject could not be taxed in normal circumstances without the consent of Parliament, but contended that the King was the sole judge of whether an emergency justified the exercise of his prerogative power to raise funds to meet a national danger.

Opinions in the Court of Exchequer split. Two judges condemned ship-money as illegal, and three others decided for Hampden on the ground that the procedure by which the Crown sought to enforce payment was inappropriate. On 10 February 1638, with a minimal difference of votes, seven to five, the Court made its decision in favour of the Crown, confirming its right 'to demand ships, men and stores – when necessary for the good and safety of the Kingdom – without Parliamentary authority'.[35] In the judgment, Justice Sir Robert Berkeley said, 'There are two maxims of the law of England, which plainly disprove Mr Holborne's supposed policy. The first is, "that the King is a person trusted with the state of the commonwealth". The second of these maxims is, "that the King cannot do wrong". Upon these two maxims the *jura summae majestatis* are grounded, with which none but the King himself (nor his high court of Parliament without leave) hath to meddle, as namely, war and peace, value of coin, Parliament at pleasure, power to dispense with penal laws, and divers others; amongst which I range these also, of regal power to command provision (in case of necessity) of means from the subjects, to be adjoined to the King's own means for the defence of the commonwealth, for the preservation of the *salus reipublicae*. Otherwise I do not understand how the King's Majesty may be said to have the majestical right and power of a free monarch.'[36]

Technically, in a formal sense, Hampden lost the case, but, in reality, didn't feel defeated.[37] On the contrary, according to Sir Lindsay David Keir, 'most men' regarded the judicial decision in the *Case of Ship-Money* 'as grotesque and dangerous', although not 'obviously and indefensibly wrong'.[38] Only three years later, in 1640, the Long Parliament would adopt the Shipmoney Act reversing the ship-money judging, and declaring the levy to have been illegal from the beginning and forbidding its future imposition. The struggle for supremacy would be concluded by the *Bill of Rights*. Article 4 of the Bill declared that it was illegal for the Crown to seek to raise money without parliamentary approval. But first it was in 1637, when *R v Hampden* created a precedent, according to which, on an initiative of a common citizen, the King's policy could be questioned in the Court. Thus, the 'royal prerogative was subject to the law'.[39]

For this study, *R v Hampden* is of special significance for two major reasons. First, it corroborates the thesis that legal regulation of 'emergency powers' became an important element of the British transition to the Rule of Law, inseparable from this transition. Second, it indicates that the principle that no emergency can justify executive usurpation of legislative authority is well-recognised in British constitutional law.[40]

However, it was not until the middle and second half of the nineteenth century that most European countries passed their first *legislation* regulating the legal regime of a state of emergency. France did so in 1848, Prussia in 1851, Austria-Hungary in 1869, Spain in 1870, Russia in 1881.

There is a certain time correlation between growing attention of European lawmakers to this legal institution and activation of the political struggle of the European proletariat. Back in 1852, in his famous book, *The Eighteenth Brumaire of Louis Bonaparte* (*Der achtzehnte Brumaire des Louis Bonaparte*), Karl Marx sarcastically observed, 'The forefathers of these worthy republicans had sent their symbol, the tricolour, on a tour through Europe. In their turn, these contemporary republicans made a discovery which spontaneously journeyed all over the Continent, but returned ever and again with renewed joy to the land of its birth, until it had acquired the right of domicile in half the departments of France. I refer to *the state of siege*. A glorious invention, this, turned to account at intervals in every successive crisis that has occurred during the revolution.'[41]

It's noteworthy to mention that – as with the original and modern meanings of 'dictatorship' – a 'state of siege' in the French context of the nineteenth century certainly differs from its contemporary meaning. If today, under national legislation of countries of the world, it's only one of the forms of a state of emergency, not necessarily the strictest one, in France a 150 years ago, it was a synonym of 'martial law'. Under it, the authority ordinarily vested in the civil power for the maintenance of the social peace and public order passed entirely to the army (*autorite militaire*), and military tribunals suspended ordinary law. In 1885, A.V. Dicey proudly wrote that Britain has 'nothing equivalent' to the 'state of siege' in France and that 'this is an unmistakable proof of the permanent supremacy of the law under our constitution'.[42]

The U.S. Founding Fathers radically broke with the European tradition of placing the war and emergency powers in the hands of the monarch and 'vested *all* executive powers in the Continental Congress'.[43] Article IX of the first national constitution, the Articles of Confederation, said, 'The United States, in Congress assembled, shall have the sole and exclusive right and *power of determining on peace and war*'[44] (*italics added – A.D.*) The authority of the Continental Congress extended to both 'perfect' and 'imperfect' wars – or to those that were formally *declared* by Congress and those that were merely *authorised*. The Federal Court of Appeals defined that the first kind of war 'destroys the national peace and tranquillity, and lays the foundation of every possible act of hostility', whereas an 'imperfect' war 'does not entirely destroy the public tranquillity, but interferes it in some particulars, as in the case of reprisals' (1782).[45] According to the U.S. Constitution of 1787, the U.S. Congress not only has the power 'to declare war, grant letters of marque and reprisal, and make rules concerning captures on land and water', it was also authorised 'to raise and support armies', 'provide and maintain a navy', 'make rules for the government and regulation of the land and naval forces', 'provide for calling forth the militia to execute the laws of the union, suppress insurrections and repel invasions', and 'to provide for the organizing, arming, and disciplining of the militia, and for governing such part of them as may be employed in the Service of the United States' (Article I, section 8).[46]

The intent of many delegates at the Philadelphia Convention not to grant the war and emergency powers to the President was not unopposed. Expressing his constitutional and political views in a series of articles, later united (with the articles by James Madison and John Jay) as the *Federalist* (or the *Federalist Papers*), Alexander Hamilton (1757–1804) categorically argued against those who considered a 'vigorous' Executive 'inconsistent' and incompatible with the 'genius of republican government'. Hamilton was certainly a defender of the 'legal' dictatorship and, like Machiavelli before him, reminded his opponents of the 'Roman story', and 'how often that republic was obliged to take refuge in the absolute power of a single man, under the formidable title of Dictator, as well against the intrigues of ambitious individuals who aspired to the tyranny, and the seditions of whole classes of the community whose conduct threatened the existence of all government, as against the invasions of external enemies who menaced the conquest and destruction of Rome' (No.70. March 18, 1788. The Executive Department Further Considered).[47]

Charles Pinckney, John Rutledge, Roger Sherman, James Wilson, Edmund Randolph, and especially James Madison disagreed with Hamilton. Madison insisted on separating the power of the President to 'conduct war' from the power of Congress to 'declare war'. According to him, 'Those who are to *conduct a war* cannot in the nature of things, be proper or safe judges, whether *a war ought* to be *commenced, continued*, or *concluded*. They are barred from the latter functions by a great principle in free government, analogous to that which separates the sword from the purse, or the power of executing from the power of enacting laws'.[48] In other words, Madison decisively adhered to 'the cardinal tenet of republican ideology that the conjoined wisdom of many is superior to that of one'.[49] As Madison explained in the *Federalist*: 'The accumulation of all powers, in the same hands, may justly be pronounced the very definition of tyranny' (No.47. The Particular Structure of the New Government and the Distribution of Power Among Its Different Parts).[50]

James Madison and Elbridge Gerry helped to reach a compromise. They moved to counterbalance the power of Congress to 'declare war' with the President's power 'to repel sudden attack'. The motion was initially adopted by seven votes to two, and in the final count, as nine to one.[51]

To complete the picture, it's necessary to mention the decision of the

U.S. Supreme Court in the case of *Talbot v Seeman* (1801) that supported and confirmed the provisions of Article I, section 8 of the U.S. Constitution. Chief Justice John Marshall wrote for the Court, 'The whole powers of war being, by the constitution of the United States, vested in congress, the acts of that body can alone be resorted as our guides in this inquiry'.[52]

That explains the position of Louis Fisher, a Senior Specialist of the U.S. Congressional Research Service and leading American expert in the subject, who argued that President Clinton's statement (at a press conference on 3 August 1994) that he was not 'constitutionally mandated' to receive approval from Congress before invading Haiti, 'would have astonished the framers of the Constitution'. It's hard to disagree with Fisher's observation: 'the trend of presidential war power since World War II – the last congressionally declared war – collides with the constitutional framework adopted by the founding fathers'. The period after 1945 created a climate in which Presidents have regularly breached constitutional principles and democratic values. Under these pressures (and invitations) – concluded Louis Fisher – 'Presidents have routinely exercised war powers with little or no involvement by Congress'.[53]

II

A state of emergency is subject to regulation by law. But what is an 'emergency' and what is a 'state of emergency? How can they be defined in legal terms?

In the previous subchapter, the author used different definitions: 'emergency powers', 'war powers', a 'state of emergency', a 'national emergency'. Do these terms mean *different* legal institutions or are they variations of just *one*? Is there a way out from this vicious circle, once described by Gerhard Casper: 'Challenged to define "emergency" one feels inclined to answer: "An emergency is an emergency, is an emergency ..."'?[54]

Two out of four explanations of the word 'emergency' (from Latin *emergentia*), contained in a fundamental 13-volume *Oxford English Dictionary*, relate to the subject of this study. One definition describes emergency as, 'the arising, sudden or unexpected occurrence (of a state of things, an event, etc.)' The next relevant definition says, 'a juncture that arises of "turns up"; a state of things unexpectedly arising and urgently demanding immediate action ... Hence sometimes used for: Urgency, pressing need'. *The New Bantam English Dictionary* gives only one definition of an 'emergency': a 'sudden or unexpected happening, demanding prompt action. Synonyms – exigency, crisis, necessity, pass, conjuncture ... These words agree in the idea of naming a pressing state of affairs.'[55]

In the legal context, the oldest law dictionaries, Gilmer's *Law Dictionary* and Kinney's *Law Dictionary and Glossary*, don't mention the term 'emergency' or its variations at all.[56] However, several others, including

Bouvier's *Law Dictionary and Concise Encyclopaedia*, Black's *Definitions of the Terms and Phrases of American and English Jurisprudence, Ancient and Modern*, Ballentine's *Law Dictionary with Pronounciations*, and *The Cyclopedic Law Dictionary*, do.[57] But in them all these terms and definitions have either extremely broad or vague descriptions. For instance, 'emergency is an unforeseen *combination of circumstances* that calls for immediate action'; or 'an *event* which . . . is *unusual and unexpected*', etc.). In other instances the definitions are too narrow and technical (referring to 'medical service', 'tort', 'negligence', 'trusts for the benefit of the widow of a testator', etc.). None of them define or consider 'emergency' as a 'constitutional mechanism' or a 'constitutional institution' (*italics added – A.D.*).

'National Emergency', as defined by the Black's *Law Dictionary*, is a 'state of national crisis; a situation demanding immediate and extraordinary national or federal action'.[58] That definition is certainly closer to the subject of this research, but it's also described as a '*crisis*' or a '*situation* demanding . . . action', rather than this very 'immediate and extraordinary national or federal *action*' or the legal (constitutional) *regime* under which such 'action' is accomplished (*italics added – A.D.*).

Out of all the definitions, only one is relevant for the purposes of this study – 'Emergency Measures', as described in Ballentine's *Law Dictionary*: '*Acts performed* in an emergency. 38 Am 1st Negl, para. 41. *Legislation enacted* in an emergency; laws necessary for the immediate preservation of the public peace, health, or safety. 28 Am J Rev edn Init & R, para. 10. *Statutes* which, because of the existence of an emergency as declared in the legislation, do by their terms take effect immediately, or from or after their passage, or from or after their approval by the governor. 50 Am J1st Stat, para. 491–493. *A municipal ordinance* relating to the preservation of public peace, property, health, safety, or morals, taking effect, according to its terms, immediately upon passage. 37 Am J1st Mun Corp, para.152'[59] (*italics added – A.D.*).

The concept of a state of emergency corresponds with the doctrine of 'civil necessity'. In private law, necessity is well-established as 'a legal defence for an action which would have been otherwise unlawful and actionable'.[60] Thus, where life is in danger, the necessity of saving it may justify action which will ordinarily be unlawful, such as throwing cargo overboard from a sinking boat in order to save the lives of passengers and crew, or a doctor performing an abortion (where an abortion is outlawed) to save the life of a pregnant woman. The doctrine is also recognised as a justification for an action necessary to preserve the life of the state or society, albeit otherwise unlawful.

When appealing to her colleagues to 'decide on our terminology: some say "a state of emergency", others "martial law", still others "a state of siege", "an extraordinary regime", and so on', and insisting that '*foreign legislation has only one term* for it: "a state of emergency"'[61] (*italics added*

– A.D.), a Soviet scholar Inga Mikhailovskaya made an apparent mistake. In reality, legislation of the countries of the world has *numerous terms* for a 'state of emergency':

- *state of emergency* (or just 'emergency') – Russia, Canada, Belarus, Georgia, Moldova, Ukraine, Latvia, Lithuania, Turkey, Hungary, Poland, Bulgaria, Finland, Albania, Romania, Slovenia, Slovakia, Portugal, Macedonia, Estonia; and its variations: internal state of emergency – Germany; national emergency – USA, Ireland, or a 'state of national emergency' (*estado de emergencia nacional*) – Ecuador; public order emergency – Canada; international emergency – Canada, USA; state of economic emergency – Colombia;
- *state of siege* – Belgium, France, Argentina, Brazil, Panama, Portugal (declared only in time of actual or imminent war or rebellion), Chile, Colombia, Venezuela, Turkey, Romania, Spain, Bolivia, Portugal, Mali, Hungary, Netherlands, Cote d'Ivoire, Gabon, Senegal, Congo;
- *state of exception* – Spain, Chile, Paraguay, Peru, Colombia (*el estado de excepcion*), Algeria (*etat d'exception*);
- *martial law* – Great Britain, USA, India, Netherlands, Poland, Lithuania, Cyprus, China, Russia, Ukraine, Cape Verde, Bulgaria, Yugoslavia, Czech Republic, South Korea, Thailand, Indonesia, Jordan, Kuwait, Philippines, Bangladesh, Pakistan, Vietnam, or 'a state of martial law' – Armenia (*la loi martiale*);
- *state of internal disturbance* (*el estado de conmocion interior*) – Colombia;
- *state of public stress* – Italy;
- *state of tension* – Germany;
- *state of assembly* (*el estado de asamblea*) – Chile;
- *state of defence* – Germany, Brazil, Costa Rica, Finland;
- *state of alarm* – Spain;
- *state of catastrophe* (*en estado de catastrophe*) – Chile;
- *state of alert* (*l'etat d'alerte*) – Gabon;
- *state of readiness* – Finland, Norway, Gabon;
- *situation of public danger* – Hungary (less serious than that required for a state of emergency);
- *state of natural disaster* – Poland;
- *state of peril* – Hungary;
- *regime of full powers* (*regime des pleines pouvoirs*) – Switzerland;
- *regime of strict necessity* (*regime de stricte necessite*) – Switzerland;
- *prompt measures of security* – Uruguay.

France, Great Britain, many countries of the British Commonwealth, and some other states by a tradition don't give a precise name to a 'state of exception' and use an indefinite term *emergency powers*.

Constitutions of nearly all countries of the world contain provisions about a *state of war* or a 'state of foreign war' (*el Estado de Guerra Exterior*) – Colombia.

However, it would be wrong to regard all these regimes should be considered *different* legal institutions. Some constitutions provide for several exceptional regimes: in Chile they are states of siege, exception, assembly, and emergency; in Spain – states of alarm, siege, and exception; in Germany – states of tension, defence, and internal state of emergency, in Hungary – states of war, emergency, extreme danger, and peril. A group of American authors have recently observed that '"inherent" powers, "implied" powers, "incidental" powers, "plenary" powers, "war" powers and "emergency" powers are used, often interchangeably and without fixed or ascertainable meanings'.[62] Black's *Law Dictionary* also recognises that 'Congress has made little or no distinction between a "state of national emergency" and a "state of war"' (*Brown v Bernstein*, D.C.Pa., 49 F.Supp. 728, 732).[63]

The last observations are right not only as far as the U.S. constitutional system is concerned. They can be easily used to describe the situation in most countries of the world. The term a 'state of emergency' (or 'public emergency') embraces the central concept of a variety of legal terms in different legal systems to identify an exceptional situation of public danger permitting the exercise of crisis-management powers. This terminology therefore covers the status of different regimes known as states of siege, alert, readiness, etc. It also includes what is described as martial rule (which itself has a variety of euphemisms, the most important being 'martial law') as it is known in the common law countries of the erstwhile British Empire and the USA, as well as a 'state of siege', as it is known in civil law countries of continental Europe and Latin America. Indeed, characteristics of a state of siege (as in Argentina) or of a state of alarm (as in Spain) are practically identical, respectively, to those as of a state of defence (as in Germany) or emergency powers (as in Great Britain and elsewhere). Thus, this is not a question of diverse legal institutions, but of *diverse forms* of a *generic concept* of a 'state of emergency' (or a 'state of exception').

The terms that are used in legislation of various countries to describe 'emergency regimes' are 'of no concern to international law' either.[64] All these regimes are covered by a generic term of a 'state of emergency', introduced when the 'life of the nation' is 'threatened', as described in multiple international covenants, charters and declarations.

By our definition, a state of emergency is a constitutionally regulated situation, when the state power is exercised in special constitutional order and in accordance with an extraordinary constitutional procedure.

Respectively, a constitutional mechanism of a state of emergency is a system of mutually correlated and co-ordinated legal norms (elements of the mechanism) regulating:

a   *goals and aims* of a state of emergency ('norms-goals', 'norms-tasks',

and 'norms-principles', as they are called in Russian Constitutional
Law);
b　*reasons and conditions* for introduction of a state of emergency;
c　*state organ* (or organs) empowered to declare a state of emergency;
d　*procedure* of its imposition, extension (or prolongation), and termina-
　　tion;
e　its *limits* (in time and space);
f　*special regime* of functioning of governmental bodies, enterprises,
　　organisations, corporations and private citizens, involving certain
　　derogations from normal human rights standards and imposition of
　　certain duties and responsibilities; limits of such derogations and
　　impositions; guarantees of human rights and freedoms and respons-
　　ibility of the officials under a state of emergency; when necessary –
　　introduction of different forms of a state of emergency in various loca-
　　tions and legal regulation of the difference between them;
g　*in federations* – temporary alterations in the distribution of functions,
　　powers and competence among the different organs of the Federation
　　and its Units;
h　*other* changes and alterations in the system of social and economic
　　relations in the country in the period of a declared state of emergency.

When speaking about a 'constitutional mechanism' of a state of emergency, I don't mean a combination of legal norms concentrated *exclusively*
in the texts of Basic Laws and Constitutions. The reason why some norms
or institutions acquire *constitutional* meaning is because of the most fundamental ('constitutional') consequences of their implementation. This interpretation allows us, for instance, to speak about a 'constitutional
mechanism' of emergency powers in Great Britain, which doesn't have a
'written constitution' or in the United States, where the constitution never
mentions a 'state of emergency' and the President's right to introduce a
national emergency is based on his 'inherent' or 'implied' powers.

Legal mechanism of a state of emergency usually belongs to a 'grey
zone' (or even a 'twilight zone') of any legal system. It is regulated by
norms of various spheres of law that include constitutional law, administrative law, criminal law, civil law, etc.

The essence and content of the institution are contradictory. On the
one hand, since it's impossible to foresee in detail all the crises and emergency situations and since they demand immediate and decisive actions
not leaving too much time for thorough juridical analysis in accordance
with a strict procedure, then the executive might be granted quite wide
and vague powers. On the other hand, such an extension of not always
precisely defined and restricted powers of the executive might create
another danger and provoke the government to 'put an end' to a critical
situation through repressive measures rather then to try to find its legal
solution.

'There is not anything in the world more abused than this sentence, *Salus populi suprema lex esto*', Mark M. Stavsky polemically generalised.[65] 'Often, the cry of freedom has been a cover for the use of force', a former U.S. Attorney-General Ramsey Clark agreed.[66] Allan Rosas expressed the same view even in a more straight-forward manner: 'That they ["public emergencies" – *A.D.*] pose a formidable risk to a system of human rights, democracy and the rule of law needs no further explanation here.'[67]

In other words, as an extremely sharp instrument, in a concrete political situation, the institution of a state of emergency can be used in pursuit of diametrically opposite goals: for maintenance or restoration of democratic foundations of social life, or for their repressive suppression and establishment of a dictatorial regime.

Contradictory character of emergency powers and national emergencies predetermined an uneasy attitude of different social groups and forces to this legal institution and to practice of its use. The situation is even more complicated, because that attitude could radically change in relatively short periods of time depending on shifting position of those very groups and forces in the system of power co-ordinates in the state. As an example, it would be appropriate to remind the readers of sharp criticism by Russian Social Democrats aimed against the emergency law, '*Ordinance on Measures for the Preservation of the State Order and Public Tranquillity*' of 14 August 1881, that was regulating an imposition of a 'state of exception' on the territory of the Russian Empire. A 'Founding Father' of Soviet Russia Vladimir I. Ulyanov (Lenin) called the Ordinance 'one of the most stable, basic laws of the Russian Empire'.[68] But when the state power fell into the hands of revolutionaries in October 1917, they automatically reconsidered their attitude to the institution, and under the slogan of the 'necessity to defend the Revolution' immediately began using it with a whole combination of the most typical 'excesses'. Symbolically, even the titles of the Communist emergency decrees of 1923 and 1926, '*On Emergency Measures for the Preservation of the Revolutionary Order*', resembled the title of the tsarist law of 1881. The only difference between them, as we can see, was a replacement of the goal of the imperial law (protection of the 'state' interests) with the necessity to preserve interests of the 'revolution'.

As a more recent example, Russian area specialists may recall a collision caused by a January 1991 decree of the USSR President Mikhail Gorbachev authorising the Soviet army and Interior Ministry troops to conduct joint patrols with local police for maintaining public order in the cities. At that time, new 'democratic' politicians of Russia, the largest and most powerful USSR republic, was actively pushing a process known as a 'parade of sovereignties' and 'war of laws' and portrayed the decree as an 'emergency measure', that potentially could be used against political opponents of the USSR President, and appealed to the Constitutional Supervision Committee[69] to study the constitutionality of the decree. In

April 1991, the constitutional watchdog reached its decision and declared that the decree was a violation of the USSR Constitution of 1977 and RSFSR Constitution of 1978. Subsequently, the decree was repealed, but half a year later (even before dissolution of the USSR), when Russian radical 'democrats' concentrated enough power in their hands, they made emergency measures the basis of their activities in political and especially economic spheres.[70]

Another important detail should not be overlooked. For many decades, there was no place in Soviet Law for an objective, unbiased study of the legal mechanism of a state of emergency. The dogmatic view on the nature of the Soviet society (especially after it was proclaimed in the new Communist Party Programme of 1961 that the Soviet society had entered the stage of 'developed socialism'), as a 'conflictless society' made any serious research of 'emergency powers' irrelevant. Indeed, what need is there of 'emergency' powers in a society of class harmony? Communist ideology made it practically impossible to study this sophisticated and contradictory legal institution *per se*, as a phenomenon (with *all* its numerous aspects and elements) that exists in nearly all legal systems of the world. Research of Soviet scholars was forced to a narrow mould of criticism of this institution in foreign legislation: as a repressive element of an alien and hostile 'bourgeois' state mechanism.

There was no lack of such criticism in publications of Soviet legal scholars and political scientists. Provisions on a state of emergency were usually described as a 'typical feature of oligarchic tendencies in bourgeois constitutions', and as a 'concentrated form of ... violent, repressive measures'. It was argued that 'by facilitating the imposition of *fascist rule* in imperialist countries',[71] emergency legislation 'legally unbinds hands of the bourgeoisie in political struggle' and enables it (the bourgeoisie) 'to ignore parliamentary democracy, bourgeois legality and existing law'. A subtitle of another article says it all: 'A State of Emergency is an Instrument of Destruction of Bourgeois Democracy'. It was finally concluded that emergency legislation and a state of emergency (as a legal institution) inevitably lead to 'frankly arbitrary rule, police repression, and governmental abuse'[72] (*italics added – A.D.*).

Already in 1989, V.N. Danilenko was still insisting that 'the institution of emergency powers of a head of the state is clearly a violation of any democratic norms and principles ... The fact of constitutional regulation of such institution is an evident sign of an erosion of one of the most important principles, laid down in the period of bourgeois revolutions and forming the basis of the regime of bourgeois democracy'. (Another legal institution, which, in Danilenko's opinion, provided 'wide opportunities for an assault on rights and freedoms' was 'judicial constitutional review'). A collective of Soviet authors came to the following conclusion in 1968: an introduction of a state of emergency creates a 'regime of complete freedom of actions, violates bourgeois legality and existing law', and 'leads to a considerable break-up of parliamentary forms of organisation of an imperialist state'.[73]

To be fair, it's necessary to admit that there was a room for similar criticism of the institution of emergency powers and a state of emergency among American authors too. President of Princeton University, Harold W. Dodds, for instance, objected to the use of any power as an emergency measure. To him it was just the 'old, old answer given throughout history by those who cannot have their own way'. Walter Lippman, in his book *An Inquiry into the Principles of the Good Society*, made an excessive liberal generalisation that 'fascism is martial law'.[74] In reality, 'fascism' is not necessarily 'martial law', and 'martial law' *per se* doesn't have much to do with 'fascism'.

Indeed, legal and political experience of a number of countries of the world, for instance, Germany in the 1930s, some states of Latin America, Asia, and Africa, knows many examples of *de jure* and *de facto* emergencies, which served as a 'smokescreen for repressive governmental policies'.[75] It's hard to disagree with a Spanish Jesuit priest and profound legal scholar Jaime Oraa when he wrote: 'In the last decades the gravest violations of fundamental human rights have occurred in the context of states of emergency. In these situations, States, using the emergency as an excuse, frequently deny the application of basic standards and take derogating measures which are excessive and in violation of international treaties on human rights.'[76]

In an advisory opinion on *Habeas Corpus in Emergency Situations*, the Inter-American Court of Human Rights stated the following: 'It cannot be denied that under certain circumstances, the suspension of guarantees may be the only way to deal with emergency situations and, thereby, to preserve the highest values of a democratic society. The Court cannot, however, ignore the fact that abuses may result from the application of emergency measures not objectively justified in the light of the requirements prescribed in Article 27 [of the American Convention on Human Rights – *A.D.*] and the principles contained in other here relevant instruments. This has, in fact, been the experience of our hemisphere.'[77]

French scholars, M. Michel Ameller (who subsequently became a member of the French Constitutional Council) and J. Vedel, argued in their works that national emergencies sometimes 'justify a step back from the constitutional legality', force 'competent state bodies, parliament in particular, out of the political game', and, as a result, lead to a 'substitution of "official" constitution' with an unconstitutional regime.[78]

Yet, two questions arise. Were the cases mentioned in the previous two paragraphs (suspension of guarantees, breakdown of constitutional legality, etc.) *caused* by the existence of legislation on emergency powers? Is it really so that arbitrary rule, governmental abuses, police repression, and extra-judicial punishment are *immanent* characteristics of a legal regime of a state of emergency, inseparable from the latter? The answer is no, of course. In reality, it is the other way round. 'Clauses in constitutions providing for regimes of exception did not cause violence and dictatorship'.[79] Regulation of the institution of a state of emergency with a parliamentary act, and not with sub-laws (executive decrees and directives or agency regulations), is usually a good evidence of fairly high legal and political levels of a society. It is also usually an indication of a high level of protection of civil rights and freedoms in such a society.

It was a horrifying discovery of the U.S. Senate Special Committee on the Termination of the National Emergency in 1973 when it was disclosed that the four proclamations of 1933, 1950, 1970 and 1971 declaring 'national emergency' in the USA (mentioned in Introduction) had brought to life 'at least 470 significant emergency powers' executive orders. Each of them 'without time limitations' delegated to the Executive 'extensive discretionary powers, ordinarily exercised by the Legislature, which affect the lives of American citizens in a host of all-encompassing ways'.[80] Among other things, the President could seize property and commodities, organise and control production, institute martial law, call to active duty 2.5 million reservists, assign military forces abroad, seize and control all means of transportation and communications, restrict travel and 'in many other ways, manage every aspect of the lives of all American citizens'. The laws made no provision for congressional oversight nor did they reserve to Congress a means for terminating the 'temporary' emergencies that triggered them into use.[81]

In 1976, U.S. Congress passed the National Emergencies Act[82] to define and restrict the use of presidential emergency powers. Its general idea was to terminate emergency authorities two years from the date the act became law (14 September 1976). In the future, the President must publish the declaration in the Federal Register. Congress can terminate the national emergency by passing a concurrent resolution. To prevent emergencies from lingering for decades without congressional attention or action, the 1976 Law included an action-forcing mechanism. No later than six months after a national emergency is declared by the President, and at least every six months thereafter while the emergency continues, each House of Congress is supposed to meet to consider a vote on a concurrent resolution to determine whether the state of emergency should be terminated.[83] The next year, one more law was passed, the International Emergency Economic Powers Act,[84] that was aimed at limiting the extensive economic powers granted to the President in peacetime emergencies by section 5(b) of the Trading with the Enemy Act of 1917.[85] The purpose of adoption of the named acts by the U.S. Congress was certainly justified and understandable.[86] That's exactly the purpose of *parliamentary legislation* on emergency powers to provide *legal* opportunities for the immediate undertaking of effective measures to normalise public life, supply people's needs and restore and maintain public order. All the basic legal relations in a period of a state of emergency must be regulated by a *previ-ously adopted parliamentary statute* not hampering the executive's ability to react promptly to a changing critical situation, but, on the other hand, rigidly and precisely specifying all admissible ways of such reaction.

It's amazing to what extent something that was written (or pronounced) some five centuries ago can still be relevant in modern times. The follow-ing passage is from Machiavelli, 'In a well-ordered republic it should never be necessary to resort to extra-constitutional measures; for although they may for the time be beneficial, yet the precedent is pernicious, for if the practice is once established of disregarding the laws for good objects, they will in a little while be disregarded under the pretext for evil purposes. Thus *no republic will ever be perfect if she has not by law provided for everything, having a remedy for every emergency, and fixed rules for apply-ing it*' (*Discourses*, I, 34)[87] (*italics added – A.D.*). Nothing can be added here. Whether we like it or not, we still live today in the shadow of this Florentine, as commentators of Machiavelli would say.

An important conclusion can be made at this point. Failure to adopt a parliamentary statute on emergency powers and national emergencies, on the one hand, may doom the government and administrative bodies to indecisiveness and inaction precisely when they must act without delay to assure national security and defend public order or the constitutional system itself, or, on the other hand, may prompt the government to take unwarranted measures in the absence of a relevant law. A parliamentary statute (which was drafted, discussed and adopted by the legislature and signed into effect by the chief executive long in advance) can help avoid both.

For this very reason, there is a growing tendency in constitutionalism in the world today to incorporate provisions on national emergencies into the texts of the constitutions, and to regulate a 'state of exception' on an even higher (than a parliamentary statute) *constitutional* level.

Authors of a Russian encyclopaedic dictionary, *Political Science*, are wrong when they say that constitutions of only two countries of the world, France and Germany, contain provisions for introduction of a 'state of emergency' (a 'constitutional dictatorship', as they call it).[88] Some 30 years ago, in my count, there were about 25 countries of the world that did *not* include emergency provisions in their constitutions (or Basic Laws): Syria, Turkey, Iran, Afghanistan, Saudi Arabia, Libya, Burundi, Kenya, Congo (with the capital of Leopoldville), Guinea, Liberia, Uruguay, and several others. Now, not more than a dozen of such national constitutions are left. They include some of the oldest constitutions of the world (those of USA (1787), Belgium (1831, 'co-ordinated' in 1994), New Zealand (Act on Con-stitution, 1852), Australia (1900), Mexico (Political Constitution, 1917), Austria (Federal Constitutional Law of 1920, in edition of 1929), Lebanon (1926), Japan (1946) and United Republic of Tanzania (1977)) or devia-tions like the Constitution of Bosnia & Herzegovina (adopted as Annex 4 of the Dayton Peace Accords, initiated in Dayton on 21 November 1995, came into effect with the signing in Paris on 14 December 1995).

The Constitution of Cuba of 1976 was probably the latest constitution that was amended with a norm regulating an introduction of a state of emergency. Article 67 empowered the President to declare a state of emergency (*estado de emergencia*) on his own authority. Articles 101 and 119 created the National Defence Council and its equivalents at the provincial, regional, and municipal levels to manage war time, military preparedness and states of emergency. New provisions were considered and adopted in July 1992, in a whole package of other amendments changing 76 articles of the Constitution overall (or 60 per cent of the whole text of the Constitution!) Other changes included abolishment of a commitment to an atheistic state, and of a social-class definition of the state. New amendments required direct elections to the National Assembly, provided guarantees of non-discrimination to religious believers, and promoted the market-oriented economic reforms implemented during the 1990s. Even anti-Castro Cuban emigres in the U.S. had to admit that the 1992 amendments were a 'significant advance over the 1976 text'. Creation of a mechanism of a state of emergency in Cuba became an integral part of such 'advance'.[89]

Incorporation of provisions regulating the institution of a state of emergency into Constitutions (that, by their nature, demanding a special, more complicated procedure of their changes and amendments than ordinary parliamentary acts) is a guarantee against possible misuse by the executive of its emergency powers. Especially when dealing with the circumstances that don't constitute emergency situations by their essence.

In this respect, like in many other cases, American constitutional law and constitutional experience is more an exception than a rule. The United States has traditionally followed the common law 'necessity' approach to dealing with emergency powers. As it has already been mentioned, unlike most of other constitutions of the world, the U.S. constitution technically does not contain a 'state of emergency' provision. There are no explicit constitutional norms providing for any general emergency rule. The only two passages in the constitution that have some relation to a state of exception are Article I, section 8(15) permitting the national government to call out the militia to 'suppress Insurrections and repel Invasions', and Article I, section 9(2), also known as the called *Habeas Corpus* Clause which provides that the writ of *habeas corpus* shell not be suspended, 'unless when in Cases of Rebellion or Invasion the public Safety may require it'.[90]

On the other hand, the U.S. constitutional system is probably the only one that contains a concept of 'inherent powers' (also known as 'prerogative powers'), as an authority vested in the national government that 'does not depend upon *any specific grant of power in the Constitution*'. A similar doctrine of 'implied powers', derived from the 'necessary and proper' clause in Article I, section 8, empowers the U.S. government to do '*all things* necessary and proper to carry out its delegated powers'[91] (*italics added – A.D.*). This principle was officially enunciated by the Supreme Court in *McCulloch v Maryland*, 4 Wheaton 316 (1819).[92]

Using their 'inherent' powers, many presidents have taken unauthorised actions to handle emergency situations, most notably Abraham Lincoln during the Civil War (initiated without declaration of war against the secessionist South). Suspension of the writ of *habeas corpus* was not the only measure undertaken by President Lincoln. He summoned troops and paid them out of the Treasury without appropriation therefore; proclaimed a naval blockade of the Confederacy and ordered their ships to be seized. Without any statutory authority Lincoln issued his famous Emancipation Proclamation and directed the seizure of rail and telegraph lines leading to Washington.[93] Subsequently, it was asserted by the U.S. Supreme Court in *Dames & Moore v Regan*, 453 U.S. 654 (1981) that the 'failure of Congress specifically to delegate authority does not "especially ... in the areas of foreign policy and national security" imply Congressional disapproval of action taken by the executive.'[94]

When describing numerous examples of wide-spread statutory unauthorised actions of the U.S. Chief Executive (like the use of federal troops by President Hayes during the Railroad Strike of 1877 and by President Cleveland in the Pullman Strike of 1895 (even though Governor of Illinois Altgeld disclaimed the need for supplemental troops), President Theodore Roosevelt's acute readiness to seize Pennsylvania coal mines if a coal shortage necessitated such action; various emergency measures of President Franklin Roosevelt,[95] etc.), American authors prefer to use a politically correct term 'executive leadership' and conclude that U.S. 'Presidents have taken prompt action to enforce the laws and protect the country whether or not Congress happened to provide in advance for the particular method of execution ... The fact that Congress and the courts have consistently recognised and given their support to such executive action indicates that such a power of seizure have been accepted throughout our history.'[96]

Overall, 'inherent powers' so often have been used throughout the U.S. constitutional history, that it was argued that 'it is unlikely that the national government, or the United States as a nation, could have emerged as a powerful force had the more limited view prevailed' that the government is to exercise only those powers expressly delegated to it in the Constitution.[97]

That's only within the framework of the 'inherent powers' concept that the following statement could be made: 'On occasion it becomes necessary for a democratic government to act without the express permission of its citizens or even all of its elected officials. Extraordinary events may create unique situations for which there are no explicit constitutional grants, public laws, or legal precedents. It is at these times that the principles of self-government are sorely tested. For it is at these times that a government must act beyond formal constitutional control for the public good or even for the sake of survival. Clearly, extraordinary powers can be abused to the detriment of liberties and civil rights; yet, necessity dictates the exercise of emergency powers, at times, in any republic.'[98]

It's hard to disagree with Daniel P. Franklin that 'necessity dictates the exercise of emergency powers, at times, in any republic'. However, the scholar seems to give an unreasonably and inadequately broad definition to the concept of 'necessity'. According to Franklin, 'it is at these times that a government must act *beyond* formal *constitutional control*' (*italics added – A.D.*). It's quite understandable that after an 'attack on America' of 11 September 2001 this approach is shared by a significant and influential segment of the U.S. political elite. Yet, the times of Oliver Cromwell who stated in his speech to Parliament on 12 September 1654, that 'necessity hath no law',[99] seem to be over. Emergency powers, including introduction of a state of exception, cannot and should not be exercised 'beyond constitutional control'. It's true that in many countries of the world, even constitutional provisions cannot always firmly and effectively contain dictatorial instincts of authorities. But that's not a justification to lift 'constitutional control' altogether. On the contrary, it's quite easy to imagine what would happen if this last obstacle, the Constitution, were to be removed from the way of some politicians and social forces thirsting for the unlimited power.

In their book, *Constitutional Law* (originally published in the 1940s, and translated into Russian in 1950), British scholars E.C.S. Wade and G. Godfrey Phillips argued that 'it was always recognised that when the state is in danger, the Executive should be *granted* special powers'[100] (*italics added – A.D.*). Sixty years later, it can be stated that this point of view is no longer based on either national legislation of an overwhelming majority of the countries of the world or on international law. It would be more adequate to say now that 'special powers' are not 'granted' to the Executive 'when the state is in danger', as if a 'danger' is a source of such powers or that a 'danger' creates them. In reality, emergency powers are usually granted to the president, or other governmental authorities, by the constitution, but they are exercised only during a declared (and strictly limited in time) period of an emergency. In other words, an emergency does not *create* new powers, but rather it provides an occasion for the *exercise* of extraordinary or special powers for specified purposes and for a specified time limit.

Already in 1964, Lord Rein made an important (for the purposes of this study) reservation. In his words, 'The prerogative certainly covers doing all those things in an emergency which are necessary for the conduct of war'. However, he added that there was difficulty in relating the prerogative to modern conditions since no modern war had been waged without statutory powers.[101] Again, not by a coincidence, this acknowledgement was made in 1964, the year when the House of Commons adopted a new

Emergency Powers Act.[102] The judicial decision in *Burmah Oil Co Ltd v Lord Advocate*, finally confirmed this tendency that 'the mobilisation of the industrial and financial resources of the country could not be done without statutory emergency powers. The prerogative is really a relic of a past age, not lost by disuse but only available for a case not covered by statute' ([1965] A.C.75, 101).[103]

Strictly speaking, just like Britain, the U.S. Constitution does *not* explicitly recognise the need for additional national powers during a state of emergency. In fact, it was as early as 1866, when the U.S. Supreme Court declared in *Ex Parte Milligan* that the Constitution is a 'law for rulers and people, equally in war and in peace', protecting 'all classes of men, at all times, and under all circumstances' (71 U.S. (4 Wall.) 2, 120–121 (1866)). The majority opinion written by Justice Davis went even further, stating that the rights contained in the Constitution with the exception of the writ of *habeas corpus*, could not be suspended by either the President or Congress (*id.* at 120). Additionally, Justice Davis questioned whether it was worth preserving the Constitution and the country by trampling upon the basic liberty and freedoms upon which society is founded (*id.* at 126).[104]

The Supreme Court reconfirmed this position in 1934, when it said: '[An] emergency does not create power. Emergency does not increase granted power or remove or diminish the restrictions imposed upon power granted or reserved. The Constitution was adopted in a period of grave emergency. Its grants of power to the federal government ... were determined in the light of emergency and they are not altered by emergency' (*Home Building and Loan Association v Blaisdell*, 290 U.S. 398, at 425 (1934)).[105] Yet, emergencies have helped to develop the use of otherwise dormant powers and the novel application of ordinary powers.

Another celebrated court decision, clarifying the question of 'special powers', when the 'state is in danger', was *Youngstown Sheet and Tube Co v Sawyer*, 343 U.S. 579, 645 (1952). With six votes against three, the Supreme Court struck down the President's Executive Order that had authorised seizure of steel mills and their operation by the national government. President Harry S. Truman acted under his inherent power as chief executive and commander-in-chief to safeguard the nation's security during the Korean War, when a strike in the steel mills threatened the supply of weapons. The Court held that the President has no authority under the Constitution to seize private property unless Congress authorises the seizure, and also that the Constitution does not permit the President to legislate.[106] However, in pronouncing Truman's seizure of the steel mills as an illegitimate use of his commander-in-chief's power in the economic sphere, Justice Jackson was prompted to concede that he would 'indulge the widest latitude of interpretation to sustain' the President's 'exclusive function to command the instruments of national force, at least when turned against the outside world for the security of our society'.[107]

Looking back at the last 15 years of Russian law, that would be fair to say that there was an apparent attempt in late Gorbachev period to introduce a concept of 'inherent powers' to the USSR Presidency. The idea was promoted by Gorbachev himself and publicly supported by the USSR Minister of Justice S.G. Luschikov. Speaking in the USSR Supreme Soviet about a possibility of adoption of another state of exception ('president's rule' in certain 'hot spots' in the Soviet Union), S. Luschikov forcefully stated that it was 'inadmissible to lay down in normative acts all details dealing with president's rule. I want to emphasise: inadmissible!' Luschikov argued that 'President bears responsibility before the state, before the USSR Congress of People's Deputies and the supreme body of authority for his actions, and that's absolutely inadmissible to tie his hands [with a written law – A.D.] prescribing what to do, what to say, to whom to appeal.'[108]

After reading those words, one could get a feeling that it was not a Soviet minister speaking, but rather U.S. President Harry S. Truman in the middle of the 1952 *Steel Seizure Case*. That's how Truman in one of his interviews of that period explained his understanding of 'inherent powers': 'The President of the United States has very great inherent powers to meet great national emergencies. Until those emergencies arise a President cannot say specifically what he would do or would not do ... There are a lot of Presidents who have had to make decisions in emergencies, and if you will read history you will find out why they had to make them. But it did not hurt the Republic. In fact, it made the Republic better.'[109]

The USSR Parliament didn't get impressed with this idea. And for good reason. Despite the strong influence made by the U.S. Constitution on many Latin American constitutions which include Argentina (1853), Mexico (1917), Brazil (1891, 1937, 1946, 1988), Venezuela (1953, 1961) as well as on constitutions of some Asian nations (Japan, Korea, Taiwan, Thailand), and Australia, none of them has borrowed either the doctrine of 'inherent powers' or the concept of 'implied powers'.[110] For these flowers belong to American soil; they wouldn't survive on foreign sand.[111]

2 Elements of the constitutional mechanism of a state of emergency

I

There are a large variety of grounds for declaring a state of emergency in legislation of the countries of the world. Not all of them, however, represent a 'grave' threat to the State. A study of 36 constitutions, undertaken in the mid-1960s under auspices of the United Nations Department of Economic and Social Affairs, was aimed at compiling an *exhaustive* list of reasons and circumstances ('sudden unexpected happenings', 'perplexing contingencies', 'sudden or unexpected occasions for action', 'exigencies', 'pressing necessities', etc.), when an imposition of a state of emergency can be justified without any doubt. Authors of the survey identified seven groups of such grounds: external threat (international conflict, war, invasion, defence or protection of the security of the state or of any part of its territory); civil war, rebellion, 'subversive actions of revolutionary elements'; violation of peace, public order or safety; danger to the constitutional order; natural disasters; danger to economic life of the state or of any part of its territory; interruption of *normal* functioning of essential spheres of economy or public services.[1]

On a national level, at the end of the 1950s and in the beginning of the 1960s, similar attempts were undertaken by German legal scholars, A. Hamann and Hans-Ernst Folz. The researchers also split all 'emergency situations' into six or seven categories. A. Hamann identified them as foreign invasion; public actions aimed at subversion of the constitutional regime; serious offences threatening public order and security; catastrophes, strikes and unrest in essential spheres of economy; disruptions in essential public services; and hardships in the economic and financial spheres.

Hans-Ernst Folz in his book, *A State of Emergency and Emergency Legislation* (*Staatsnotstand und Notstandsrecht*), published in Germany (Köln–Berlin–Bonn–München) in 1961, proposed a more elaborate list of reasons allowing introduction of a state of emergency. His conditions included: presence of an external danger to the state (acts of military danger or military invasion, or co-ordination of activities of 'subversive elements' within the country from the territory of a foreign state); 'domestic unrest' of different kinds, revolts, rioting, and mutinies, 'constitutional necessity' caused by a disruption of normal functioning of any constitutional organ or a conflict (in federal states) between the Centre and a subject of the federation; disruption of normal functioning of the governmental authorities caused by a strike in the civil service; refusal to pay taxes (tax strike); hardships in the sphere of economy and finances and labour unrest; catastrophes, epidemics and national disasters.

Folz assumed a possibility of a combination of two or more reasons identified by him as well as a possibility of emergence of new reasons and circumstances that could justify an introduction of a state of emergency.

Agreeing with a possibility of emergence of such new reasons, a French administrativist A. Matio proposed another approach to the subject of this research. In his book, *A Theory of Emergency Circumstances*, Matio concluded that 'it is not possible to foresee in a long advance precisely what emergency circumstances can occur'. For that reason Matio argued against attempts to compile an *exhaustive* list of emergency situations when an imposition of a state of emergency can be allowed and justified. His position is shared by some other authors, including Zubair Alam, who suggested that a constitution cannot provide for all eventualities and that emergencies are, by definition, situations which cannot be predicted and, respectively, that the powers of various constitutional bodies cannot be prescribed in advance.[2]

Indeed, not all of those 'model' reasons and grounds presented in the works of A. Hamann, H.-E. Folz, experts of the United Nations, and some other authors, are really reflected in legislation of the countries of the world. In most cases, the definition is limited by 'war', or 'danger of war', and 'foreign invasion'. Legislation of other countries contains a wider list of emergency circumstances, including armed violence, internal disturbances, danger to independence, territorial integrity, state institutions, economic stability, public order and safety, plus natural disasters. Constitutions of Germany and nearly all former socialist countries of Europe, as well as of Mongolia (1960) and China (1982), named one more reason: the necessity to accomplish 'international treaty commitments and obligations' in the sphere of mutual defence against aggression. In Germany this provision is known as a 'union clause'.

A rare condition for imposition of a state of exception ('state of siege') was contained in the Constitution of the Turkish Republic (adopted by the Supreme National Assembly on 20 April 1924) and highly influenced by some European constitutions and the first Soviet Constitution of 1918. Under the constitution, the executive power of the Republic (Council of Commissars, one of the borrowings from the Soviet Constitution), formed by the President from members of the Supreme National Assembly, could declare a 'local or national' state of siege not only because of war, danger of war, and rebellion, but also in case of 'intensive and real plots of betrayal of the Fatherland and the Republic' (art.86). Similarly, the 1935 Constitution of the Republic of Poland allowed the Council of Ministers (with the consent of the President; in the whole territory of the State or 'in the endangered part') to declare a state of emergency in case of 'internal disturbances or *widespread conspiracy of a treasonable character* menacing the order and safety of the State or the safety of its citizens' (art.78(1)) (*italics added – A.D.*). The provision was not preserved and was excluded from the texts of the Constitutional Law of 19 February 1947, '*On Structure and Competence of Supreme Bodies of the Polish Republic*', and the socialist Constitution of Poland (adopted on 22 July 1952).

The contemporary constitution of Turkish-occupied part of Cyprus (so-called 'Turkish Federated State of Cyprus') gives quite original reasons for a martial law proclamation (for a period of two months or less): 'The creation of circumstances necessitating war, the carrying out of a revolution, the endangering of the existence of TFSC, internally or externally, and widespread acts of violence aimed at the elimination of the liberal and democratic law and order recognised by the Constitution of TFSC' (art.98(1)).[3]

There are two main ways of imposing a state of emergency: by a decree issued by the Executive or by a parliamentary act depending on which of the two branches of government originates the decision. Carl J. Friedrich called it an 'emergency action' of an executive or legislative 'nature'.[4]

That would be right to say that there is a consensus among the majority of both Russian and international legal experts on this point. German jurists D. Bartzsch, H. Schtrebel, F.A. Heidte, for instance, agreed that it should be the executive power to introduce a state of emergency when there is a danger to the state calling for immediate actions. 'In dire straits, a nation cannot afford the luxury of the parliamentary slowness', warned a Russian philosopher in Argentina, ideologue of 'people's monarchy', Ivan Solonevich. The same position was shared by French scholar M. Michel Ameller, when he said, 'Ordinary procedure is unacceptable in times of crisis, when the mechanism of the government must act with maximum promptness'.[5]

Indeed, in most countries of the world (first of all, in presidential and semi-presidential republics)[6] the right to proclaim a state of emergency is vested in the Chief Executive or the head of state. That's understandable. Although in recent years presidentialism has been sharply criticised by Western (as well as Russian) academic community,[7] with few voices raised in its defence,[8] the presidential form of government currently enjoys widespread popularity throughout the world, expanding to African (e.g. Namibia, Zambia, Zimbabwe), Asian (e.g. Kyrgyzstan, Philippines, South Korea), and most former Soviet and Eastern European 'democratising' nations (e.g. Russia, Ukraine, Belarus, Poland).[9]

A (rather incomplete) survey of the Inter-Parliamentary Union, contains a list of 58 countries, where a power to declare a state of emergency is vested in the President.[10]

The French constitutional model, regulating emergency powers, is a typical example of that model. The French form of government gives a certain priority to the executive branch of government over the legislative one. The President's powers are very wide even in ordinary and normal circumstances. The Constitution of the Fifth Republic (adopted by the referendum on 28 September and promulgated on 4 October 1958) also grants President emergency powers 'to take the measures' that are 'commanded' by the 'circumstances'. Such circumstances include 'grave and imminent' threats to the 'institutions of the Republic, independence of the nation, the integrity of its territory or the fulfilment of its international commitments', as well as 'interruption' of the 'regular functioning of constitutional governmental authorities' (art.16).[11]

Similar or identical regulations are adopted in the countries of former French and Belgian colonial empires, whose constitutions were based on the model of 'rationalised parliamentarism' of the Fifth French Republic. They include Algeria, Cameroon, Cape Verde, Cote d'Ivoire, Morocco, Senegal, Togo, Tunisia, and some other states of Tropical Africa (so-called 'new Francophone states'), as well as Sri Lanka.

For instance, the Constitution of the Gabonese Republic (Law No.3/91, adopted on 26 March 1991) in general repeats the same 'circumstances' (a 'grave and immediate' threat to 'the institutions of the Republic', 'independence of the nation', its 'territorial integrity', 'the execution of its international engagements' or interruption of the 'regular operation of constitutional public powers') allowing the use of presidential emergency powers, with one addition. Emergency measures can also be taken by the President ('by ordinance', 'with the least delay'), when there is a menace to the 'superior interests of the nation' (art.26). What constitutes such 'superior interests' of the Gabonese nation is a question to which the constitution of the country fails to give an answer.

'When circumstances demand', the President of Gabon can also proclaim by decree three different forms of a state of exception: a 'state of siege' (*l'etat de siege*), a 'state of alert (*l'etat d'alerte*), and a 'state of emergency' (*l'etat d'urgence*), 'which shall confer upon him special powers'. The constitution doesn't define the difference between these forms of a state of emergency, and doesn't say what kind of 'special' powers can be conferred upon the President, and under what conditions – all those questions are left for determination by a regular law (art.25). The situation becomes even more complicated, because another article of the constitution mentions, but doesn't define either, the fourth form of a state of emergency – a 'state of readiness' (*l'etat de mise en garde*). In this case as well, a regular parliamentary law 'shall fix the rules concerning' this new form of a state of exception (art.47).[12]

A certain concern needs to be expressed at this point. Much criticised at the time of drafting of the current Constitution of France, Article 16 has been invoked only once in 1961 to suppress the rebellion of several French army units in Algeria.[13] Since then it has become a 'dead letter' of the French Constitution. Two factors: economic and political stability (that was never drastically shaken under the Fifth Republic, either in the days of the 'student revolution' of 1968 or at any other time), and the French party system (approximating the Anglo-Saxon two-party system), have become the most effective safeguards against invocation of a state of emergency in France. However, the *model* itself, as laid down in Article 16 of the French Constitution, with its concentration of emergency authority in the executive and weak control functions of the legislature, might be quite dubious and open to abuse in countries without in-built democratic structure of France and its liberal tradition of self-reservation of power.

Needless to say the Chief Executives in 'superpresidential' republics of Latin America enjoy similar or even bigger discretionary powers. Quite often they are used under a pretext of necessity to 'reaffirm and strengthen the presidential regime to save democracy'. President of Colombia Alberto Lleras (1958–1962) was certainly right when saying that 'weak and anarchic governments are the prelude to dictatorships'.[14]

In Ireland, Spain, Canada, Cyprus, Lebanon, France, Latvia, and some African countries, a state of emergency can be declared by the government or Council of Ministers.

An original model was proposed in Poland in the 1940s. Under the Constitutional Law, '*On Structure and Competence of Supreme Bodies of the Polish Republic*' (adopted on 19 February 1947, as a temporary fundamental act until adoption of a new constitution), a 'state of exception' or a 'state of war' could be declared neither by the Legislature (*Sejm*), nor President or Government (Council of Ministers), but by another supreme governing body – State Council (art.16d), which consisted of the President of the Republic (as its Chairman), elected by the legislature; leaders of the *Sejm* ('Marshall' and three 'Vice Marshalls'); and Chairman of the Supreme Auditing Chamber (art.15(1)). The decision on an imposition of any form of a state of emergency could be made in a 'Resolution' of the State Council on a 'proposal' by the Council of Ministers. The resolution was to be forwarded for adoption by the session of the *Sejm* and was automatically repealed if it had not been submitted to the *Sejm* or if the latter failed to adopt it (art.19(2)).[15]

Only in about a dozen countries, including the United States, Germany, Israel, Angola, Malta, Czech Republic, Paraguay, Yugoslavia, Slovenia, Bulgaria, Spain, and Argentina, Parliament itself is empowered to introduce a state of emergency. In some countries, however, this power depends on the circumstances or the kind of a state of emergency involved.

For instance, under the Constitution of the Federal Republic of Yugoslavia (uniting Serbia and Montenegro; adopted on 27 April 1992), if the Union Federal Assembly (*Skupschina*) 'is not able to convene', an 'imminent threat of war', 'state of war', or 'emergency' can be proclaimed by the Federal Government after previous 'consultations' ('subject to the opinion') with the President of the Republic and 'presidents of the Federal Assembly chambers' (art.99(10)).[16]

In Slovenia, a state of emergency can be proclaimed 'when a major and general danger threatens the existence of the state'. An emergency proclamation, as well as a proclamation of war, and 'introduction and repeal of measures necessitated' by such proclamations are decided by the State Assembly on the 'proposal' of the Government. The State Assembly is also the organ that decides 'on the use of defence forces'. The President can take decisions on these questions only when the Parliament can't meet. However, his decision must be sent to the State Assembly for confirmation 'immediately' after it convenes (art.92).[17]

According to the new Constitution of Argentina (adopted on 24 August 1994), in the event of internal disorder or foreign attack 'endangering the operation of this Constitution and of the authorities created thereby', a state of siege can be declared in such Province or territory (art.23). In the first case ('internal disorder' or 'internal disturbance'), a respective decision can be taken by the Congress (art.75(29)), whereas the President of the Nation can declare it in the event of foreign attack. However, even in this case he needs 'consent' of the Senate. In the event of internal disorder, the President has the power to impose a state of siege only when Congress is in recess, 'since this is a power belonging to that body' (art.99(16)). The Congress needs to approve or suspend such imposition (art.79(29)). The Parliament also has a right 'to dispense Federal intervention into a Province or into the City of Buenos Aires' (art.75(31)).[18]

Similarly, the Government of Spain is empowered by the constitution to introduce two relatively mild forms of an emergency, whereas the House of Representatives reserves for itself a power to introduce its severest form – a state of siege.

Article 116 of the Spanish Constitution (adopted by the referendum on 6 December 1978; entered into force on 29 December 1978; and amended on 27 August 1992), provides for an introduction of three different forms of a state of emergency: state of alarm (*el estado de alarma*), state of exception (*el estado de exception*), and state of siege (*el estado de sitio*). The constitution determines different procedures of their imposition, duration, and, what is especially important, their legal consequences. A separate act, the Organic Law 4/1981, distinguishes various reasons and circumstances under which all three forms of a state of emergency can be proclaimed.

A 'state of alarm' is declared by a governmental decree, 'agreed upon by the Council of Ministers', in the case of natural disasters, epidemics, or interruption of the normal functioning of essential services of the community. A state of alarm can be introduced for a maximum period of 15 days. It can be extended only under 'authorisation' of the House of Representatives, which must be convened 'immediately for that purpose'.

The decree must also determine the 'territorial area to which the effects of the declaration shall be excluded' (art.116(2)).

When the public order, civil freedoms or normal functioning of democratic institutions are menaced, the Government can issue a decree introducing a 'state of exception'. Unlike with the state of alarm, this form of emergency can be declared only 'after authorisation by the House of Representatives'. Its maximum duration is twice as long, 30 days, and 'it may be extended for a like period'. According to the constitution, the 'authorisation and proclamation of a state of emergency must expressly determine its purposes, the territorial area to which it is extended and its duration' (art.116(3)).

A 'state of siege' may be declared under even more serious and grave circumstances, including revolt, imminent danger to state sovereignty, territorial integrity, or to the Constitution of Spain. This form of emergency is imposed not by the government, but by the House of Representatives itself (by the 'absolute majority' of votes), at the 'exclusive proposal' by the Government and without any restrictions concerning its duration (art.116(4)).

The same article contains another paragraph prohibiting dissolution of the House of Representatives while any form of the emergency is in effect. Both chambers of the parliament, the House of Representatives and the Senate, are automatically convoked if they are not in a period of sessions. 'Their functioning, like that of the other constitutional powers of the State, may not be interrupted during the effectiveness of these states' (art.116(5)); 'the declaration of the states of alarm, emergency, and siege shall not modify the principle of the responsibility of the Government or its agents as recognised in the Constitution and in the laws' (art.116(6)), the Spanish Constitution stipulates.[19]

In the majority of countries, it is the Chief Executive that decides by himself whether there are sufficient legal grounds to impose a state of emergency. In many countries of the world, however, a state of emergency cannot be declared until after consulting various government bodies.

In France and several African countries (including Benin, and the Central African Republic) the President can exercise his special powers only after 'consultations' with the Prime Minister, chairpersons of both chambers of parliament, and with the Constitutional Council (in some countries, like Gabon, with the Constitutional Court). The President of Algeria declares a state of exception 'in consultation' with the National People's Assembly (lower chamber of the parliament), and Presidents of the Council of the Nation (upper chamber) and the Constitutional Council, and with 'the consent' of the High Council of Security and the Council of Ministers (art.93). Under the present constitution, the President of Portugal cannot introduce states of siege (*do estado di sitio*), or emergency (*do estado di emergencia*), without previously consulting the Government (art.141), whereas in the past he was to consult with the State

Council. The President of India issues an emergency declaration on the 'advice' of the Cabinet, while the Venezuelan President does so at a session of the Council of Ministers. The President of Zaire, and Governor-General of Mauritius, can declare a state of emergency 'upon the advice' of the parliament, President of Mali – upon consultations with the government, President of Somalia – with the National Defence Council, President of Chad – with the Government and the Office of the Superior Council of the Transition. In Gabon, the acts of the President of the Republic, including his emergency decrees, shall be countersigned by the Prime Minister and the 'ministers charged with their execution' (art.27). The President of Brazil can initiate the process of introduction of a form of a state of emergency only 'after having heard from the Council of the Republic and the National Defence Council' (art.136, 137).

In light of what has been said, a recommendation of the International Committee on the Enforcement of Human Rights Law gets an essential significance. After six years of study by a special subcommittee (chaired by Subrata Roy Chowdhury of India), and two additional years of revision by the full International Committee on the Enforcement of Human Rights Law, the 61st Conference of the International Law Association (held in Paris from 26 August to 1 September 1984) approved by consensus a set of so-called *Minimum Standards of Human Rights Norms in a State of Exception* (also known as the Paris Minimum Standards). The Committee stated that 'among the two political organs [i.e. the Parliament and the Executive – *A.D.*] responsibility for the declaration of emergency belongs to the legislature'.[20]

The recommendation may seem paradoxical only at first glance. Actually, parliamentary control is a necessary (although not in all countries – imperative) element of the legal institution of a state of emergency. Indeed, a decision by the executive to declare a state of exception, as a rule, must be approved by parliament. The time limits for presentation of the emergency proclamation to the legislature vary from 24 hours (i.e. in Russia, under the 1991 Law 'On a State of Emergency', Azerbaijan, Brazil, Uruguay), 48 hours (i.e. Costa Rica) or three days (i.e. in Uzbekistan) to 30 (i.e. in India, Pakistan, Sudan) and even 45 days (as in Nicaragua).

Some Fundamental Laws set even stricter controls. According to the current Constitution of the Republic of Paraguay (approved by the National Constituent Assembly on 20 June 1992), for instance, a state of exception (*el estado de excepcion*) can be introduced by Congress or the Executive; in the second case, an emergency proclamation issued by the President has to be not only submitted to the Congress, but approved (or rejected) by it within 48 hours (art.288).[21]

If the Parliament is in recess, it shall be promptly convoked (within five days in Brazil and Great Britain); and after that adopt or reject the proclamation of emergency (within ten days in Brazil). In his 'emergency clause'

Bernard H. Siegan, an American professor of law (at the University of San Diego), who provided constitutional advice to the drafters of the new Bulgarian Constitution of 1991, recommended that an emergency proclamation of the President (as well as partial or general mobilisation of the armed forces) shall require parliamentary confirmation 'within five days'.[22]

Of course, there are exceptions to this rule. Constitutions of Nepal and Turkey-occupied Cyprus are extreme cases in this respect. The Constitution the Kingdom of Nepal (issued on 9 November 1990) mandates that the King's proclamation, or order, on a state of emergency 'shall be *laid before a meeting* of the House of Representatives for approval within three months from the date of issuance' (art115(2)). Being the longest term by itself, the provision is further aggravated by the fact that the drafters of the constitution 'forgot' to set the time limit within which the House of Representatives should *actually adopt* the emergency proclamation[23] (*italics added – A.D.*). The Constitution of the Turkish Federated State of Cyprus (adopted on February 13, 1975) only mentions that a governmental proclamation of martial law 'shall be laid forthwith before the Assembly of TFSC for approval'. However, it's silent regarding how soon the proclamation should be actually 'laid forthwith before the Assembly'. In addition, the Constitution fails to set the time limit for the proclamation's approval, as well as to say how soon the Assembly shall be convened, if martial law is proclaimed when it is in recess (art.98(2)).[24]

On average, legislation of the countries of the world proscribe that a decree on the declaration of a state of emergency is to be approved or rejected within 14 to 30 days.

Finally, at least three constitutions – of Portugal, Brazil, and Suriname, – although empowering the Presidents of these Republics to declare emergency (states of siege and emergency in Portugal; a state of siege in Brazil; war, danger of war and states of siege and emergency in Suriname), provide for a previous (!) and not *post factum* authorisation of this measure by the Parliaments of these countries: Assembly of the Republic, National Congress, and National Assembly (respectively).

According to the Constitution of Portugal of 2 April 1976 (considerably revised in 1982, 1989, and 1994), if the Assembly of the Republic is not in session and 'it is impossible to call it into session at once', 'authorisation' is to be received from the Standing Committee of the Assembly (art.141).[25]

Under the Constitution of the Republic of Suriname (adopted on 30 October 1987), termination of any of these special regimes is also impossible without previous consent of the National Assembly. However, the Constitution of Surinam makes a significant exception: parliamentary 'consent' is not required, when, 'as a result of *force majeure*, consultation with the National Assembly has appeared to be impossible' (art.102).[26]

The Brazilian Constitution doesn't contain such '*force majeure*' clause. The model that it proposes is really sophisticated and includes four stages. First, the President must 'hear' from the Council of the Republic and the

National Defence Council about a necessity to declare a state of siege. Second, the President requests 'authorisation' to decree a state of siege from the National Congress explaining the reasons for such measure. Third, the National Congress takes a respective decision by an absolute majority of votes. Only after that can the President actually introduce an emergency regime (art.137).[27] Since adoption of the constitution in 1988, Brazil hasn't known either war or foreign aggression, so this model hasn't been tested in practical life, but it's obvious that it wouldn't survive in most other states of the world and could even jeopardise survival of those states themselves.

Constitutional law of the countries of the world, as a rule, contains norms prohibiting dissolution of the supreme legislative and representative bodies under a state of emergency (e.g. Article 16 of the French Constitution (1958), Article 296(1) of the Constitution of the Republic of Cape Verde (1990), Article 28 of the Constitution of the Central African Republic (1995)). On the contrary, several constitutions prolong the term of the parliament when a proclamation of emergency is in operation. Poland's constitutional law of transitional period, for instance, implied that 'during the State of Emergency the Diet shall not dissolve itself, and, if the term is expired, it shall be prolonged for a three-month period after the end of the State of Emergency (Act of 7 April 1989, on Amendment to Constitution, art.32 I (4)).[28] In India, duration of both chambers of the parliament (*Lok Sabha* and *Rajya Sabha*) is extended for a period 'not exceeding one year and not extending in any case beyond a period of six months after the Proclamation has ceased to operate' (art.83). A similar provision is contained in the Constitution of the Islamic Republic of Pakistan allowing *Majlis-e-Shura* (Parliament) to extend the term of the National Assembly for the same period of time as in India (art.232(6)).[29]

A decision concerning prolongation of a state of emergency is usually taken by the parliament too. The number of such extensions might be limited by the Constitution.

In some countries of the world (for instance, in Belgium and Brazil) an imposition of one form of a state of exception is preceded by another form (less severe by the character of its legal consequences) or stipulated by it.

Neither the original text of the constitution of Belgium (issued on 7 February 1831), nor its revised edition (signed on 17 February 1994, redefining the country as a federal state (art.1) unifying two indigenous groups – the Walloons and Flemish[30]) contains any norms regulating a state of exception. However, World War I made the government correct this deficiency and develop some legal mechanism to deal with emergencies. As a result, on 11 October 1916, a Decree-law on a State of War and a State of Siege was adopted.

According to the act, a 'state of war' is declared by a King's decree. By this decree, the King is empowered to mobilise army and exercise police functions in the country, which he can delegate (to a larger or smaller extent) to the governors of provinces and commissars of municipalities.

Another, more important for this study, legal consequence of a declaration of a 'state of war' is a 'state of siege' that can be imposed by the King upon advice of the Council of Ministers in the whole country or in some parts of its territory. In this case, the Minister of Defence acquires responsibilities of civil authorities on preservation of the public order and proper functioning of essential services. On the territory, declared under a state of siege, military authorities have a right to exercise some discretionary powers. These powers include the ability 'to deport criminals, aliens, persons suspected to be in relations with an enemy, as well as any other persons whose presence can hamper military operations'. Military authorities can also search the houses and exercise a personal search; look for and confiscate weapons and ammunition; ban meetings that can cause disturbances; introduce censorship of correspondence, including private correspondence; ban publications and distribution of printed materials and other information that can be considered 'favouring an enemy' and having 'bad influence on the spirit of the army and the population'.

The Decree-law of 1916 provided for the trial of persons guilty of offences against its regulations. The usual penalty was an imprisonment for three months and a fine not exceeding 300 franks. A more severe punishment could be used against those printing or distributing banned printed materials, instigating panic, etc. In those cases, the offenders could be tried by courts of military jurisdiction and imprisoned for one year and pay a fine not exceeding 1,000 franks.

Last time the Decree-law was implemented during World War II: a state of war was declared in Belgium on 27 August 1939 and lifted on 1 June 1949. Furthermore, a state of siege was imposed on all the territory of the kingdom on 11 May 1940, and repealed on 25 January 1946.[31]

The Constitution of Belgium prescribes that it 'may not be suspended, entirely or in part' even under a state of war or a state of siege (art.187, originally art.130).[32]

A new Constitution of the Federative Republic of Brazil (adopted on 5 October 1988; with later amendments), also provides for a consequent introduction of two forms of emergency: a 'state of defence' (*do estado de defesa*) and a 'state of siege' (*do estado de sitio*).

A 'state of defence', as a milder form, can be declared in order 'to preserve or promptly to re-establish public order or social peace threatened by grave and imminent institutional instability or affected by large scale natural calamities' (art.136). Its duration may not exceed 30 days, and it may be extended only once for another 30 days, 'if the reasons justifying the respective decree persist' (art.136(2)).

However, in case of 'ineffectiveness of measures taken during the state of defence', it can be changed for a 'state of siege', a much more severe emergency regime, also introduced with the beginning of war or as a response to foreign aggression (art.137). Like the first form of emergency, a state of siege (unless it's caused by war or foreign aggression) is declared for 30 days, but in this case, the constitution doesn't restrict how many times it can be extended (each time for another 30 days) (art.138).[33]

As a legal institution, a state of emergency generally reflects the type and social orientation of regimes. For instance, not a single constitution of European socialist countries contained a provision concerning introduction of a state of emergency (in any of its forms) by the supreme representative body of the state. It was usually decreed by the President or the State Council.

Constitutions of so-called 'revolutionary democratic' states (Angola, Mozambique, Benin, Sao Tome and Principe, the Congo, Somalia) not only vest the President with considerable emergency powers, but also secure the 'leading and guiding' role of the ruling (in most cases, the only) Party, headed by the President. Following the USSR model, such constitutions prescribe that the ruling Party determines 'the main political orientation of the state and society' (Constitution of the People's Republic of Mozambique of 1975, art.3), or that it is 'responsible for the political, economic and social leadership of the State' and 'constitutes the organised vanguard of the working class' (Constitution of the People's Republic of Angola of 1975, art.2). The ruling Party of the 'revolutionary democratic' states is defined either as 'the vanguard of the working masses', 'the highest form of the political and social organisation of the people' (Constitution of the People's Republic of the Congo of 1979, art.36(2)), or 'the only legal party', having 'supreme authority of political and socio-economic leadership' (The Constitution of the Somali Democratic Republic of 1979, art.7).[34]

The principle of parliamentary supremacy in such countries is usually seriously eroded or explicitly restricted (often – on the constitutional level). For instance, a decision of the Somali President to declare states of war and peace can be made only after 'authorisation' by two organs: the Central Committee of the Party and the People's Assembly (art.82(12)). In the 1970–1980s, Presidents of the Congo and Togo could introduce of a state of emergency only after consultation with the Politbureau or Central Committee of the ruling Party. Besides, according to the same Constitution of the Congo of 1979, a decision on extension (for a period longer than 12 days) of a state of emergency could also be taken only by the Central Committee of the Congolese Workers' Party (art.71).[35]

Constitutions of the world vary in detailing provisions on a state of exception: from just a few words and a couple of articles to a whole chapter (as in the Constitution of India of 1950 and some Latin American constitutions). That's important to note that detailing emergency powers on a constitutional level is not necessarily an indication of a balanced, 'liberal' or non-repressive character of the institution. In the end, the character of a constitutional mechanism of a state of emergency in a given country is predetermined by a more general question: whether the process of constitution-making was democratic or not. In particular, how a constitution was *drafted*, whether it was *discussed* by the population or not, and whether citizens' proposals were actually taken into consideration to improve the draft, or was the constitution simply *granted* to the country, *imposed* on it by its not necessarily legitimate rulers (foreign invader, dictator, military junta, etc.). As an example of such negative experience of constitution-making, a comparativist can recall that the Constitution of Chile, which was adopted under Pinochet in 1981, also claimed to be based on the 'rule of law' principle.

II

Constitutional legislation of a large number of countries of the world (including Russia, the United States, France, Belgium, China, Netherlands, Turkey, Peru, Egypt, Argentina, Colombia, Portugal, Poland, Romania, Zimbabwe, Nicaragua, Vietnam, and Jordan) sanctions introduction of not only a 'national' emergency, but also of 'regional' or 'local' emergencies in some 'parts of the territory' of the country.

The Constitution of the People's Republic of China of 1982, for instance, authorises the Standing Committee of the National People's Congress, as the permanently working 'highest organ of state power' (art.57), 'to decide on the enforcement of martial law throughout the country or *in particular provinces, autonomous regions or municipalities directly under the Central Government*' (art.67(20)). Similar powers concerning 'enforcement of martial law *in parts of provinces, autonomous regions, and municipalities directly under the Central Government*' (art.89(16)) are granted to the State Council (or the 'Central People's Government') of PRC, the 'highest organ of state administration' (art.85)[36] (*italics added – A.D.*). The Constitution of Nepal allows 'His Majesty' to declare a state of emergency 'in respect of the whole of the Kingdom of Nepal or *of any specified part* thereof' (art.115(1))[37] (*italics added – A.D.*). Presidents of Brazil and Bolivia can introduce, respectively, a state of defence and a state of siege 'in certain restricted locations' (art.136), in the first case, and 'in such portion of the territory as may be necessary', in the other (art.111).[38]

Most of the international human rights agreements contain norms allowing, in exceptional circumstances, to make derogations from some of their provisions. Such agreements include the European Convention for the Protection of Human Rights and Fundamental Freedoms of 1950 (hereafter the ECHR), the European Social Charter of 1961 (ESC), the International Covenant on Civil and Political Rights of 1966 (ICCPR), the American Convention on Human Rights of 1969 (ACHR).[39] Within a European context of so-called political commitments, similar norms are contained in the Documents of the Copenhagen (1990) and Moscow (1991) Meetings of the Conference on the Human Dimension of the CSCE (Conference on Security and Cooperation in Europe) (hereafter the CSCE Copenhagen and Moscow Documents).

The standard condition in these instruments is the existence of a 'public emergency' (ECHR, art.15; ESC, art.30; ICCPR, art.4R, the Copenhagen and Moscow Documents, para.25 and para.28, respectively), or 'war, public danger, or other emergency' (ACHR, art.27). However, three main conventions – the ECHR, ESC, and ICCRP – establish an 'additional standard': in order to justify derogations, a public emergency should 'threaten the life of the nation' as a whole, and not of some part of the territory of the country, even if it's heavily populated.

Besides those covenants, the question regarding the additional standard was considered in a number of official studies representing *communis opinio doctorum*, or an 'authoritative opinion', based on the doctrine of international law and international practice. For instance, a recognised specialist in international law, expert of the Sub-Commission on Prevention of Discrimination and Protection of Minorities (Commission on Human Rights, UN Economic and Social Council) Erica-Irene A. Daes acknowledged in her study, *The Individual's Duties to the Community and the Limitations on Human Rights and Freedoms under art.29 of the Universal Declaration of Human Rights* (1983) that 'the emergency must be nationwide in its effects ... in the sense of article 4, paragraph 1, of the Covenant'.[40] Nicole Questiaux, author of another expert report, *Study of the Implications for Human Rights of Recent Developments Concerning Situations Known as States of Siege or Emergency* (1982), interpreted a threat to the 'life of the nation' as 'a threat to the very existence of the nation, that is to say, to the organised life of the community constituting the basis of the State, whether this means to the physical integrity of the population, to territorial integrity or to the functioning of the organs of the State.'[41]

The most comprehensive explanation to the formula 'public emergency threatening the life of the nation' was elaborated in the so called *Siracusa Principles on the Limitation and Derogation Provisions in the International Covenant on Civil and Political Rights* named after the location (Siracusa, Sicily) of a symposium dedicated to a close examination of the conditions and grounds for permissible limitations and derogations enunciated in the ICCPR in order to achieve an effective implementation of the rule of law. The symposium was convened in 1984 by the International Commission of Jurists, the International Association of Penal Law and some other organisations with participation of 31 distinguished experts in international law, including E.-I.A. Daes, Secretary-General of International Institute of Human Rights Alexandre Kiss, Senior Advocate of the Supreme Court of India Subrata Roy Chowdhury, and Director of the Institute of Criminal Law Andrzej Murzynowski (Poland).

Principle 39 of the Siracusa Principles defines a 'Threat to the Life of the Nation' as one that:

a affects *the whole of the population* and either the whole or part of the territory of the State, and

b threatens the physical integrity of the population, the political independence or the territorial integrity of the State or the existence or *basic* functioning of institutions *indispensable* to ensure and protect the rights recognised in the Covenant' (*italics added – A.D.*).

Unfortunately, the Siracusa Principles were translated and published in Russia (in a periodical of the Moscow State University) with an apparent mistake that seriously tainted the real meaning of Principle 39. The formula 'affects the whole of the population *and* either the whole or part of the territory of the State' (*italics added – A.D.*) was translated as 'affects the whole of the population *or* either the whole or part of the territory of the State' (*italics added – A.D.*).[42]

As it was described in the commentary to Principle 39, by an expert of the Inter-American Institute of Human Rights (Costa Rica) Daniel O'Donnell, 'Threat to the Life of the Nation' contains four elements. 'There must be a danger which: (a) is present or imminent, (b) is exceptional, (c) *concerns the entire population*, and (d) constitutes a threat to the organised life of the community'[43] (*italics added – A.D.*).

Special emphasis was given to the point that natural disasters, major strikes, internal dissent, and conflicts and unrest not meeting all the above-mentioned criteria do not 'constitute a *grave and imminent* threat to the life of the nation' and cannot justify derogation measures (Principle 40).[44] One example of an impermissible measure is a state of emergency 'of a preventive nature'[45] (*italics added – A.D.*). Another illegitimate measure might be a state of emergency 'intended to protect a particular government's hold on power where there is no threat to constitutionally recognised institutions'.[46] And finally, 'economic difficulties per se cannot justify derogation measures' (Principle 41).[47]

Public emergencies and their correlation to provisions of the European Convention for the Protection of Human Rights and Fundamental Freedoms of 1950 were considered in four major cases: *Greece v United Kingdom* (1958–1959), *Lawless v Ireland* (1961), *Greek Case* (1969) and *Ireland v United Kingdom* (1978).

In the case of *Lawless v Ireland* of 1961, both the European Commission and European Court confirmed that a 'public emergency' is 'an exceptional situation of crisis ... which affects the whole population and constitutes a threat to the organised life of the community of which the State is composed'.[48]

In the *Greek* case of 1969, caused by a joint statement of the governments of Norway, Sweden, Denmark and the Netherlands on the coup d'etat and imposition of a state of emergency (on 21 April 1967) in Greece, the European Commission refused to accept reliance by the military junta on a 'public emergency' clause and formulated four conditions:

- the emergency must be actual and imminent;
- its effects must involve *the whole nation*;
- the continuance of the organised life of the community must be threatened;
- the crisis or danger must be exceptional[49] (*italics added – A.D.*).

The decision of the European Commission on this case was supported by the Committee of Ministers of the Council of Europe.

This approach, however, is not limited to the European continent. In its 1983 report on the situation in Nicaragua, the Inter-American Commission on Human Rights observed that the emergency 'should be of a serious nature created by an exceptional situation that truly represents a threat to the organised life *of the state*'[50] (*italics added – A.D.*).

The CSCE Copenhagen and Moscow Documents refer to a 'state of public emergency' without stipulating explicitly that it should threaten the life of the nation. However, both Documents affirm the limits provided by the international law, in particular the relevant international instruments, by which the participating States are bound (this refers above all to the ECHR and the ICCPR). Moreover, the Moscow Document spells out that a state of public emergency 'is justified only by the most exceptional and grave circumstances, consistent with the State's international obligations and CSCE commitments' (para.28.1).[51]

The cited conclusion of the last Document was especially symbolic, because it was adopted by the Moscow CSCE Human Rights Dimension Meeting on 3 October 1991, some six weeks after the failed 'coup' in the USSR. One of the first acts of the Moscow *putschists*, who tried to seize power on 19 August 1991, was to declare a state of emergency in some parts of the then Soviet Union for six months. In fact, the very name of the group, which united the USSR Vice President, Chairman of the Council of Ministers, Ministers of Defence, State Security, Internal Affairs, etc., was 'State Committee for the State of Emergency in the USSR'.

On the morning of 21 August 1991, Asbjorn Eide, a member of the UN Sub-Commission on Prevention of Discrimination and Protection of Minorities, declared before the Sub-Commission that the action taken by the coup plotters was 'unconstitutional and null and void', since the emergency had not been declared by the lawful government, but by a 'group of persons' who illegally seized power. He particularly articulated that the public emergency did not meet the requirements of Article 4 of the ICCPR, since the situation was not endangering *the life of the nation*. According to Eide, 'the only threat had been to the power and influence of the group of persons forming 'State Committee for the State of

Emergency in the USSR'. But it would be a clear violation of several provisions of the International Bill of Human Rights for a disaffected group of politicians to overturn the democratically elected authorities and impose a state of emergency in order *not to save the nation* as required by Article 4, but to consolidate their own rule. They might in due course threaten *the life of the nation*, but they were themselves now the cause of that threat, which would disappear if they desisted from the violent behaviour'[52] (*italics added – A.D.*).

So, in light of what has been said above, how do provisions of national legislations providing for imposition of a state of emergency on a 'part of territory of the country' correlate with the international law principle that a public emergency is justified when exceptional circumstances 'threaten the life of the nation', and not some 'part of its territory'?

Introduction of a 'regional' or 'local' state of emergency is not necessarily a violation of the 'additional standard' of the ECHR, ESC, ICCPR and some other instruments. Regional or local public emergencies are quite defensible in those cases when the reason for the imposition of a state of emergency was *of a national character*, like a danger to the sovereignty of the state, its independence, territorial integrity, etc. In this author's opinion, the 'additional standard' should not be understood in the sense that the extraordinary circumstances must be such as to require the proclamation of a public emergency on the whole territory of a state. If the circumstances are local, and not national by their character, then it's not necessary for the government to use the extreme mechanism of a state of emergency at all. The authorities have enough other means of administrative and criminal law to deal with contingencies: declaration of a 'zone of disturbances', imposition of a curfew, etc.; in federal states – declaration of a federal intervention, introduction of a direct (president's) rule.

The other thing is that sometimes it's quite difficult to distinguish precisely between emergency circumstances of a 'national', and 'regional' (or 'local') character. For instance, was it justified for Egypt to declare a national emergency after the beginning of the Operation 'Desert Storm' in the Persian Gulf in January 1991? Or was it defensible for Colombia in 1972 to introduce a state of siege in two departments (Antiochia and Santadera) of the country affected with violence of antigovernment guerrilla groups?

If in the first case the author doesn't have doubts about adequacy of the decision of the Egyptian government, the second case can hardly be qualified as having a 'national' character. The proportionality of the decision by Colombian President Misael Pastrana (1970–1974) to the seriousness of the situation and its 'national' character can certainly be questioned, especially if we take into account that he didn't even submit his decree introducing a state of siege aimed at 'restoration of the public order' for adoption by the Congress, although it by itself was a grave violation of the constitution.[53]

Decision of the President of the Philippines Marcos to introduce a state of exception and suspended the writ of *habeas corpus* following the explosion of a grenade in Manila during an election rally (on 21 August 1971) does not need additional comments here.

III

Carl J. Friedrich was certainly right, when (following Machiavelli) he asserted that 'a government which cannot meet emergencies is bound to fall sooner or later. There is no object in arguing against such emergency powers on the ground that they endanger the constitutional morale, and hence the maintenance of the constitutional order'.[54] Normally, an emergency declaration gives a way to extraordinary means of the state administration – introduction of special temporary regime of regulations in all or most spheres of societal life, including:

- redistribution of powers between branches of government,
- alterations in the competence of the Centre and the Units (in federal states),
- temporary restrictions (or suspension) of certain social, economic, political and other rights and freedoms of citizens, and imposition of additional duties on them.

Issuance (and in most cases, parliamentary approval) of an emergency proclamation (decree, order) leads to a considerable extension of the powers of the executive, administrative bodies, and law enforcement agencies. The Chief Executive acquires additional or exceptional powers in social, economic, political, defence, and other spheres of state mechanism.

The most detailed regulations of emergency powers are contained in the constitutions of some Latin American countries.

The Constitution of Bolivia (adopted on 2 February 1967, and considerably revised by later amendments) contains a whole chapter on 'Preservation of Public Order' (Chapter IV), regulating a 'state of siege'. Under a state of siege 'the executive may increase the armed forces and call into service such reserves as he deems necessary' (art.112(1)). He can also 'order such advance collections of taxes and national revenues as he deems necessary, as well as negotiate and demand loans, provided ordinary resources are insufficient. In the case of forced loans the executive shall fix and distribute them among the taxpayers in accordance with their economic capacity' (art.112(2)). In case of international war 'censorship of correspondence and all publication media may be established' (art.112(4)).[55] Law No.1585 '*On Reform to the Political Constitution of the State of Bolivia*' of 12 August 1994, seriously changed many norms of the Constitution of 1967, but didn't affect its emergency provisions.

In Ecuador (1979) the president may declare the advance collection of taxes, impose censorship and suspend constitutional guarantees (art.78n).

One of the most dramatic uses of state-of-siege powers in Colombia was the enactment of a tough statute on security by President Julio Cesar Turbay (1978–1982) shortly after his inauguration. Ostensibly decreed to be employed as a tool against drug trafficking, it was used primarily against the growing guerrilla threat and against student and labour activists. The new statute increased the police powers of the armed forces and the types of crimes by civilians to be tried by military justice, extended sentences for such crimes as kidnapping and extortion, and limited press reports on public disturbances. An increase in military actions against guerrilla groups, and allegations of human rights violations, led to fears of the 'Uruguayisation' of the country, meaning a gradual military take-over, as in Uruguay in 1973. But the state of siege was eventually lifted, and the effect of the statute on security automatically evaporated nearly at the end of Turbay's term.[56]

According to some constitutions, in extraordinary circumstances exceptional powers are acquired not by the Chief Executive (or head of state), but by emergency organs of power (like the Joint Committee in Germany, or War Delegation in Sweden), which are specially formed to deal with war and other emergencies.

Creation, membership, and functioning of the War Delegation (*krigsdelegation*) in Sweden is regulated by the Instrument of Government and the *Riksdag* Act, fundamental constitutional laws of the country (adopted on 27–28 February 1974).

According to the *Riksdag* Act, the War Delegation is a 'parliament in miniature'. It consists of the Speaker (*talman*) and 50 members, 'elected by the Riksdag for the election period of the *Riksdag*'. A member of the Parliament is eligible to be a member of the War Delegation 'notwithstanding his being a member of the Government'. The *Riksdag* Act makes an exception for 'deputy members' who cannot be appointed to the War Delegation (Ch. 8, art.12).

If the country is at war or just 'exposed to the danger of war', 'if circumstances so warrant', a War Delegation replaces the Parliament and exercises the powers, which in ordinary circumstances belong to the *Riksdag* (Instrument of Government, Ch. 13 'War and Danger of War', art.2(1)).[57]

Generally, the War Delegation is independent in determination of its 'working methods' (art.3(2)) with one major exception – it can not declare new elections for the Parliament (art.3(1)) which is a prerogative of the *Riksdag* itself. For instance, if Sweden is exposed to the danger of war when ordinary elections are due to be held, only the *Riksdag* may decide to defer the elections; 'such a decision shall be reconsidered within one year and at intervals thereafter not exceeding one year' (art.12). The decision that the Parliament can resume its functions has to be taken by the War Delegation and the Government – either jointly or separately (art.2(3)).

In exceptional circumstances, when the country is at war and neither the Parliament nor the War Delegation can carry out its duties, the Government must assume these duties 'to the extent it considers necessary to protect the Realm and bring hostilities to an end' (art.5(1)). Pursuing that goal, the Government may do nearly anything. Among other things, it may issue regulations by statutory order in a particular matter 'which shall otherwise be set forth by law in accordance with fundamental law' (art.6(1)), or it may even agree to a cease-fire without seeking the approval of the Parliament and without consulting the Foreign Affairs Advisory Council, 'if deferment of the agreement would endanger the country' (art.9). However, it cannot enact, amend, or repeal 'any fundamental law, the Parliament Act, or any act concerning elections for the Parliament' (art.5(2)), and, like the *Riksdag*, it cannot make decisions in occupied territory (art.10(1)). In those cases, when the Government cannot carry out its duties, the Parliament, but not the War Delegation, may decide on the formation of a Government and may determine the Government's 'working methods' (art.4).

The constitution prohibits holding elections for the Parliament or for local legislative assemblies in occupied territory (art.10). If the country is at war, the Monarch, as the Head of State, is to accompany the Government. In addition, should he find himself in occupied territory or 'separated from the Government', he shall be deemed 'to be prevented from carrying out his duties as Head of State' (art.11). Finally, it shall be obligatory to 'any public body' in the occupied territory to act in the manner which best serves the defence and resistance activities, as well as the protection of the civilian population and Swedish interests at large. 'In no circumstances may any public body make any decision or take any action which imposes on any citizen of the Realm the duty to render assistance to the occupying power in contravention of international law' (art.10(2)).[58]

Emergency powers under a 'state of defence' (*Verteidigungsfall*) in Germany are granted to the Joint Committee. Two-thirds of its members are deputies of the House of Representatives (*Bundestag*) and one-third of the Senate (*Bundesrat*). *Bundestag* delegates its deputies 'in proportion to the relative strength of its parliamentary groups', and they cannot be members of the Government. The Constitution demands that each State is to be represented in the Joint Committee 'by a Senate member of its choice; these members are not bound by instructions' (art.53a). The Government must inform the Joint Committee 'about its plans in respect of a state of defence' (art.53b).

With an absolute majority of the votes cast (not of *all* members), the Joint Committee may 'determine' that 'insurmountable obstacles' prevent the timely assembly of the House of Representatives or that there is no quorum in it. Such 'determination' leads to acquiring by the Joint Committee of the 'status' of both chambers of the Parliament; it replaces *Bun-*

destag and *Bundesrat* and 'exercises their rights as one body' (art.115e(1)). 'Should the necessity arise' the Joint Committee can also elect (by a simple majority of its members) a new Chancellor (upon President's proposal) or vote no confidence in him 'by electing a successor with a two-thirds majority of its members' (art.115h(2)).

Functions and powers of the Joint Committee are not absolute. The competence of this 'emergency parliament' does not include the right to amend the Basic Law or to abolish its application, totally or partially (to 'deprive it of effect or application either in whole or in part') (art.115a(2)). Furthermore, the Committee has neither the power to transfer sovereign rights of the Federal Republic to international organisations nor the right to reorganise the federal territory with respect to the States (*Lander*). The Federal Constitutional Court Act may be amended by the Joint Committee only when it's required, in the opinion of the Federal Constitutional Court itself, to 'maintain the capability of the Court to function'. Neither the constitutional status, nor the performance of the constitutional functions of the Federal Constitutional Court, and its judges, may be 'impaired' (art.115g).

Duration of validity of the statutes adopted by the Joint Committee or of other 'extraordinary legal provisions' is limited to six months after the termination of a state of defence (art.115k(2)), if until then it won't be repealed by the House of Representatives, with the consent of the Senate. 'Any measures taken by the Joint Committee or the Government to avert a danger has to be revoked where the House of Representatives and the Senate so decide' (art.115l(1)).[59]

A different model was provided by the first post-monarchic Constitution of the People's Republic of Albania (proclaimed on 14 March 1946). Instead of creating any emergency bodies of power, Article 66 allowed the Government, if necessary, by its decree to form a 'smaller' Council of Minister, which would 'deal with some questions of . . . national defence'. The constitution didn't define the competence of this 'smaller' Council. It was to be regulated by the Government itself. An identical provision was included into the next Constitution of Albania (adopted on 4 July 1950, art.70),[60] but was abandoned in the process of drafting the next constitution.

This time, the new Constitution of the People's Socialist Republic of Albania (adopted on 28 December 1976) provided for an establishment of a special organ, Council of Defence, 'to guide all power and resources of the country, their organisation and mobilisation in order to protect the Fatherland'. The Council was chaired by the First Secretary of the ruling Workers' Party of Albania, who was also Commander in Chief of the Armed Forces. Upon his 'proposal', the Presidium of the People's Assembly formed the Council of Defence (art.89). A state of emergency or a state of war (the latter could be declared in case of foreign aggression or the 'necessity to fulfil international treaty commitments'), as well as general or partial mobilisation (under the Constitution of 1950, only 'general') could be proclaimed by the People's Assembly (art.67) convened twice a year (art.70). If it was 'impossible to summon' the Assembly, a state of emergency, a state of war or mobilisation could be introduced by a permanently working Presidium of the Assembly. If in time of war it was impossible to convene the People's Assembly, its Presidium (consisting of the Chair, three Deputy Chairs, Secretary, and ten members (art.75)), was empowered to assume the Assembly's duties and responsibilities, except amending the Constitution (art.78).[61]

Creation of the Council of Defence, possessing 'emergency powers', was also provided by the Constitution of the People's Republic of Hungary (PRH) of 1949 (as amended by Law No. 1 of 1972).[62] According to Article 31(1), the Council could be formed by the PRH Presidium (permanent organ, elected by the State Assembly, the 'supreme organ of state power and people's representation' of Hungary (art.19(1))) and assuming 'all rights based on people's sovereignty', guaranteeing constitutional regime and determining 'organisation, direction and conditions of administration' (art.19(2)). The Defence Council could be formed under two major circumstances. The first of them was more than concrete: war. The second one was much more vague and defined as a 'serious threat to the security of the state'. Both presence and absence of such a threat were to be outlined by the PRH Presidium (consisting of the Chair, two Deputy Chairs, Secretary and 17 members (art.29(1))). The same Presidium was empowered to make respective declarations (art.31(2)).

Provisions on the National Defence Council (NDC) were further elaborated in the acting Constitution of the Republic of Hungary, adopted as a 'transitional' document at the Round Table of 1989–1990. NDC can be set up by the Parliament (as the 'supreme organ of State power and popular representation in the Republic' (art.19(1)), 'ensuring the constitutional order of society' (art.19(2))) in two cases: of war or of the 'immediate threat of armed attack by a foreign power' (art.19(h)). If Parliament 'is prevented from making the decisions concerned', NDC can be set up by the President (art.19/A (1)).

NDC is headed by the President, and includes as its members the Speaker of Parliament, the leaders of the parliamentary factions, the Prime Minister, the ministers, and the commander and chief of staff of the Army (art.19/B (2)). The Constitution doesn't say much about the functions of the Defence Council. It only provides that NDC exercises the 'rights of the President of the Republic', of the Government, and the 'rights temporarily vested in it by Parliament' (art.19/B (3)), including the 'deployment of the armed forces outside or inside the country and the introduction of the emergency measures' (art.19/B (1)). It may also issue decrees suspending 'certain laws' or deviating from 'certain legal provisions' (art.19/B (4)). It can even suspend emergency measures the President of the Republic has called for (art.19/C (3)), but it cannot suspend the

Constitution itself (art.19/B (4)). Neither NDC nor any other government body may 'limit' the operation of the Constitutional Court (art.19/B (6)). Decrees issued by NDC go out of force as soon as the given state of emergency is over (art.19/B (5)).[63]

In many countries of the world, including Great Britain, Sri Lanka, Thailand, Kenya, and some Latin American republics, introduction of a state of exception leads to granting the Chief Executive a right to issue normative acts (decrees, regulations, orders, ordinances) equal in their effect and significance to laws. Sometimes they take a form of whole 'codes' (comprised of up to 70 articles, like in Sri Lanka, or 35 regulations, like in Britain) covering various legal relations in the society under a state of emergency. In some cases such normative acts of the executive branch of government, issued for the duration of an emergency proclamation, and repealed when the emergency is lifted, might have even stronger effect than parliamentary statutes, thus violating a recognised hierarchy of sources of law (Constitution – laws – by-laws).

Moreover, in some cases emergency decrees might change or alter not only acts of ordinary legislation, but even restrict or suspend constitutional provisions. Thus, Article 55(1) of the old Constitution of Nepal (1959) allowed the King by his proclamation to partially or completely suspend 'any provisions' of the constitution itself.[64]

Several acting constitutions still keep this norm. When martial law or a state of emergency is proclaimed, the President of Zaire gets a power 'to take all measures required by the circumstances'. He may restrict the exercise of individual liberties and certain fundamental rights, and suspend 'in all or in part of the national territory, and *for the duration and for the infractions which he determines*, the *substitution of ordinary jurisdiction* for that of *military jurisdiction*'. The only exemption that the constitution makes is that the President may not 'infringe upon rights to defence and to appeal' (*italics added – A.D.*). The Constitutions of Somalia and Algeria say, respectively: 'In the event of a state of war the President shall assume power over the entire country, and those articles of the Constitution which shall be incompatible with such a situation shall be suspended' (art.83(2)); 'during a state of war', the 'Constitution is suspended and the President of the Republic assumes all the powers' (art.96).

Experience of many countries of the world shows that the declaration of a state of exception to wage a war, repel foreign aggression, or curb destructive social processes through constitutional mechanism of emergency powers may be an earnest (almost the only one in some circumstances) way of:

a   preserving the independence of the state and its territorial integrity,
b   maintaining or even re-establishing the existing constitutional order, government structures, legality, law and order, and
c   defending political and social liberties of the people.[65]

Or it may not. The answer to this question may be found not in the sphere of differences and peculiarities of legal regulations of emergency regimes in various countries of the world, but in the sphere of social 'aims' and 'goals' of a state of emergency.

With the exception of situations like war, repulsion of foreign aggression or elimination of the effects of natural disasters and calamities or technological catastrophes, the social function of the institution is usually two-fold: first, to suppress resistance or protest (either organised or unorganised, spontaneous) of some groups or strata of the population in the interests of others, holding a leading and guiding position in the state. Second, to guarantee the social peace and public order in the interest of society as a whole. The unity of these functions consists in the fact that they are exercised simultaneously and aimed at maintaining the *status quo* in the society and state.

A social meaning of such *status quo* might vary in different countries. On the one hand, it could be a protection of a legitimate rule against subversive or illegal actions of the opposition, when timely measures for the maintenance of legality, law and order may head off much greater bloodshed. On the other hand, it could be a reaction of an authoritarian or totalitarian regime to a mass movement demanding democratic changes in the legal and political system of the country. However, in both cases an imposition of a state of emergency usually leads to introduction of restrictions on some fundamental civil rights and freedoms or their temporary suspension.

As a rule, this means:

- a temporary withdrawal of guarantees for the immunity of the individual and the inviolability of the residence;
- increased responsibility under criminal, administrative or disciplinary measures or prosecution coupled with a simultaneous restriction of judicial guarantees (a circumstance which legalises simplified or accelerated court proceedings, execution of searches, arrests and detentions);
- a ban on release on bail; recognition of statements made by defendants before trial as proof of their guilt; recourse to coercion;
- curbs on:
  - freedom of speech, including freedom of the press and information, as well as the privacy of correspondence;
  - freedom of assembly, public meetings and demonstrations;
  - freedom of associations;
  - the right to strike;
  - freedom to choose a place of residence and freedom of movement, in particular on account of the imposition of a curfew, establishment of special restricted areas;
  - economic rights and freedoms, such as freedom of private property, freedom to choose and practise a profession (including the

practice of 'compulsory industrial conscription', 'labour mobilisation' or the formation of 'labour armies'.

- Imposition of other civil duties and obligations, introduction of a system of compulsory government contracts, etc.

For instance, Article 358 of the Constitution of India (1950), Articles 25 and 68 of the Constitution of Zimbabwe (1978) and Article 28 of the Constitution of Nigeria (1960) empower the authorities to suspend all or some individual rights and fundamental freedoms of citizens. The Portuguese Constitutional Law No. 3 of 14 May 1974, provided for 'complete or partial suspension of constitutional guarantees in one or several parts of national territory' in the case of introduction of a state of siege (art.7(12)).[66] According to Articles 121(7) and 140(4) of the Constitution of Costa Rica (adopted on 8 November 1949, with consequent amendments), 'the rights and guarantees' can be suspended by the Legislative Assembly (by two-thirds of votes) or the President (during adjournment of the Parliament). The President can exercise his authority under a more than ambiguous pretext – 'in case of clear public necessity'.[67] In Mexico, under the Political Constitution of 1917, in the event of invasion, serious disturbance of the public peace, or *any other event* that may place society in great danger or conflict, the President may suspend constitutional guarantees with consent of Congress or its Permanent Committee, and Congress shall delegate authority it deems necessary to the President (art.29) (*italics added – A.D.*).

Classic of American political philosophy of the twentieth century John Rawls postulated in his work, *A Theory of Justice* that 'liberty can be restricted only for the sake of liberty itself'. Unfortunately, neither Rawls himself nor his commentators have elaborated this thesis in the context of emergency powers and a state of exception.[68] However, restriction of liberty for the sake of liberty ('lesser liberty today – bigger liberty tomorrow') is questionable as *an abstract principle* that is detached from *particular circumstances*, along with *concrete reality* and *practical meaning*.

Contemporary international law, including international conventions on human rights (the ECHR, ESC, ICCPR and ACHR), also recognises the admissibility of temporary restrictions on civil rights and freedoms in exceptional circumstances, like an 'emergency' (ACHR) or 'public emergency' (ECHR, ESC, ICCPR), 'threatening the life of the nation' (ECHR, ESC, ICCPR) or 'the independence or security of a State Party' (ACHR). In other words, when a threat is posed to national independence, security, or life of the nation itself, especially in periods of war or national emergencies, the state can adopt measures limiting certain rights and freedoms. 'The flame of individual rights and justice must burn more palely when it is ringed by the more dramatic light of bombed buildings', Lord Pierce said in *Convay v Rimmer* [1968] A.C.910, 982.[69]

Indeed, it's generally accepted that 'no modern political society gives unfettered rein to individual rights or society's rights. Neither does the international system require states to destabilise their domestic orders to secure human rights'.[70] In face of threats to its security, particularly in time of national emergency, the State may take restrictive action for the 'maintenance of the public order in the wide sense, as for the control of crime, the protection of public health, the observance of certain accepted moral standards, or the protection of the rights and freedoms of others'. However, 'it is no less generally recognised', wrote J.E.S. Fawcett, member of the European Commission of Human Rights, 'that it is often through precisely action of this kind that human rights are violated'.[71]

This explains why the international conventions set strict limits to such derogations. The derogation clause of human rights treaties has been described as the 'cornerstone' of the entire system for protecting human rights, and as the most important provision of human rights treaties.[72] In the words of Jaime Oraa, 'one of the most important problems in the international protection of human rights is that of identifying the standards governing these rights in situations of emergency. Public emergencies present a grave problem for States: that of overcoming the emergency and restoring order in the country while at the same time respecting the fundamental human rights of individuals'.[73]

Article 4 of the ICCPR, and Article 27 of the ACHR, lay down three sets of conditions. The derogations:

a   must be 'strictly required by the exigencies of the situation',
b   may not be inconsistent with the state's 'other obligations under international law', and
c   may not involve discrimination on certain specified grounds (race, colour, sex, language, religion or social origin).

Article 15 of the ECHR and Article 30 of the ESC contain two first conditions but do not expressly prohibit discrimination.

The conventions also set a list of 'non-derogable rights' that cannot be restricted or suspended *even* under a state of emergency. ICCPR defines them as: the right to life (art.6); the right to be free from 'torture or cruel, inhuman or degrading treatment or punishment' (art.7); the right to be free from slavery and 'forced or compulsory labour' (art.8); prohibition of imprisonment 'merely on the ground of inability to fulfil a contractual obligation' (art.11); the principle of non-retroactivity of penal laws ('No one shall be held guilty of any criminal offence on account of any act or omission which did not constitute a criminal offence, under national or international law, at the time when it was committed') (art.15); the right to 'recognition everywhere as a person before the law' (art.16); freedom of thought, conscience and religion (art.18). Four of these rights, covered by Articles 6, 7, 8 and 15 of the ICCPR, are contained in all other major international law instruments and documents (ECHR, ACHR, Siracusa (1984) and Paris (1984) Principles, Moscow Declaration (1991)) and constitute the 'irreducible core' of non-derogable human rights.

When it's necessary for a member state, which has ratified the above-mentioned international conventions, to take measures derogating from its obligations under the Conventions, it must 'immediately' inform the world community (through the Secretary-General of the United Nations) of the provisions from which it has derogated and 'of the reasons by which it was actuated'. A further communication through the UN Secretary-General is to be made 'on the date on which it terminates such derogation' (ICCPR, art.4(3); ECHR, art.15(3)).[74]

The very character of international humanitarian law as a whole, and obligations assumed by states in signing international law documents, imply, among other things, that derogations shall be reduced to the absolute minimum and that the criteria of declaring a state of emergency shall be restrictive and explicit. Fried van Hoof, Dutch professor of international law from Utrecht, testified:

> Situations which are not entirely normal, but which do not directly threaten the life of the nation, either occur in many States so often that, if emergency situations are interpreted broadly, the emergency situation would almost become the *normal* situation.

In van Hoof's opinion, this result would be contrary to the 'purpose and meaning' of the ICCPR. What is even more troublesome, 'even in normal situations the Covenant leaves States ample room for coping with actual internal disturbances and with situations that may lead to such disturbances. It allows States to restrict the exercise of individual rights and freedoms, if required for the protection of national security, public order, etc., thus leaving certain powers to the States to respond to internal disturbances'. Van Hoof concluded:

> A State which deals with these non-emergency situations with further restrictions than these normal measures, does not fulfil the requirements of the Covenant concerning the protection of human rights and freedoms.[75]

In her *Study of the Implications for Human Rights of Recent Developments Concerning Situations Known as States of Siege or Emergency* submitted to the 35th Session of the Sub-Commission on Prevention of Discrimination and Protection of Minorities, ECOSOS Human Rights Commission, in July 1982, Nicole Questiaux listed six principles which states should follow in declaring a state of emergency:

1   *The principle of formal proclamation* of a state of emergency (para.43);

2 *The principle of notification* of the world community 'immediately' (as the ICCPR and ACHR stipulate) or at the earliest possible date of the emergency proclamation, the reasons for it and the nature of the measures being adopted (para.44);

3 *The principle of exceptional threat*: the circumstances that are indicated must constitute a 'grave and imminent' danger threatening the state and existence of the nation; it is necessary that 'the situation of danger must be such that the normal measures and restrictions authorised by the instruments in normal times manifestly no longer suffice to maintain public order' (para.55(2));

4 *The principle of proportionality*: the emergency measures adopted by the state must be commensurate with the exigencies of the moment; they must correspond to the dangerousness of the crisis situation and must not go beyond the strict limits required by the situation (para.60);

5 *The principle of non-discrimination*: the measures adopted under a state of emergency shall not involve discrimination based 'solely' on the ground of race, colour, sex, language, religion or social origin (para.64);

6 *The principle of inalienability of certain fundamental rights* (right to life, prohibition of torture, slavery, retroactive penal measures, etc.) (para.67).[76]

As it has been discussed above, national legislation not always contains effective safeguards against abuses of civil and political rights and freedoms under emergency. That explains why the necessity to improve national constitutions, and laws, has been increasingly emphasised by human rights experts. The Special Rapporteur of the UN Sub-Commission on Prevention of Discrimination and Protection of Minorities, Leandro Despouy, initiated work on draft guidelines for the development on legislation on states of emergency. The effort has not failed. Inclusion of an express list of non-derogable rights into a number of new constitutions of the former Soviet republics and countries of Eastern Europe is one of the most positive and encouraging events of contemporary constitutionalism world-wide. Sometimes the constitutions of those countries name even more rights and freedoms as non-derogable than respective international law instruments do.

The Constitution of the Republic of Slovenia (adopted on 23 December 1991) became one of the very first of such constitutions. Although Article 16 starts with the words, 'human rights and basic liberties specified in this constitution may exceptionally be temporarily suspended or limited during war and states of emergency', it continues on to say: 'The specifications of the previous paragraph do not allow any temporary suspension or limitation of rights specified under Articles 17 [inviolability of human life], 18 [prohibition of torture], 21 [protection of human personality and dignity],

27 [assumption of innocence], 28 [principle of legality in criminal law], 29 [legal guarantees in penal processes] and 41 [freedom of conscience].'[77]

'Non-derogable clauses' are also *contained* in the constitutions of Russia (1993), Belarus (1994), Armenia (1995), Kazakhstan (1993), Hungary (as amended in 1989–1990), Poland (1997) and *not contained* in the new constitutions of Romania (1991), Slovakia (1992), Azerbaijan (1995), Uzbekistan (1992). To be sure, the law itself cannot remove the causes of the rise of emergency situations, but it can and must avert some of them or substantially limit their dangerous impact on people's health and lives. Yet, the necessity to develop legislation regulating a state of emergency in Russia, as well as other former Soviet republics and elsewhere, and the desire to apply it as effectively and securely as possible in dealing with crises, conflicts, national disasters, etc. (and not to abuse rights and freedoms of the population) does not eliminate a long-range task of the human race, that is to build a social, economic and political order that would reduce to a minimum the need to resort to the legal mechanism of a state of exception as a means of solving problems facing the state and society in the twenty-first century. Even though setting such goals at this moment may be wishful thinking.

3 Legal regulation of emergency powers in Imperial Russia

In the whole body of the Russian Imperial legislation (of the 17th–early 20th centuries), one can hardly find a statute that has been as much misinterpreted and misrepresented by either Russian (and Soviet) or Western commentators, as the emergency law of 1881. Coincidence of views of Bolsheviks and some foreign scholars on this law is astonishing. A founder of the Soviet state Vladimir Ulyanov (a.k.a. Lenin) called it 'Russia's *de facto* constitution',[1] and Richard Pipes – 'the most important piece of legislation in the history of imperial Russia ... The real constitution under which ... Russia has been ruled ever since'.[2] In his denunciation of the emergency law, Pipes cited Alexei A. Lopukhin,[3] a former procurator, head of the Police Department (1902–1905) and Governor of Estlandia (1905) who got 'disillusioned', passed secret information to the revolutionaries, was tried for revealing a state secret, and spent three years in a Siberian exile.[4] (A microscopic term compared to punishments for similar crimes in Europe or America). What Pipes didn't mention is that Lopukhin's report with his criticism of the emergency law ('a remarkable pamphlet', as Pipes called it) was first published in Geneva in 1905 with an introduction ... by the same Bolshevik leader Vladimir Ulyanov ('N. Lenin').[5]

Another American researcher alleged that Russia's 'rulers ... were nearly all apparently uncomfortable with the maintenance of that unpopular legislation, especially since their European role models no longer invoked such rules'.[6]

In reality, neither the fact of issuance of the emergency law in Russia, nor its substance, nor its use was unique. As it has already been indicated, adoption of special statutes regulating the legal regime of a state of emergency was a common trend of European law-making in the middle and second half of the nineteenth century. Such 'European role models' of Russia as France, Prussia, Austria-Hungary and Spain passed first statutes in this sphere in 1848, 1851, 1869 and 1870, respectively.

In France only it was repeatedly invoked throughout the second part of the nineteenth century, including the period of 1871–1876 when nearly all territory of the country was under a state of siege (*etat de siege*), and led to hundreds of times bigger repressions than in Russia. A new French law on a state of siege was adopted on 3 April 1878, next year after issuance of the first Russian law on the procedure of military assistance to civil authorities[7] and three years before issuance of the first Russian law on a state of emergency.

On 19 October 1878, a notorious emergency Anti-Socialist Law was adopted in Germany. In the next eight months (until 30 June 1879) the government used the act to shut down 217 workers' unions, and ban 127 periodicals and 278 non-periodical publications.[8] All in all, in 12 years of the law's existence, a state of siege was declared and repeatedly extended against 'socialists' in Berlin, Potsdam, Leipzig, Hamburg, Scharlottenburg, districts of Telt, Niderbarnim, Ost-Havelland. Hundreds of workers' unions were closed down (352 in 1878–1888), thousands of meetings and assemblies prohibited, more than 10,000 house searches exercised, 1,299 publications (both periodical and non-periodical) banned, more than a 1,000 persons extradited, more than a 1,000 years of prison sentences announced.[9] We should not forget that the Prussian emergency law of 1851 not only allowed the German government to periodically introduce a 'state of war' (*kriegszustand*), suspend most basic constitutional rights, subject civilians to military courts, and transfer important aspects of government powers from civilian to military authorities at that time, but served as a legal antecedent of notorious Article 48 of the Weimar Constitution.

A scholar of emergency regimes in Latin America of the nineteenth century correctly argues that 'parallel studies of Spain, France, Italy, Germany, Portugal, and the United States would find regimes of exception, methods of suppressing ethnic and religious minorities, political opposition to rising labor movements, and claims of defending the constitutional order'.[10] Needless to say, that European states resorted even more cruelly, massively and regularly to emergency measures in their colonial possessions in Africa and Asia.[11]

Russian understanding of the essence of emergency powers was by no means unique either. It was similar to generally accepted views on this subject in the European ('continental') legal tradition.

'In life of each state such critical moments occur', – Professor of St. Petersburg University N.M. Korkunov[12] wrote in his *Comparative Study of State Law of Foreign Countries*, – 'when integrity and even existence of a state can depend on a single minute, when the state cannot think about some far away general goals, but rather save itself by any means'. After that, N.M. Korkunov made a logical conclusion, comparable by its laconic definition to the famous Cicero's maxim: 'Self-restriction of the power with law cannot go to such extreme, when the state would bring its own existence as prey to this principle'. The scholar argued that just like 'a right of self-defence' is recognised and enjoyed by 'private persons', the same right should be exercised by 'state authorities' and concluded: 'In cases of extreme external or internal danger, state power should undertake emergency measures of defence, including temporary restrictions of civil rights'.[13]

'State necessity is superior to individual freedom', – agreed his colleague Professor of St. Petersburg University, deputy of the III and IV Dumas, and member of the Central Committee of the Constitutional Democracy Party ('kadet') Vladimir M. Gessen.[14] – 'If in normal circumstances of state and social life a contemporary state recognises and guarantees individual freedom, then in emergency circumstances it makes it subordinate to the interests of security and maybe even of the existence of the state'.[15]

The views, reflected in the citations of Korkunov and Gessen are hardly different from the dominating position on the subject of this study in the European law of the second half of the nineteenth century represented in works of such German, French and Swiss legal scholars as Edgar Loening, Johann Kaspar Bluntschli, Lorenz von Stein, and Maurice Block.

'When existence of the state or its peace are in danger, salvation of the state from dire straits is the most important task of the state power', – a classic of German administrative law E. Loening wrote in his book *Lehrbuch des Deutschen Verwaltungsrechts*, (Leipzig, 1884), and continued: 'In order to be able to accomplish this task, state authorities must be granted wide powers. Limitations, imposed by legislation protecting personal freedoms, must be temporarily abolished.'

'A state is a being of so high level, that maintenance of its existence, which is the first duty of the government, can in extreme cases justify violation of individual rights and suspension of normal state of affairs', argued Swiss jurist and political scientist J.K. Bluntschli. In his book *German State Law* (*Algemeines Staatsrecht*, Munich, 1863), Bluntschli analysed Cicero's concept of necessity and concluded: 'When existence of a state is in danger and its salvation is impossible without restrictions of existing rights of certain people or even whole classes of the population, the government can not and should not, when respecting these rights, doom the state to death; decisively following the principle *salus populi supremo lex esto*, it must do everything to save and defend the state'. Bluntschli repeated the argument of John Hampdon's counsel Holborne and elaborated it: 'In order to save the ship during storm, a skilful captain without hesitation throws the property of passengers to the sea; in order to bring victory to the army in the battle or guarantee its safe retreat, a commander sometimes has to send some battalions to certain death, if that's the only thing he can do. A statesman, a leader of the state cannot act otherwise, when the state is in grave danger.'[16]

Analysis of the Russian emergency law of 1881 should be started with putting it into a more general context of Russian law of pre-Soviet period, with a special reference to those facts that are often ignored or dismissed as not fitting into an image of Russia as a land of a 'thousand years of terror and repressions'.[17]

The last half-century of the Imperial rule has a deserved reputation of the 'Golden Age' of Russian law. Law of 17 April 1863 abolished corporal punishment in the civil institutions, army, and fleet (save through peasant courts). Anatole Leroy-Beaulieu (1842–1912), a French scholar, member of the Academie des Sciences Morales (since 1887), Professor of the Free School of Political Science (and its Director in 1906–1912), and author of a three-volume study *The Empire of the Tsars and the Russians*, termed the Russian criminal code of the nineteenth century 'probably the mildest code in Europe'.[18] Leroy-Beaulieu was not the only foreign observer who came to such a conclusion. Before him, Albert F. Heard, an author of two remarkable articles in *Harper's New Monthly Magazine* in 1887–1888[19] (and apparently living in Russia during those years), used the same words to characterise the Russian penal code as 'one of the mildest in Europe'.[20]

In the opinion of Marc Szeftel, one of the most distinguished American specialists in the Russian Imperial Law, Russia's Charter on Criminal Procedure (*Ustav ugolovnogo sudoproizvodstva*)[21] of 20 November 1864 'may be considered as the Russian parallel to the Habeas Corpus Act'.[22] In the last decades of the Imperial rule, 'the Russian legal profession flowered, producing distinguished practitioners, judges, and legal scholars, successfully challenging in several celebrated jury trials an absolutist autocracy',[23] another American scholar correctly observed.

Whereas in England at the end of the eighteenth century, according to William Blackstone, the number of 'capital statutes', or the laws imposing capital punishment 'without benefit of the clergy', was 160,[24] and by the beginning of the nineteenth century it has reached 223,[25] capital punishment was abolished from Russian codes during the 13th and most of the 12th and 14th centuries, under Elizabeth from 1742 to 1754, and up until 1775 when Catherine the Great used it against six participants of the Emelyan Pugachev rebellion. From then on until the execution of the five leaders of an armed mutiny (so-called Decembrists)[26] in July 1826, nobody was executed for political offences either.[27] Since 1812 the death penalty applied for some military crimes, but not for common crimes like murder or rape, though this was frequently the case abroad.[28]

According to probably the most comprehensive study on capital punishment in Russia, a 500-page work by S. Usherovich, the number of persons executed (for both criminal and political offences) during the reign of Alexander I (1801–1825) was 24, of Nicholas I (1825–1855) – 41, and of Alexander III (1881–1894) – 33[29] (including 14 terrorists).[30] Vadim Kozhinov continued the list adding 31 terrorists executed under the reign of Alexander II (1855–1881). All in all, between mid-18th and late 19th centuries, the number of those sentenced to death and executed in the Russian Empire was equal to 135 in 'mainland' Russia and about 1,500 in Poland (after the Polish rebellion).[31]

For comparison, it was in 1785 that the last 'witch' was sentenced to death and executed in Switzerland.[32] In the years of Jacobean terror in

France (1793–1794) from 70,000 to 500,000 people were arrested, and 17,000 of them were sentenced to death and executed on a guillotine.[33]

In just one week of revolutionary events in Paris in June 1848, the number of those sentenced to death and executed under French martial law was equal at least to 11,000. A contemporary French historian, however, testified that the actual number of victims was much higher: the municipal council of Paris paid the expenses of burial of 17,000 corpses; but a great number were killed out of Paris. The ultimate number of those who were killed or died as results of wounds in those days could be as high as 20,000.[34]

Similarly, there are no exact figures of how many people perished as a result of violent suppression of the Paris Commune in May 1871. It is estimated that between 17,000 and 30,000 Parisians became victims of the Thier regime. The figure of 30,000 seems to be consistent with figures quoted in news reports of the time. Approximately 50,000 Communards were arrested, 11,000 were tried, of these 5,000 were transported to penal colonies of New Caledonia. Hundreds of people who managed to escape went into exile in Switzerland, Belgium, Britain and other European countries. Overall, about 100,000 men and women were killed, died as a result of wounds or were exiled to the colonies.[35]

It was long after the end of the Cold War that a Western scholar could recognise the obvious: 'Anyone imagining the course of Russian pre-modern history to have been particularly barbarous or bloodstained should remember the near absence, in comparison with Western lands, of witch-hunting, crusading, institutionalised capital punishment (abolished under Elizabeth in the mid-eighteenth century). The brutal episodes in the reigns of Ivan the Terrible or Peter the Great were traumatic because uncharacteristic.'[36]

As in other countries of Europe, adoption of a special statute regulating emergency powers and states of emergency was a natural and inalienable element of Russian transition to constitutional monarchy and the rule of law.[37] It became possible after Alexander II (1855–1881), known in Russian history as the Tsar-Liberator, abolished serfdom in 1861 and instituted Russia's first significant abridgement of monarchical authority and its earliest affirmation of the civil rights of persons by means of his Reform of Province and District (*Gubernia i Uezd*) Self-Government and Judicial Reform of 1864. The latter crucial act effectively created an independent judiciary, thus significantly weakening the autocrat. It also restricted arbitrary arrest, established strict criminal procedure and placed the investigation of all crimes under the supervision of the Procuracy (*prokuratura*), an agency of the Ministry of Justice. It is indicative, that a leading Soviet historian P.A. Zaionchkovskiy had to recognise that 'the apogee of administrative-police arbitrariness' in Russia happened, not *after* adoption of emergency law of 14 August 1881, but *before* it – at the end of 1879.[38]

On 24 January 1878, a member of the 'Land and Freedom' (*Zemlia i volia*) terrorist group (founded in late 1876) Vera Zasulich made an attempt on life of General Fyodor F. Trepov, Governor of Russia's capital St. Petersburg (son of emperor Nicholas I, born out of wedlock), and severely crippled him.[39] On 4 August 1878, Sergei Kravchinsky stabbed to death the Chief of Russian Gendarmerie N.V. Mezentsev. Next year, in August 1879, the 'People's Will' (*Narodnaia volia*) revolutionary movement was created. Their programme included plans to assassinate ten to 15 'pillars of the current government' in order to provoke panic, paralyse the autocracy, and pave the way for revolution.[40] Alexander II survived six assassination attempts. On 19 November 1879, terrorists bombed the tsar's train and killed and wounded dozens of innocent people. Another well-known failed attempt was an explosion in the Winter Palace, the tsar's residence, detonated by Stepan Khalturin on 5 February 1880. The powerful blast destroyed two floors, killed and wounded about 70 people, but the tsar and his family escaped again. The explosion proved to be the last straw. A week later, Alexander II created a Supreme Executive Commission for the Preservation of the State Order and Public Tranquillity (*Verkhovnaia Rasporiaditel'naia Komissiia po okhraneniu gosudarstvennogo poriadka i obschestvennogo spokoistvia*) and authorised the head of the Commission, Count Mikhail Loris-Melikov, to 'give any regulations and take any measures ... for the preservation of state order and public tranquillity in St. Petersburg and other localities of the [Russian] Empire'.[41]

In the next year, the police arrested nearly all of the major activists of the 'People's Will'. The organisation did not carry out any terrorist acts between February 1880 and 1 March 1881, when the seventh and the last desperate attempt at regicide became a 'success'. The Russian tsar Alexander II was murdered.[42]

Life and history can really be richer than human imagination. Could anybody envisage that a few hours before his assassination, Alexander II had given his Royal approval to a plan of the creation of a 'Constitution' (known as 'Constitution of Count Loris-Melikov') and an elective proto-parliament ('Joint Commission') with consultative functions?[43] The project was to be considered by the Council of Ministers on 4 March, but assassination of the tsar drastically changed the mood and postponed long-awaited and much needed constitutional reforms in the country.[44]

On 14 August 1881, five-and-a-half months after the assassination of the Russian tsar, his successor Alexander III signed an act drafted by the Committee of Ministers. It was the law '*On Measures for the Preservation of the State Order and Public Tranquillity*' (*O merakh k okhraneniiu gosudarstvennogo poriadka i obschestvennogo spokoistvia*).[45]

In its opening paragraphs, the decree asserted that ordinary laws had proved insufficient to preserve order in the empire so that it had become necessary to introduce certain 'extraordinary' procedures. Contrary to what is said by critics of emergency legislation in the Russian Empire, the Ordinance of 1881 did *not* increase discretionary extraordinary powers of the administration. It actually limited and diminished them, because the adoption of the Ordinance meant an annulment of all previous emergency decrees (*ukaz*), which had been issued amid the terrorist campaign to murder Alexander II at the end of the 1870s and invested vast arbitrary power in the Governors-General.[46] As it was acknowledged in an official report of 1895, by adoption of the 1881 Emergency Law the authorities hoped to systematise ('to unify') the 'repressive measures employed against anti-government elements',[47] rather than to introduce any *new* measures.

The Emergency Law established two forms of a state of emergency or a 'state of exception' (*iskluchitel'noe polozhenie*), as it was called in Russia: 'reinforced security' (or 'reinforced protection', *usilennaia okhrana*) and 'extraordinary security' (or 'extraordinary protection', *chrezvychainaia okhrana*). It also contained 'rules for places not declared in a state of exception' (art.28–31). The law fully concentrated the struggle against subversion in the hands of the Ministry of the Interior (MVD) where it has largely remained since.

Reinforced security (RS), as a milder form of a state of emergency, could be declared by MVD upon a request of city and provincial governors. The Governors-General were also able to impose it on their own authority, but such a decision was still subject to approval by the MVD (art.7). RS could be introduced for a period of up to one year.

Extraordinary security (ES) required both the Committee of Ministers' and the Emperor's sanction (art.9), and lasted only six months. Re-establishment of any form of a state of emergency required a formal reapplication (art.12).

In regions under a state of *reinforced security*, the Governors-General (or Governors in provinces lacking one, art.14), while retaining the powers enumerated above, were authorised:

- to issue binding orders enforceable with penalties of up to three months' imprisonment or a 500 rouble fine (art.15);
- to forbid social, public, and private gatherings;
- to shut down commercial and industrial enterprises either for a specific period or for the duration of the emergency;
- to deny individuals the right to reside in their jurisdictions (*vospreschat' prebyvanie*) (art.16);
- to transfer to military courts *any* case in the interest of preserving order (art.17).

Police and gendarmerie were permitted:

- to detain any person 'inspiring substantial suspicion' from the point of view of state security, but for only two weeks (one month with permission from the governor), or

- to search any premises on pure suspicion of involvement in the commission of state crime (art.21).

Finally, provincial and city governors were authorised to declare any non-elective local officials employed by the *zemstva*, city governments or courts as 'untrustworthy' or 'politically unreliable' (*neblagonadezhnyi*) and to order his instantaneous dismissal. (art.20).

Under a state of *extraordinary security*, the Governors-General retained all of the prerogatives conferred by reinforced security and were furthermore authorised:

- to create special military-police units with broad powers for the restoration of order;
- to transfer to military courts whole categories of state crimes;
- to sequester any private property or source of income 'harmful to state or public security';
- to issue binding administrative orders and to impose fines of up to 3,000 roubles for failure to comply with them;
- to declare any crimes liable to administrative punishments of the magnitude just mentioned;
- to remove from office any civil servant (even locally elected officials, as distinct from hired employees) up to and including rank four (*deistvitel'nyi statskii sovetnik* or *General-Maior*);
- to prohibit *zemstvo* and other public-institution meetings;
- to suspend newspapers and other publications; and
- to close schools and other educational institutions for up to one month (art.26, pts.a–i).

Unlike the 5 April 1879 law on the Governors-General, the Emergency Law contained no carte blanche provision that allowed them to take 'any measures deemed necessary for the preservation of tranquillity'.

The section establishing 'rules for places not declared in a state of exception' was a peculiar feature of the Emergency Law, distinguishing it from similar legislation in other European countries of the nineteenth century. It empowered *all* police and gendarme authorities in any locality of the Russian Empire:

- to search, arrest and detain for up to seven days persons suspected of involvement in the planning or perpetration of state crimes, or of belonging to illegal organisations;
- to propose the exile (*vysylka*) of such persons for up to five years (arts.29, 32–36);
- upon obtaining the consent of the Ministry of Justice, to transfer to military courts specified state-crime cases, as well as cases of violent resistance to, or physical attacks against, administrative officials in

their line of duty (art.31), if only a state of reinforced or extraordinary security was declared *anywhere* in the Empire.[48]

Ninety-five years later, a norm similar to the last provision of the Russian Emergency Law was included into the Constitution of India. The Constitution (Forty-Second Amendment) Act (adopted on 18 December 1976) consisted of 59 articles and was the biggest amendment ever made to the Indian Constitution. (It was also larger than constitutions of some countries of the world). Articles 48, 49, and 52 of the act made a number of changes to Part XVIII of the Constitution ('Emergency Provisions'). According to them, even if a state of emergency is *not* declared in some 'part of the territory of India', an emergency regime (including extension of powers of federal authorities, suspension of certain rights and freedoms, etc.) can still be extended to 'any State or Union territory', 'if and in so far as the security of India or any part of the territory thereof is threatened by activities or in relation to the territory of India in which the Proclamation of Emergency is in operation'.[49]

In other words, if a state of emergency is declared in Amritsar (in Punjab), an emergency regime can be extended to Delhi, located in several hundred miles from Punjab, if the President of India 'is satisfied' (upon an 'advise' of the Prime Minister, as determined by the Constitution (art.74)) that events in Amritsar 'threaten' 'security' of the capital of India. Similarly, if a state of exception was declared in Moscow, an emergency regime could be extended to Vladivostok in the Russian Far East, on the Pacific coast.

In sum, the Emergency Law of 1881:

a   placed the system of extra-legal arrest and punishment under the supervision of the home minister (but granted him fewer prerogatives than the director of the Supreme Executive Commission of 1880);
b   extended the right to arbitrary arrest to the regular police (but strictly defined the period of detention); and
c   empowered Governors and Governors-General to subject political suspects to administrative exile (but less extensively and with shorter terms of exile than under the 5 April 1879 law on the Governors-General) and to transfer them to military courts.

Although the Law was defined as 'temporary', it was renewed in 1884 for another period of three years and then regularly afterwards.

As far as the implementation of the Emergency Law of 1881 is concerned, on 4 September 1881 a state of 'reinforced security' was declared in ten provinces (most notably, in St. Petersburg and Moscow), and several smaller localities in three other provinces of the Russian Empire. (Compare to 21 provinces and Poland affected by the edict of 5 April 1879!)[50] In 1901–1902, the reinforced security was extended to include two full provinces, and parts of six other provinces, plus three major cities.

War with Japan (1904–1905) and especially the first (failed) Russian 'revolution' of 1905–1907 made the government, on the one hand, to implement the Emergency Law more actively, and, on the other hand, initiate drastic legal and social reforms, culminating in the Emperor's Manifesto '*On Improvement of the State Order*' of 17 October 1905, instituting constitutional monarchy with the first elected Russian Parliament (State Duma).

By January 1907, in Daly's count, martial law was in effect in 57 different localities across the empire, including 21 provinces, 25 districts, nine cities, and along two railroads, where it remained in force until gradually lifted between 1908 and 1913, especially in 1908–1909.[51] In 1906–1907, a state of extraordinary security was established in Moscow, St. Petersburg and 15 other localities.

Overall, Michael Gernet (1874–1953), a distinguished Russian scholar and author of a fundamental, five-volume study of the Russian penitentiary system counted 60 *guberniyas* and *oblasts* which had been placed under reinforced and extraordinary protection in 1905–1907, and 25 *guberniyas* and *oblasts* where martial law had been introduced. However, by 1914 there was no martial law anywhere in the Russian Empire, extraordinary protection was in effect only in one isolated case (in Yalta and its district, around the Emperor's summer residence in the Crimea on the Black Sea) and reinforced protection – in just a few localities.[52]

The normalisation of the situation was abruptly interrupted and drastically changed because of the immanence of the war with Germany. The assassination of Archduke Franz Ferdinand in Sarajevo (on 28 June 1914) provided Austria-Hungary with an excuse to take aggressive actions against Serbia. Bound by treaty to Serbia, Russia announced mobilisation of its vast army in her defence, and simultaneously introduced martial law (in its eastern and southern provinces) or a state of extraordinary security throughout the whole Empire. The decision was quite understandable given a forthcoming (on 1 August 1914) Germany's declaration a war against Russia.

It's a debatable question – whether or not a broad imposition of a state of emergency (in its different forms) in Russia in the years of the first revolution of 1905–1907 was justified. There are two main reasons that probably allow us to give an affirmative answer.

The first of them is more of a 'technical' character; it concerns the quantity of law-enforcement personnel of the Russian Empire. Police forces in tsarist Russia have always been microscopic, miserably diminutive and chronically understaffed. It is important to remember that at the turn of the twentieth century, rural areas of the largest country on earth (populated by more than 90 million peasants at that time) were policed by only 8,456 ordinary police sergeants and constables. In 1900, a regular rural policeman could have a 'beat' of 1,800 square miles and 50,000–100,000 people.[53] Even in 1914 there were fewer than 15,000 gendarmes throughout the empire.[54] Jonathan W. Daly makes an interesting comparison noticing that in 1897 France had about 40 per cent more policemen than Russia, even though France at that time was a 'country with three times fewer people and forty times less territory'.[55]

Indeed, Vera Figner, a famous revolutionary, 'symbolising', in words of another legendary terrorist Boris Savinkov, 'the best traditions of the revolutionary movement',[56] recalled that 'in Petersburg itself, propaganda, agitation, and organisation were carried on on a broad scale. The lack of police-nagging and of round-ups by the Gendarmerie ... was very favourable to work among the students and the workers'.[57]

Figner's testimony is definitely reliable. One may recall a sad recognition of a deputy head of tsarist 'secret police' (so-called Third Department) Shultz that 'it was impossible to find police-spies and plain-clothed agents in Russia'.[58] And how large was the total staff of the central apparatus of the Third Department itself, known to modern readers thanks to numerous 'terrifying' stories about it running like a trend through writings of many Western and liberal Russian authors? At the time of its creation on 3 July 1826, the Third Department had 16 (!) persons, at the height its activity in 1873 it had 58, and when the Department was abolished by Alexander II (on 6 August 1880), it had 72 persons, including full-time officers, agents and contractors.[59] 'A ridiculously small number for even the remotest Cheka [Lenin's secret police, future KGB – *A.D.*] provincial headquarters in the country', Alexander Solzhenitsyn sarcastically observed.[60] Solzhenitsyn's observation remains valid even if we take into account that the head of the Third Department was automatically becoming the chief of the Gendarmerie Corps. In 1826, the Corps consisted of not more than 4,278 persons for the whole empire.[61]

Russian penitentiary system was too soft and ineffective. Quite typical is an example of Felix Dzerzhinsky, future founder and first head of Cheka. Between 1897 and 1917 (to be precise, in 1897, 1900, 1905, 1906, 1908, and 1912) he was arrested six times; three times he was sentenced to Siberian exile and each time escaped penalty, once after serving just seven days of a life sentence.[62] Over the course of a single year beginning in October 1905, there were 1,951 robberies (with seven million roubles confiscated); in 1,691 of these cases, the revolutionaries escaped detention.[63]

On 1 March 1917, several days after the beginning of the so-called 'Bourgeois Revolution in Russia', Moscow mob stormed Butyrki prison and released its inhabitants, including Dzerzhinsky, who had been serving his sentence there. A very informative study by Lennard Gerson contains an apparent mistake when the author writes about '*hundreds* of *political* prisoners ... released from their cells' in Butyrki in March 1917[64] (*italics added – A.D.*). Most inhabitants of prisons were ordinary criminals – murderers, thieves, burglars, etc. Alexander Solzhenitsyn gave an exact figure (taken from local newspapers of that period) of political prisoners released from the Tambov Prison: 'The February Revolution, which opened wide the doors of the Tambov Prison, found there political prisoners in the number of ... seven (7) persons'.[65] It's very unlikely, that Butyrki contained many more 'political prisoners' than the Tambov Prison or any other jail in Russian provinces. The fact itself that Dzerzhinsky was known in Butyrki as 'Prisoner 217' does not necessarily mean that there were 'hundreds of political prisoners' in that or any other prison of Russia.

That elegance and easiness with which Dzerzhinsky, Trotsky, Stalin and many other revolutionaries in Russia were able to escape Siberian exile is also an unquestionable proof of mildness and 'liberalism' of penitentiary system in Tsarist Russia, – especially comparing to the one later created by Bolsheviks.[66]

The second reason justifying a broad imposition of a state of exception in 1905–1907 is more substantive. In the beginning of the twentieth century, social and political threats to the Russian state order were truly grave. It would be fair to say that it was the bloodiest period in the whole previous history of Russia, except time when the country was at war. Critics of Russia never miss this opportunity to remind us of the number of people sentenced to death in the 1900s. Indeed, according to official statistics, in seven months of existence of 'field courts-martial' (19 August 1906–April 1907) they sentenced 683 persons to death. They were not the only institution that could try and sentence offenders to death. According to S. Stepanov's calculation, the general number of capital punishments in 1906–1907 was equal to 1,102, and in 1906–1909 – 2,694. P.Koshel's numbers are smaller: 1906 – 245, 1907 – 624, 1908 – 1,340, and 1909 – 540.[67] After the peak of 1907–1909, the number of death sentences gradually handed down: in January–March of 1910 – to 116 (as compared with 0 to 12 annually before 1906).[68] Of course, not all of those persons were actually executed. In many cases death sentences were changed to long prison terms. According to official *Russkie vedomosti*, for instance, out of 71 sentenced to death in March 1910, the number of executed was 15.[69]

As a comparison with the Stalin period, according to the latest and most reliable statistics (based on archival evidence), in 1921 through 1953, the repressive agencies (Cheka, OGPU, NKVD and MVD) persecuted 4,060,306 people for political reasons. As many as 799,455 people of them were sentenced to capital punishment (shooting). The tidal wave of persecutions swept the country in 1937–1938, when 1.3 million Soviet citizens were sentenced to hard labour under the notorious Article 58 of the Criminal Code ('counterrevolutionary crimes'), and more than a half of them (682,000) were executed. At least 40 million people were sentenced to different prison terms in 1923–1953. As many as 2.6 million languished in prisons in 1950, and another 2.3 million lived in special settlements (data of late 1940s).[70]

Still, the figure of 2,694 (sentenced to death in 1906–1909) is really terrifying, for it was larger than the number of people, who had been executed in all previous history of Russia. The fact that the number of executions in the Russian Empire in 1906–1909 was more than ten times smaller than in Paris in May 1871 is hardly an excuse here.

What is an explanation, however, is the number of victims among Russian citizens who were assassinated by terrorists. The 'systematic extermination of the most evil or prominent individuals in the government' and the 'mass extermination of the government and in general of individuals by whom is preserved or might be preserved one or another structure that we deplore' had traditionally been major goals of revolutionaries in Russia since 'Land and Freedom'.[71] In 16 months only (February 1905 to May 1906), 1,273 'exploiters' and 'tsarist dogs' were murdered, including: eight Governors and Governors-General, five Vice Governors and Counsellors, four Generals, 51 land owners, 54 entrepreneurs, 29 bankers, 21 *polizeimeisters*, 554 policemen and police officers, 265 gendarmes and gendarme officers, 257 guards, 85 civil servants, 12 clergymen.[72] According to official statistics, in 1906–1909 this figure was equal to 5,946.[73] The general number for the 1900s was approximately 17,000 (!),[74] including Minister of People's Education (former Professor of Roman Law and President of the Moscow State University) Nikolay Bogolepov (14 February 1901), Ministers of the Interior Dmitry Sipyagin (2 April 1902) and Viacheslav von Plehve (15 July 1904), Great Duke (uncle of Emperor Nicholas II, the Governor-General of Moscow) Sergei Alexandrovich Romanov (4 February 1905), and finally – after nine previous attempts – the Prime Minister of Russia (and simultaneously Minister of the Interior) Peter Stolypin (1 September 1911).[75]

The first Russian Constitution (Basic State Laws of 23 April 1906) reformed, *inter alia*, the legal mechanism of a state of emergency. Article 15 of the Constitution drastically reduced the number of those who possessed a right to introduce a state of emergency. Before April 1906, martial law could be declared not only by the Emperor, but also by the Chief Commander of the Army, while reinforced protection (not extraordinary protection!) could be declared by the Minister of the Interior. The declaration of either form of a state of emergency became a privilege of strictly 'Supreme Administration' from April 1906 on: 'Our Sovereign the Emperor declares localities to be under martial law or in a state of exception' (*iskluchitel'noe polozhenie*). The last article in Chapter 2 of the Constitution ('On Rights and Responsibilities of Russian Subjects') left to 'special laws' the determination of what rights and freedoms could be suspended on a territory declared 'under martial law or a state of exception' (art.41). Since neither Article 15, nor Article 41 defined conditions under which a state of emergency was to be declared, the evaluation of those conditions, as well as deciding whether and when to place a locality under any form of a state of emergency remained within the Emperor's discretion.

Like most other constitutions of the countries of the world, adopted in the nineteenth to early twentieth centuries, the Basic State Laws of the Russian Empire of 1906 also contained a provision confirming the right of the 'Sovereign Emperor' as the head of the state to exercise 'legislative action' if it was required by 'extraordinary circumstances' (art.87).

The institution of emergency decrees, as a surrogate form of a 'state of emergency', was a component of the constitutional law of many countries of the world: Austria (Law of 1867 amending the Basic Law on the Empire Representation, No.141 R.G.B.), Bulgaria (Constitution of 1879, art.47, 48, 76), Denmark (Constitution of 1849, art.25), Spain (Constitution of 1876, art.17), Portugal (Constitution of 1826, art.145 (34)), Turkey (Constitution of 1876, art.36), Montenegro (Constitution of 1905, art.75), Japan (Constitution of 1889, art.8), Argentina (Constitution of 1860, art.23, 53, 67 (26), 89 (19)). The institution of emergency decrees was an integral part of legal systems of the majority of German states, where it was known as *Nothverordnungen*: Angalt (Constitution of 1859, art.20), Baden (Constitution of 1818, art.66, 67), Braunsweig (Constitution of 1832, art.120–122), Waldek (Constitution of 1852, art.7), Wurtemberg (Constitution of 1819, art.88, 89), Gessen (Constitution of 1820, art.73, and Constitutional Law of July 29, 1862), Lippe (Constitution of 1836, art.5), Oldenburg (Constitution of 1852, art.137), Reiss (Constitution of 1852, art.66, 67), Saksen-Altenburg (Constitution of 1831, art.211) and Saksen-Weimar (Constitution of 1850, art.61), Saksonia (Constitution of 1831, art.88), Schaumburg-Lippe (Constitution of 1868, art.31, 32), Schvartzburg-Zondersgauzen (Constitution of 1857, art.39), and Schvartzburg-Rudolfstadt (Constitution of 1854, art.25, 43).[76]

Emergency decrees had the power of laws (parliamentary statutes). The reasons for their issuance were usually very vague and ambiguous. Only the Constitution of Portugal defined such reasons as 'rebellions, foreign invasions'; the government could resort to emergency decrees, if that would be necessary for 'security of the state'. In other countries the reasons for their issuance were usually defined as 'maintenance of public security or control of the emergency situation' (Prussia), urgent necessity, 'maintenance of the public peace and security' and 'avoidance of public disaster' (Japan), 'the public good, security of the dukedom or other extremely important circumstances' (Angalt), 'unquestionable necessity to protect the state and guarantee the public safety' (Turkey), 'extreme circumstances' (Austria), 'state security' (Baden, Wurtemberg, Gessen, Saksen-Altenburg), 'state security and emergency circumstances' (Spain), threat to the state security 'from within or from outside' (Montenegro), 'events of domestic or external danger to the state' (Bulgaria) and completely undefined 'urgent necessity' (Schwartzburg-Rufolfstadt), 'happenings demanding immediate actions' (Denmark, Schwartzburg-Zondersgauzen' and 'extreme events calling for urgent actions' (Waldek), 'state necessity' (Lippe) and 'interests of public good' (Braunschweig, Reiss, Saxen-Weimar, Saxonia).

Under the constitutions of Denmark and Prussia, emergency decrees could not contravene the Basic Laws of the countries. Constitutions of Oldenburg, Reiss and Schwartzburg-Zondersgauzen provided that emergency decrees could not introduce any changes in the Basic Laws. Constitutions of Saxen-Weimar and Saxonia extended such prohibition to making amendments to electoral legislation. Constitution of Waldek made two more additions to the list and said that emergency decrees could not touch upon the courts system, guarantees of personal rights and taxation. Constitutions of Bulgaria also prohibited introduction of 'taxes or state duties' with emergency decrees. Only Constitutions of Baden, Montenegro and Japan didn't contain any restrictions on the sphere of regulation with emergency decrees.

The majority of the constitutions provided that emergency decrees could be issued only when the legislature was in recess, and when 'circumstances' didn't allow to convene it (Bulgaria, Turkey). In some countries (Austria, Bulgaria, Braunschweig, Waldek, Prussia, Reiss, Saxen-Weimar, Saxonia, Schwarburg-Rudolfstadt) emergency decrees were to be countersigned by the Cabinet of Ministers. In Braunschweig after an emergency decree is issued, it was to be approved by a Select Committee of Landtag (Ausschuss). Finally, according to the Constitution of Oldenburg an emergency decree was to be countersigned and approved by the Cabinet of Ministers, although the second condition was not so categorical: 'if there is no urgency.'

The decrees were to be presented to the legislative assembly for consideration and adoption. It was to be done: 'immediately' (Braunschweig), 'as soon as possible' (Spain) or 'as soon as [the legislative assembly] is convened' (Brazil, Portugal, Prussia. Saxonia, Schwartzburg-Rudolfstadt), in the earliest session (Bulgaria, Waldek, Denmark, Oldenburg, Reiss, Saxen-Weimar, Montenegro, Schaunburg-Lippe, Schwartzburg-Zondersgauzen, Japan) or within some defined time after the beginning of its work. The Constitutions of Angalt and Turkey contained only general norm about the necessity to pass on 'temporary' decrees for adoption by – respectively – the Landtag and the House of Deputies without any established periods of time.

Comparative analysis of the constitutional provisions, contained in Article 87 of the Russian Constitution of 1906, shows that Russian emergency regulations were better defined and less 'authoritarian' than respective provisions of many European constitutions. Emergency decrees of the Russian Emperor could be issued only 'whilst the State Duma is in recess', and they could not introduce any changes or alterations 'in the Fundamental Laws, in the statutes of the State Council and State Duma or in the regulations governing elections to the Council and the Duma'. Unlike in Gessen, for instance, where the emergency decrees were to be presented for adoption by the Legislature 'within one year', the Basic Law of Russia established a much more reasonable term: 'Should such a measure not be introduced into the Duma as a bill within two months from the date of its next meeting ... it loses force'.[77] In this respect, only the Constitution of Austria could be considered more 'liberal' – it demanded an approval of an emergency decree within four weeks.

At the turn of the twentieth century, Russia was passing through a painful period of long-awaited large-scale social reforms and rapid economic growth. 'Give us twenty years of peaceful development, – Prime Minister of Russia Peter Stolypin declared in his famous speech, – and you won't recognise the country'. 'We need great Russia, not great calamities', was his credo. Four years before his assassination, in a speech in the Duma (on 13 March 1907) Stolypin defended the use of emergency measures, including martial courts, against revolutionary terrorists. The words of Stolypin deserves a full citation for they contained the most complete rationale for the use of emergency powers in pre-Bolshevik years:

> We have heard here accusations against the government ... We have heard that it is a shame and disgrace for Russia that such measures as field courts-martial have been resorted to ... But when in danger, the state must revert to the most rigorous, the most exceptional measures in order to avert disintegration. This was, this is, and this will be so always and everywhere. This is the principle of human nature that lies in the nature of the state itself. When a house burns, gentlemen, you break into a strange department, you break the doors, you break the windows. When a person is sick, he is treated by poisons. When a murderer attacks you, you kill him. This system is recognised by all states ... Gentlemen, there are fateful moments in the life of a state, when ... one must choose between the integrity of theories and the integrity of the fatherland ... I am asking myself ... has the government the right with regard to its faithful servants, who are subjected to deadly danger every moment, to make an open concession to the revolution? After having considered this question, after having weighed it thoroughly, the government came to the conclusion that the country expects from it a demonstration not of weakness but of faith. We wish to believe, we must believe, gentlemen, that we will hear words of appeasement from you, that you will stop the bloody madness [of the revolutionary terror – A.D.], that you will pronounce the word which will force us all to start, not the destruction of Russia's historical building, but its rebuilding, remodelling and adornment.[78]

It's always a problem and a challenge for any transforming and modernising (or, in Stolypin's words, 'rebuilding and remodelling') society to keep preserving law and order using exclusively liberal methods. The last observation is particularly relevant to the situation in such an enormous multi-ethnic, multi-religious, and multi-linguistic country as the Russian Empire at the end of the 19th and in the beginning of the 20th centuries.

In the final count, it is not 'excessive' use of emergency powers in pre-revolutionary years in Russia that should be criticised, but, on the contrary, a lack of sufficient and effective employment of it.

What amazes observers is that 'Russia's rulers permitted unrest and disorder – in the midst of a major war – to grip the entire country before taking decisive measures'. Until 1905, a strong form of a state of emergency ('extraordinary security') was never introduced, and scarcely any 'political criminals' received a punishment harsher than administrative exile. The Russian 'government unsheathed its mightiest weapons only as the crisis reached its apex ... Then, almost as if to compensate for earlier dilatoriness, it resorted to the harshest form of emergency legislation: martial law' (*voennoe polozhenie*).[79]

Of course, as it was advocated in a report of the Council of Ministers of 5 March 1906, states of reinforced security and extraordinary security were preferable to martial law since the latter removed administrative oversight from regular, civilian channels of authority. However, frequent use of the legal mechanism of a state of emergency (in all of its form, including martial law and reinforced or extraordinary' security) was certainly a defensible measure in the times of grave and imminent danger to the Russian society and state of that period.

When writing about the Russian Emergency Law, Richard Pipes agreed with Peter B. Struve, that 'the real difference between Russia of that time and *the rest of the civilised world* lay 'in the omnipotence of the political police' which had become the essence of the Russian monarchy'[80] (*italics added – A.D.*).

In reality, at the turn of the twentieth century, Russia was no longer an absolute monarchy, given the independent judiciary, free press,[81] elective parliament and local self-governments. In the opinion of William E. Butler, one of the most authoritative English-speaking specialist in Russian law, Criminal Code (*Ugolovnoe ulozhenie*) of 1903 'represented the most advanced statement of criminal jurisprudence in Europe'; and a draft Civil Code (*Grazhdanskoe ulozhenie*) of 1910–13 'achieved the same standard of technical and substantive proficiency'.[82]

As it was mentioned before, the 1906 Basic State Laws contained a separate chapter 'On Rights and Responsibilities of Russian Subjects' whose 15 articles (arts.27–41) could be called the Russian Bill of Rights. They included all customary freedoms except the right of petition.

According to the Constitution, no one could be:

a 'prosecuted for a criminal action otherwise than in a manner determined by law' (art.30);
b 'placed under guard [arrested] otherwise than in the cases determined by law' (art.31);
c 'tried and punished except for criminal actions foreseen by penal laws in force at the time of the perpetration of these actions' (art.32).

'Everyone's domicile' and 'property' were declared 'inviolable' (arts.33, 35). 'Every Russian subject' had the right:

a   'to choose freely his place of residence and his occupation, to acquire and to transfer property and to travel freely [without molestation, *besprepyatstvenno*] beyond the limits of the State' (art.34);
b   'to hold meetings, peacefully and without arms, for purposes not contrary to laws' (art.36);
c   'within the limits fixed by law', to 'express his thoughts orally and in writing, as well as disseminate them in print or otherwise' (art.37);
d   'to form societies and unions for purposes not contrary to laws' (art.38);
e   to 'enjoy freedom of religion [*svoboda very*]' (art.39).

Foreigners who sojourned in Russia also enjoyed 'the rights of Russian subjects within the limitations fixed by the law' (art.40). Trial by jury was not specifically mentioned in this list of rights, but it had already been a part of Russian legislation since 1864.[83]

Even before adoption of the Constitution of 1906, the police and inter-rogating officers were operating under constraints. 'After the judicial reform of 1864, and *definitely after 1881*, the security police had no judicial or punitive functions', D.Lieven rightly asserted[84] (*italics added – A.D.*). A.I. Spiridovich recalled that 'the arrest of each person, even under the *Okhrana*'s [emergency – *A.D.*] rights, had to have serious causes', and that the arrest in particular of a member of the *intelligentsia* or a student would lead to immediate telephone calls from the Procuracy asking for reasons; in the event of a prolonged period of detention under arrest, the Procu-racy would press hard for the suspect's release'.[85] In an objective assess-ment of an American scholar, 'the late imperial Russian polity was a regime in transition from absolutism to constitutionalism' and the Emer-gency Law was a 'sign of that progression', a sign of Russia's 'uneasy trans-ition from an absolutist to a constitutional order'.[86]

Marc Szeftel's criticism of the Emergency Law for the fact that it allegedly 'obviously *failed its purpose*, when it became evident that it could not *prevent* the major disorders of 1905'[87] (*italics added – A.D.*) is hardly relevant. In fact, Szeftel's comment is a mirror reflection of those dogmatic Communist scholars' fault-findings which were cited in Chapter 1 of this work. Indeed, the Soviet jurists argued that emergency legislation and a state of emergency (as a legal institution) inevitably 'lead' to 'arbitrary rule, police repression, and governmental abuse', whereas Szeftel claims that the emergency law failed to 'prevent' disorders.

In reality, no statute can *guarantee* the successful resolution of *any* crisis, exigency or emergency; but what a law *can* and *should* do is to provide a 'structure politically conductive to a solution'.[88] This is not a 'purpose' of the legal mechanism of a state of emergency in *any* country of the world to 'prevent' disorders. Moreover, as it was indicated in the above-mentioned 1980 Report of the U.N. Special Rapporteur on Chile and as it was confirmed in the 'Siracusa Principles' (Principle 41), a state of emergency 'of a preventive nature' is an 'impermissible measure'.[89] In Professor Szeftel's defence, however, it might be stated that his excellent book was published four years before issuance of the U.N. report and eight years before formulation of the 'Siracusa Principles'.

Again, it was not harshness and toughness of the Russian emergency law or alleged 'administrative arbitrariness' in its implementation that accelerated the end of the Russian Empire and that deserve condemnation, but rather neglect and carelessness of the authorities (especially, of the State Duma) and their inability to apprehend real and actual danger presented to the state and society by revolutionary terrorism.

P.N. Durnovo, head of the Police Department (1884–1893) and the Ministry of the Interior (1905–1906) repeatedly underlined the many weaknesses of law-enforcement agencies in Russia and five years before the revolution (on 26 January 1912) rhetorically exclaimed: 'Let any of us ask himself if order is guaranteed under the present extremely weak police force'.[90] In February of 1914, in his famous memorandum (called by D.Lieven 'the most impressive document produced by an imperial official in the last years of the old regime')[91] Durnovo warned that the war with Germany, which actually was to begin in five months, would lead to radical social revolution, if necessary protective measures won't be undertaken. Mikhail Menshikov, a leading Russian journalist of the pre-Bolshevik period (executed in 1918) in a series of articles titled 'An Offensive Struggle' of 1911 criticised the government and noted that even an official legal term 'protection' (*okhrana*) bespoke of a totally inadequate ('defensive') rather than a more decisive ('offensive') character of the counter-terrorist and counter-revolutionary measures in the country.[92] Neither of those warnings, nor Machiavelli's prophecy about the states that will be ruined 'when grave occasions occur', if 'in time of danger' they 'cannot resort to a dictatorship', was ever appreciated by the government of Nicholas II.

Extreme liberal reforms of the Provisional Government (formed after the February 1917 'bourgeois revolution') and irresponsible concession of the last tsar to declare his abdication had a suicidal effect and removed the last obstacles on the way of the Bolsheviks to power. No surprise, that democratic 'achievements' of the Provisional Government were warmly praised by the leader of the October Revolution Vladimir Lenin who called 'new' Russia, 'the freest, most progressive country in the world'.[93] 'Thanks' to, first, lack of political will of the tsarist regime and its shy unwillingness to decisively fight grave enemies of the Russian society and, second, fatal misunderstanding of national interests of Russia by the Provisional Government (February–October 1917), mechanism of self-preservation of the Russian state was never effectively implemented and was ultimately destroyed – with Russia herself.

4 Emergency powers and states of emergency in Soviet and contemporary Russian law

I

No parliamentary statute existed in the Soviet Union before 1990 for dealing with emergencies arising as a result of popular unrest or in the wake of a natural disaster.

The last USSR Constitution of 1977 (sometimes called 'Brezhnev's Constitution') didn't contain any provisions dealing with a 'state of emergency'. It distinguished between two regimes of exception: a 'state of war' (*sostoianie voiny*) and a 'state of martial law' or just 'martial law' (*voennoe polozhenie*). Questions of peace and war, including a power to declare war, were assigned to the exclusive jurisdiction of Union authorities (art.73(8)). To be precise, that was a prerogative of the USSR Supreme Soviet. Article 121(17) provided that 'during the time between the sessions of the Supreme Soviet of the USSR' Presidium of the USSR Supreme Soviet was to proclaim 'a state of war in the event of a military attack on the USSR or when necessary to fulfil treaty obligations concerning mutual defence against aggression'.

In contrast to the 'state of war', the Presidium of the USSR Supreme Soviet was entitled to proclaim martial law in specific localities or in the whole country when it was demanded by the USSR defence interests (art.121(15)).

General rules regarding a 'state of martial law' were contained in a Decree of the USSR Supreme Soviet Presidium of 22 June 1941, '*On Martial Law*'.[1] Even though it was introduced on the day when Nazi Germany began its undeclared aggression against the Soviet Union, the 1941 decree didn't deal exclusively with the defence of the country during the Great Patriotic War (1941–1945). The decree stayed in effect long after the end of the war and termination of a state of martial law. Subsequently, it was partially superseded by new legislation, notably by the Statute '*On Military Tribunals*' of 1958 (in a new edition of 1980). According to the 1941 decree, the proclamation of a state of martial law in the USSR (or in some of its areas) was to lead to the following consequences: competence and responsibility in matters of public order and state security are transferred to military authorities; military authorities acquire broadly defined powers to take over ('requisition without compensation') means of transportation, and to conscript civilian labour force; in all fields of administration under military control, the military authorities may back up their orders by the imposition of administrative fines and short-term detentions.

Speaking about requisition, we must remember that the socialist legal doctrine prescribed that the right of the Soviet state to seize any property in the USSR was superior to any individual's right of ownership over the property in question. Aware of the potential for misuse of this right, the Soviet state consented to certain self-imposed limitations. Accordingly, under the *Civil Code of the Russian Federation* (art.149) requisition was defined as the seizure by the state of an owner's property in the interests of the state or the public, with reimbursement for the value of the property. Requisition was permissible only in the instances specifically designated and pursuant to established procedure. Instances under which requisition was permissible could be found both under federal and union republican law. In all of those instances, the taking of property was permitted only if it was 'in the public interest' or if there were no other adequate alternatives to requisition. The determination of whether a planned requisition was in the public interest, or whether an adequate alternative to requisition existed, fell within the exclusive prerogative of the state. No such determinations could be challenged in a court.

Existence of a declared state of martial law during the Great Patriotic War didn't preclude the USSR Supreme Soviet Presidium from occasionally proclaiming an additional state of exception – a 'state of siege' (*osadnoe polozhenie*) – within certain defined territories: Moscow, Crimea, Stalingrad Oblast', etc.[2] A state of siege could be regarded as a stricter form of a state of martial law having more extreme consequences, for instance, entitling the military to shoot looters, spies, saboteurs, etc. on the spot.

The 1988 constitutional amendments broadened the justification for martial law to include ensuring the domestic security of the country's citizens, while adding the requirement that the Presidium of the USSR Supreme Soviet (and subsequently – the USSR President) had to consult with the relevant republican Supreme Soviet Presidium before taking an action.[3] This power of the supreme Union authorities was never used.

A new regime of exception – a 'state of emergency' – was introduced to the USSR constitutional law as a result of the most fundamental constitutional reform of the *perestroika* period. In December 1988, the USSR Law '*On Changes and Amendments of the USSR Constitution (Fundamental Law)*'[4] changed about a third (!) of the whole text of the USSR Constitution introducing permanently working legislature and other innovations for the Soviet transition to the rule of law. Establishment of a constitutional mechanism of a state of emergency became an integral part of such transition. Similar changes were made to the constitutions of the USSR republics, including the RSFSR Constitution of 1978. As a result of this radical reform of December 1988 and numerous subsequent changes, the Constitutions of the USSR and Russia effectively stopped being 'Brezhnev's' and became the most democratic constitutional documents in the history of the country, including the current Constitution of 1993.

In 1990, further amendments established Presidency in the USSR (in Russia it happened in 1991) and transferred emergency powers of the USSR Supreme Soviet Presidium to the new office. In addition, the President was given the authority to proclaim 'temporary presidential rule' (*vremennoe prezidentskoe pravlenie*) as a form of a state of emergency.[5]

The Act '*On the Legal Regime of a State of Emergency*' (*O pravovom regime chrezvychainogo polozhenia*),[6] was adopted by the USSR Supreme Soviet on 3 April 1990, to fill an apparent legal vacuum. Its 17 articles defined the nature of a state of emergency, and provided enabling legislation that gave the Union authorities the operational language, definitions, and procedures for using emergency powers, as Article 1 stated, 'in accordance with the USSR Constitution'.

Interpreted strictly, the law on a state of emergency could not be invoked against peaceful demonstrations or other legitimate actions. In reality, however, as Gorbachev made clear in his comments on the situation in Lithuania, he put so broad a construction on the 'safeguarding of citizens' security' that the letter of the law was essentially vitiated. In general, the act allowed the central authorities to override the constitutional and legal protection of Soviet citizens. A number of Soviet and foreign legal and political experts disagreed with the official interpretation of the act as the 'extreme legal form for ensuring the safety of citizens and normalising conditions'.[7] They called the 1990 Act 'draconian', and concluded that 'a measure that should provide a legal basis for the actions of the government in the event of a natural disaster or of large-scale public disorders has been formulated in such a way as to give the authorities *carte blanche* to flout basic human rights'.[8]

Ironically, the Act was used against its strongest supporter – USSR President Gorbachev himself – during the August 1991 putsch, when an extra-constitutional Committee for the State of Emergency (GKChP), 'temporarily' replaced Gorbachev (on the verge of signing a new Union Treaty, and in the wake of a 10 per cent reduction of GDP in the first half of 1991, and a more than 50 per cent growth of prices) by the USSR Vice-President Gennady Yanaev and announced a state of emergency in Moscow and 'some areas' of the country for a period of six months.[9]

Nevertheless, adoption of special legislation on emergency powers and a state of emergency was a sign of serious political changes in the Soviet Union, a breakthrough on the way of Soviet transition to the rule of law. Legislation on emergency powers and states of emergency could not be drafted and adopted before the beginning of *perestroika*, because there was no necessity of a *legal* regulation of such questions in the authoritarian regime of 'de facto emergency' that existed in the former Soviet Union for about seven decades.

Just like it happened with introduction of Presidency, adoption of a special USSR act on a state of emergency created a precedent that was followed by the largest of the Union republics – Russia. On 17 May 1991, the Russian Federation Supreme Soviet passed its own act, '*On a State of Emergency*' (*O chrezvychainom polozhenii*).[10] Observers of the New York-based Lawyers' Committee for Human Rights acknowledged that 'like many other laws' adopted by the Russian parliament in 1990–1993, the Emergency Law 'relie[d] heavily on international human rights norms, and in particular on the International Covenant on Civil and Political Rights'.[11]

Very symbolic is the fact that the Law was drafted by the parliamentary Committee on Human Rights rather than by the Committee on Law and Order, or by the Committee on Defence and Security, or, for that matter, by some executive agency. Indeed, the Russian Law of 1991 was probably one of the most liberal acts in this sphere in the world. The act introduced strong safeguards against its possible abuse by either branch of the government, especially in case of a collision between the branches themselves. So it was not a surprise that in September–October 1993, an emergency regime (which included dissolution of the Russian parliament and a partial suspension of the Constitution), and *de facto* state of emergency, were imposed by President Yeltsin, not in accordance with the 1991 Russian Law, but rather in violation of it.

As required by international law instruments (discussed in Chapter 2), no regime of emergency powers can be instituted unless it is 'necessary or even indispensable' to the preservation of the state and its constitutional order. Given the danger, it is demanded that emergency powers should be the last resort and that the executive should bear the burden of showing this kind of necessity. As it was shown before, an absolute majority of constitutions include clauses for determining when these powers can be triggered. Though these 'trigger clauses' are often not drafted with clarity, the concepts of 'imminent danger' and 'self-defence' are universally present either implicitly or explicitly.

The 1990 Soviet legislation defined a state of emergency as follows: 'A temporary measure declared, in accordance with the USSR Constitution and the present law, in the interests of safeguarding the security [or "safety", *bezopasnost'* – *A.D.*] of the USSR citizens in the event of natural disasters, major accidents or catastrophes, epidemics, outbreaks of epizootic disease, and also mass disorders' (art.1).

Article 1 proclaimed that the goal of a state of emergency was 'the swiftest possible normalisation of the situation and the restoration of legality and law and order'. In other words, following the letter of the law, explicit goals of state of emergency in the country could not be preservation of the state itself and constitutional order (or restoration of constitutional normalcy), but rather 'security' (or 'safety'), 'normalisation of the situation', 'legality', and 'law and order'. More notably absent was any provision limiting declaration of emergency powers to situations of an imminent danger.

In contrast, Article 56 of the 1993 Russian Constitution provided that emergency powers could be declared in order to 'ensure the safety of citizens and the protection of the constitutional system'.[12] By including language about preserving the Constitution, Article 56 could be considered a major step forward from the 1990 Soviet legislation. However, absent again was any provision limiting declaration of emergency powers to situations of imminent danger.

For comparison, let's briefly return to the French legal experience in this sphere. Constitutional Law of France has special relevancy to this analysis since the USSR Presidency (introduced by a constitutional amendment in 1990) was based mainly on the French model. Article 16 of Constitution of France (of the Fifth Republic, 1958) requires that the President may exercise his emergency power only when 'the institutions of the Republic, the independence of the nation, the integrity of its territory or the fulfilment of its international commitments' are threatened in a 'grave and immediate' manner and the 'proper functioning of the constitutional governmental authorities' is interrupted (sec.1). In addition, the same article provides that the goal of such emergency powers must be to 'ensure within the shortest possible time that the constitutional governmental authorities have the means of fulfilling their duties' (sec.3).

In 'defence' of the Soviet legislation, one may argue that although the French Constitution uses more definite and precise language and limitations in declaring emergency powers, it is still rather open ended. The meaning of 'institutions' of the republic and 'international' commitments seems rather vague and open to a great latitude of interpretation. However, the danger of uncertainty of the language of the French norm is minimised by provisions requiring consultation with the Prime Minister, Constitutional Council, and chairs of both chambers of the parliament (sec.1), immediate meeting of the parliament *ipso jure* (sec.4) and a ban on dissolution of the National Assembly (sec.5).

One of the most important conclusions of Clinton Rossiter's classic study of emergency powers was that 'the decision to institute a constitutional dictatorship should never be in the hands of the man or men who will constitute the dictator'.[13] Rossiter was not alone in this respect. The same position was expressed by Carl J. Friedrich: 'There should be clear and adequate provision for constitutionally safeguarded emergency powers. These powers should be exercised not by those who proclaim the emergency, but by others, duly designated in the basic law'.[14] In other words, the right *to declare* a state of emergency should not belong to those who will be authorised *to exercise* emergency powers. Apparently, this kind of limitation may be able to compensate for a more vague 'trigger language'. If, for instance, only the legislature can introduce a state of emergency, then it might have the same kind of limiting effect as a narrowly drafted trigger clause.

Article 2 of the 1990 USSR legislation specified three kinds of states of emergency.

- The first one could be declared *'on the territory of a Union or autonomous republic or in various locations'* by the *legislature* of a Union or autonomous republic (ASSR) with a notice being given to the USSR Supreme Soviet, the president of the USSR, and, in the case of an ASSR, to the legislature of the Union republic concerned.
- The second one could be declared by the *USSR President* in *'various locations'* of the USSR 'upon a request or with a consent' of the Supreme Soviet Presidium of the respective Union republic. If necessary, a state of emergency can be introduced without such a 'consent' by a two-thirds majority of the USSR Supreme Soviet over the objections of the republic involved.
- The third one was an *all-Union* state of emergency, which could be declared only by *the USSR Supreme Soviet.*

At first glance, one could argue that Article 2 compensated for the extreme vagueness of Article 1. However, this argument would assume a separation of powers. In reality, back in 1990 (especially before elections in Union and autonomous republics), that would be difficult to suggest that the Supreme Soviet (especially the USSR Supreme Soviet which was formed as a result of partially free and fair elections of 1989) was really independent of the USSR (Gorbachev's) presidency.

According to Article 3, the declaration of a state of emergency was to be accompanied by an announcement specifying: the reasons (*motivy*) for the measure, the period it was to last, and the area to which it was to apply. The article, however, created a massive loophole and provided that each of those conditions could be modified at its discretion by the body that had declared the state of emergency, thus seriously diminishing the value of this provision.

Under Article 16, the USSR Ministry of Foreign Affairs was to 'immediately inform' the UN Secretary-General of an introduction, extension or termination of a state of emergency.

In contrast, under the Russian 1991 law, a state of emergency could be introduced by either executive or legislative branches of government – the President and the Presidium of the Supreme Soviet – with the 'immediate notification' of the other of them (art.5). The act introduced an effective mechanism of checks and balances. If a state of emergency had been imposed by the President, the Supreme Soviet was to review the decree within 24 hours if in session, or within 72 hours if not in session. It was to approve the decree by resolution, or the decree would automatically lose its force (art.11 and 12). The President could not extend a state of emergency beyond the stated time periods without the Supreme Soviet's authorisation. The law set out maximum time limits for a state of emergency, such as 30 days for the republic as a whole, or 60 days for a portion of the republic. Those periods could be extended only by a new authorising resolution of the Supreme Soviet (art.13).

Once a state of emergency is declared, an important question is *how* and *to what extent* the government may legitimately re-constitute itself. As with other emergency power provisions, the answer lies in the goal of such powers that, again, is as swift a return to constitutional normalcy as possible. The author fully concurs with a statement by Questiaux that 'there must be no alteration in the bases of the institutions whose functions are modified to meet the needs of the moment, so that they can revert to their original function when the crisis has been overcome'[15] and would like to emphasise that any necessary modifications to constitutional institutions should be clearly grounded in the constitution or statutory law.

Article 5 of the 1990 Russian Act stated that the higher organs of state power were empowered to 'revoke any decision of lesser organs operating in localities where a state of emergency' had been declared. It also gave broad power to the 'higher-level authorities' to set up alternative administrative bodies ('special temporary agencies') 'to coordinate' the situation, thus effectively suppressing normal operations of republican and local governments. Unfortunately, the statute failed to indicate any limits to the jurisdiction of these 'agencies' or to explicitly specify if their existence was limited by the duration of the state of emergency.

The new Russian Constitution of 1993 took an altogether different and more vague approach to institutional adaptation during a state of emergency or martial law. The constitution is silent on the creation of 'special temporary agencies'; and it's certainly a step forward that it forbids the president to dissolve the Duma during a state of emergency. However, the constitution, by its silence, appears to leave wide open exactly *what* changes in governmental and constitutional structure the president can make. The document states only that 'the regime of martial law shall be defined by the federal constitutional law' (art.87(3)) and that a state of emergency is to be instituted 'in accordance with the procedure stipulated by federal constitutional law' (art.88). Yet, the Constitution fails to define, or simply hint at, what such 'regime' and 'procedure' should be. To evaluate these provisions in a vacuum, outside the *realpolitik*, they seem to be extremely vague and open ended.

Also absent from the 1990 Act, and the 1993 Constitution, is any provision like Article 150(7) of the 1977 Malaysian Constitution, which requires that: 'At the expiration of a period of six months beginning with the date on which a Proclamation of Emergency ceases to be in force, any ordinance promulgated in pursuance of the Proclamation and, to the extent that it could not have been validly made but for this Article, any law made while the proclamation was in force, shall cease to have effect, except as to things done or omitted to be done before the expiration of that period.'[16]

This kind of provision can be really important in limiting a possible abuse of emergency powers by the executive, especially in a legal and political system that lacks a strong legislature and truly independent judiciary, as in Russia. While illustrations from nations like the United States show that the judiciary is not always willing to invalidate government abuses in times of dire emergency,[17] such courts will not usually tolerate gross excesses in situations of non-emergency. The kind of 'restoration provision' found in the Malaysian Constitution would be extremely helpful to such courts to restrict enforcement of emergency powers in more 'normal times'.

For purposes of this study, it is assumed that the goal of a society, based on the rule of law is the creation and preservation of ordered liberty. An emergency powers scheme with the most restrictive declaration requirements, time limits and institutional alteration provisions can still cause harm that outweighs those hazards and perils which it is designed to protect against. While a society periodically has to fight fire with fire, measures such as arbitrary detention or torture can undermine the very utility of invoking emergency powers.

The 1990 USSR legislation made an attempt to specify rights and guarantees that were subject to derogation during a state of emergency. Article 4 established a list of 20 measures that could be applied 'depending on the concrete circumstances, the organs of state power and administration'. Taken together, and even more so by extension, they gave the authorities the power to take over virtually all institutions in the territory affected: to suspend activities of any 'political and social organisations, mass movements' (sec.18), impose quarantines (sec.13), introduce censorship and restrict or ban use of audio and video equipment, copying machines (sec.14, 15), prohibit assemblies, meetings, demonstrations and strikes (sec.6, 10), seize resources (sec.9), exercise business reorganisation (sec.8) and shift workers from one area to another (sec.11), engage in search-and-seizure operations without a warrant (sec.20), temporarily deport population (sec.2), enforce protection of certain objects and areas (sec.1), temporarily confiscate weapons and other materials (sec.5), restrict movement and transportation (sec.3, 16), and to ban any 'armed formations' (sec.19).

Article 6 empowered the authorities to transfer workers and employees 'without their consent', and Article 7 specified that a total curfew may be imposed. In addition to a regular criminal liability, Article 8 prescribed administrative fines (of up to 1,000 roubles) and detention (of up to 15 days) for violations of Article 7 and sections 3, 4, 6, 10, 12–16 of Article 4.

The next two articles introduced more severe penalties for 'dissemination of provocative rumours, actions that provoke a disruption of law and order or that stir up national discord and the active hindering of citizens and officials in the exercise of their lawful rights and the performance of their duties, as well as persistent failure to obey lawful orders or demands' by members of law-enforcement agencies, 'or any other actions of this sort that violate public order or tranquillity' (art.9). Such persons could be fined up to 1,000 roubles or held for up to 30 days. Finally, persons involved in 'leading a banned strike' or 'otherwise preventing' an emergency regime from 'operating normally' were announced liable to criminal penalties, including fines of up to 10,000 roubles, two years of 'corrective labour', or three years of imprisonment. Besides, Article 14 allowed the central authorities to change the territorial jurisdiction in all civil and criminal cases.

The USSR and Russian acts on a state of emergency have certain similarities. Both of them (art.11 and 21, respectively) permitted the use of military personnel, as well as the military formations of the Ministry of the Interior and KGB upon a decision of the USSR Supreme Soviet or the USSR President (in Russia's case – RSFSR Supreme Soviet or Russian President). Articles 12 and 18 of the USSR and Russian laws respectively provided for the establishment of a joint command in such situations. In addition, Article 13 of the 1990 Law empowered the USSR Minister of Defence to draft specialists in the reserves for up to two months to deal with natural disasters or accidents. He was presumably not permitted to do so in cases of public unrest. Article 15 of the Russian law provided for compensation to victims of disasters.

While there were no any additional provisions in any other Soviet legislation of that period shedding light on emergency powers in the USSR, as they were laid down in the 1990 Act, one could certainly argue that the statute contained an exhaustive list of restrictions and limitations (especially those in Articles 4 and 9 of the Act) that could be imposed in a state of emergency. The problem was that, even though 'exhaustive', the list was awfully broad. It is hard to imagine what rights and freedoms could not be affected if the government would have decided to use that legislation. The phrasing of a provision prohibiting any 'actions' that could 'provoke a disruption of law and order' seems to be especially vague and ripe for use as a vehicle for abuse (art.9).

Perhaps the most dubious provision of the USSR 1990 Act was contained in Article 16, which specified that 'in cases where the organs of state power and government are not functioning properly in places where a state of emergency has been declared, the president of the USSR can introduce temporary presidential rule'.

Under the provisions of the article, the president of the USSR could 'suspend' the authority of regional bodies and appoint an alternative power structure that would exercise all the powers specified in Article 4. Moreover, this body, and presumably its creator, could make proposals for changing virtually everything in a republic and could take direct control over any enterprises, institutions, and organisations in the relevant area. The only restriction on this virtually unlimited grant of power to the president was a provision saying that he couldn't violate the 'sovereignty or the territorial integrity of the Union republic concerned'.

Looking back at the legal development in relations between the Union and its republics, it can be argued that the above-mentioned provision of Article 16 led to undesirable (for the Union authorities) consequences and became one of those actions of the USSR law-makers that facilitated the 'war of laws' and 'parade of sovereignties' in the country (even though such 'parade' was triggered not by the Union authorities). The mode of thinking of the republican leaders – especially after parliamentary elections in the Union republics (first of all, in Russia) in the spring of 1990 – was quite understandable. If 'sovereignty' of the Russian Federation or any other Union republic is one of only two consti- tutional prerequisites that can not be challenged by the Union authorities (the other one being, again, the 'territorial integrity' of a Union republic), then – let it be – let's enhance our sovereignty to the hilt and adopt a special declaration of 'state sovereignty' guaranteeing independence and 'sovereignty' of our republic in its relations with the Union. To the hilt indeed, for our *Declaration on State Sovereignty of Russia*' (adopted by the Russian Congress of People's Deputies on 12 June 1990) would: (a) proclaim the 'supremacy' of our republican Constitution and legislation 'throughout the territory of the RSFSR', and (b) suspend 'the effect of acts of the USSR which are contrary to the sovereign rights of the RSFSR' (art.5).[18]

Although the Russian Law of 1991 specified the same restrictions (as the USSR Act of 1990) that could be imposed on Russian citizens in a state of emergency – special regime of exit and entry; increased security; restrictions on assembly and the right to strike; restrictions on transporta- tion; a curfew and restrictions on the press and media, etc. (art.23 and 24), – there was a major and principal difference between the Russian and USSR laws. The Russian Act clearly and in explicit terms proclaimed that a state of emergency could not be the basis for derogation of 'fundamen- tal' rights protected by the ICCPR, including the right to be free from torture; cruel, inhuman, or degrading punishment; or freedom of thought, conscience, or religion (art.27). In fact, the 1991 Russian Act '*On a State of Emergency*' became the very first law among any other similar legislation in the USSR republics that included a 'non-derogable clause'.

The Russian law set other limits on the state of emergency:

- prohibiting introduction of emergency courts (art.34) and death penalty ('the death penalty may not be imposed during the state of emergency, or for 30 days after its conclusion' (art.36));
- making changes to the Constitution or to electoral laws, prohibiting elections or referenda until the end of a state of emergency (art.38);

- in accordance with the ICCPR, obliging the President to inform the UN Secretary-General (within three days of the imposition of a state of emergency), to provide the latter with the detailed information about the reasons for an introduction of a state of emergency and about the restrictions that were to be imposed in the republic (art.41).

Thus, the 1991 Russian Act represented an outstanding legal development and a remarkable improvement over the USSR legislation.

The 1993 Constitution has kept and repeated the best provisions of Part 5 'Guarantees of Rights and Responsibility of Citizens and Officials in a State of Emergency' of the 1991 Russian Law. Article 56 enlists the rights and freedoms that cannot be affected by a state of emergency and deserves a title of the 'non-derogable clause' of the Russian Constitution. Though the respective rights are listed in negative terms, the article is certainly more explicit and more protective than the provisions of the USSR Act of 1990.

Article 56(3) specifies 16 rights that 'shall not be subject to restriction'. Included in this list are: the right to life (art.20); protection of human dignity and ban on 'torture, violence or any other harsh or humiliating treatment or punishment ... medical, scientific or other experiments without his or her free consent' (art.21); 'right to privacy, to personal and family secrets, and to protection of one's honour and good name' (art.23(1)); prohibition to 'collect, keep, use and disseminate information on the private life of any person without his consent' (art.24(1)); freedom of information (art.24(2); freedom of conscience and freedom of religious worship, 'including the right to profess, individually or jointly with others, any religion, or to profess no religion, to freely choose, possess and disseminate religious or other beliefs, and to act in conformity with them' (art.28); right to occupation (art.34(1); right to housing (art.40(1)).

The article also includes the most basic and fundamental criminal procedural rights: 'everyone shall be guaranteed protection of his or her rights and liberties in a court of law' (art.46); 'no one may be denied the right to having his or her case reviewed by the court and the judge under whose jurisdiction the given case falls under the law' (art.47); right to legal counsel (defence attorney) from the moment of detention or indictment (art.48); presumption of innocence (art.49); prohibition to be repeatedly convicted for the same offence and right to have the sentence reviewed by a higher court (art.50); right not to testify against himself or herself, for his or her spouse and close relatives (art.51); protection of the 'rights of victims of crimes and abuses of power' (art.52); right to compensation by the state for the 'damage caused by unlawful actions (or inaction) of state organs, or their officials' (art.53); prohibition of retroactive force for laws 'instituting or aggravating the liability of a person'; no one may be held liable for an action which was not recognised as an offence at the time of its commitment' (art.54).

Naturally, not all rights and freedoms can be protected in a state of emergency. Among them are freedoms of speech, association, democratic elections, and various social and economic rights, including social security, education and health care.

However, as with other provisions in the Constitution (whose alleged goal is to protect individual rights against government abuse), the problem is that the President is the body that has the right to declare a state of emergency under Article 88, and under Article 80(2) he is also the one who serves as the 'guarantor of the Constitution of the Russian Federation, and rights and freedoms of man and citizen'. According to the latter article, it's the President again who 'shall take measures to protect the sovereignty of the Russian Federation, its independence and state integrity'. Without a well-established system of checks and balances and separation of powers, as is the case in the post-1993 Russia, one has to seriously question the enforceability of all the rights and freedoms guaranteed in Chapter Two of the Constitution, including Article 56.

Moreover that the 'non-derogable clause' of the Russian Constitution (art.56(3)) concerns *exclusively* a state of emergency, and *not* the other regime of exception – martial law. No provision in the Constitution explicitly provides for non-derogable rights during martial law. A newly adopted Federal Constitutional Act No.1-FKZ '*On Martial Law*' (*O voennom polozhenii*) of 30 January 2002 didn't eradicate that deficiency and only proclaimed that 'in the period of martial law citizens enjoy all rights and freedoms established by the Constitution of the Russian Federation except those rights and freedoms that are restricted by this Federal constitutional act and other federal legislation' (art.18(1)).

As it was mentioned in the Preface of this study, in the last 15 years states of emergency and emergency regimes have been introduced by the USSR and republican authorities approximately 30 times. In general, emergency powers have been invoked at three different levels of the constitutional systems of the USSR and former Soviet republics.

At the *all-union level* that happened in Lithuania. When (on 11 March 1990) this Baltic republic declared its 'independence' from the USSR, President Gorbachev first unsuccessfully appealed to the leadership of the unruly republic not to violate the constitutional subordination in the Union and then invoked his new constitutional powers to impose an economic embargo, a form of political coercion, on the secessionist republic. The embargo was in effect for several months in 1990. On 7 January 1991, the USSR President ordered Soviet airborne troops into Lithuania (as well as into Latvia, Estonia, Armenia, Georgia, Moldavia and some areas of the Ukraine) to 'enforce the draft', and on 13 January, Soviet armed units assisted a shadowy Lithuanian 'National Salvation Committee' in taking over several strategic buildings in Vilnius, the Lithuanian capital. Reportedly, 13 or 14 people were killed and some 100–150 others wounded. In a characteristic manner, Gorbachev denied that he had given prior authorisation for the crackdown in Lithuania, but defended it as a 'necessary defensive action' and denied any responsibility for the events in Vilnius.

At the *union republic level*, on 22 September 1988, the USSR Supreme Soviet declared a 'state of exception' (*osoboe polozhenie*) and curfew in the Nagorno-Karabakh Autonomous Oblast' (NKAO) and Agdam raion (district) of Azerbaijan (east of Karabakh), which by then had been rent by interethnic conflicts for months.[19] On 23 November 1988, the Presidium of the USSR Supreme Soviet issued a decree '*On Immediate Measures for the Establishment of Public Order in the Azerbaijan SSR and Armenian SSR*' extending the state of exception to Baku, capital of Azerbaijan, and some other cities and districts of the republic as well as to Yerevan, the Armenian capital. Simultaneously, federal Ministry of the Interior troops were deployed to Yerevan, Baku, and Karabakh. These measures failed to produce the desired results, and 'in view of the continuing tension in interethnic relations in and around NKAO and in order to prevent their further aggravation and to stabilise the situation in the region' the Presidium of the USSR Supreme Soviet on 12 January 1989 decreed the introduction of a 'special form of administration' in accordance with Article 119(14) of the USSR Constitution. All government powers over the autonomous region were transferred to the Committee for the Special Administration of the NKAO headed by Arkady Volsky,[20] a member of the CPSU Central Committee of Gorbachev's draft (since 1986) and a former economic aide to CPSU General-Secretaries Yuri Andropov (1983) and Konstantin Chernenko (1984). In May 1989 federal Army troops were deployed in Stepanakert, the Karabakh 'capital'.

Although the very first paragraph of the decree of 12 January 1989 described the measure as 'temporary', it set no time limit. In several cases this distressing tradition continued even after adoption of the parliamentary statute in 1990. For instance, a decree of the Presidium of the Supreme Soviet of Kirghiz SSR of 7 June 1990, declaring a state of emergency in Frunze, capital of Kirgizia, didn't specify the period the state of emergency was to last.[21] That was an obvious violation of Article 3 of the 1990 USSR Law.

Looking back, it would be fair to say that quite often (if not usually) imposition of a state of emergency was a reaction to civil unrest and other forms of internal strife that had led to grave violations of human rights. In some cases declaration of a state of emergency provoked clashes between civil population and illegal paramilitary formations on the one side, and internal troops and/or army on the other. 'Black January' in Azerbaijan is a typical example here. Responding to an official declaration (on 1 December 1989) by the Armenian Supreme Soviet (legislature) that Azerbaijan's province of Karabakh was an 'integral part' of Armenia, the Popular Front of Azerbaijan (PFA), then a nationalist opposition political party with a militia, began a railroad blockade of Armenia and NKAO, severely restricting delivery of food and fuel. On 13–14 January 1990, anti-Armenian violence broke out in Baku, where PFA was in control, and resulted in between 60 (officially) and 100 deaths. Radical PFA members led attacks on the Communist Party and government buildings in Baku and other cities. Outposts of the USSR border guards were attacked on the Soviet-Iranian border. On 15 January, the USSR Supreme Soviet Presidium continued experimenting with its emergency powers and introduced a new regime of exception (the third one within 16 months!), this time a 'state of emergency'.[22] Among other measures, the Union authorities declared a curfew and dispatched thousands of federal troops to Baku to restore normalcy and protect safety in the area. Their attempts to disarm militias and dismantle barricades and other makeshift devices proved to be ineffective. According to official reports, 124 people were killed and some 700 wounded.[23] What was viewed as a 'Soviet intervention' further alienated the Azeri population from Moscow and later helped the Popular Front leader Abul'faz El'chibey temporarily come to power in the republic.[24]

As an example of a regime of exception *within a union republic*, we should consider a state of emergency that was introduced on 12 December 1990 (in accordance with Article 113(7) of the 1978 Georgian Constitution) on the territory of one of the autonomous regions of Georgia with a large concentration of non-Georgian population – South Ossetian Autonomous Oblast'.

Disintegration of the USSR (in December 1991) along *administrative* (often illusionary) demarcation lines rather than *state* (national) borders led to a division of several ethnic groups living on the territory of the Soviet Union between new 'independent' countries. The Ossetian nation, in this respect, was divided between the Russian Federation (North Ossetia) and Georgia (South Ossetia). However, reporters of a respectable newspaper *Wall Street Journal*, made a mistake when claiming that South Ossetia (and Abkhazia, another region of Georgia) 'broke away from Georgia in wars that followed the collapse of the Soviet Union in 1991'.[25] In reality, the conflict in South Ossetia had deeper roots and was caused by a general discriminatory policy of the government of Georgia against ethnic minorities. The Ossetian side claims, for instance, that if in the 1920s there were as many Ossetians in North Ossetia as in South Ossetia, by 1991, that proportion had changed to 350,000 Ossetians in the North and only 68,000 in the South.

The situation was ignited more than two years before disintegration of the Soviet Union by the language act (adopted in August 1989) that made Georgian the 'official' language in the republic (including schools and other educational institutions) and plans of further 'Georgianisation' of the region. Trying to prevent this, the South Ossetia Oblast' Council requested the Georgian Supreme Soviet to grant South Ossetia the status of an 'autonomous republic' (a higher level of self-administration than an 'autonomous oblast''). The leader of Georgian nationalists, Zviad Gamsakhurdia, replied by calling the South Ossetians 'ungrateful guests' of Georgia, alluding to the (Georgian) claim that they have lived in the area for 'only a few centuries'.

As a next step, the Georgian government refused even to use the name 'South Ossetia' and began referring to the region as 'Samochablo' (an old Georgian name of that region) or the 'Tskhinvali Region' (after the regional capital city Tskhinvali).[26] In November 1989, groups of Georgian youth held a 'march on Tskhinvali'. Arrival of some 15,000 armed men on trucks, buses and cars led to severe clashes and injuries of hundreds of people. In September 1990, the government of South Ossetia proclaimed independence of the 'Soviet Republic of South Ossetia' (within the USSR), and in October boycotted Georgia's elections that brought Gamsakhurdia and the 'Round Table Free Georgia' coalition to power.

On 11 December 1990, the Gamsakhurdia government stripped South Ossetia of *any* autonomous status, and a day later, imposed a state of emergency on the stated grounds that two Georgians and one Ossetian had been murdered in Tskhinvali under mysterious circumstances.[27] Deployment of 3,000 to 6,000 Georgian militia to Tskhinvali under a pretext 'to maintain order' in the region was viewed by the South Ossetians as an 'intervention' and 'occupation'. A resulting resistance led to three weeks of urban warfare (with all its elements like armed barricades, shooting, burning of houses, and a division of the town into Georgian- and Ossetian-controlled zones) until the Georgian militia was pushed out of the city. First declared for one month in the city of Tskhinvali and Javsky district, the state of emergency was repeatedly extended. The continuous struggle (including armed clashes and shelling of Ossetian villages) and economic and military blockade of the area made thousands of Ossetians flee their region and find shelter in North Ossetia, on the territory of the Russian Federation.

A *coup d'etat* of Edward Shevardnadze (and his allies, notorious criminals Tenghiz Kitovani and Jaba Ioseliani) against Gamsakhurdia (December 1991–January 1992) didn't change the nationalities policy of Georgia. In fact, as it was revealed in a report of a Swedish–American factfinding mission to Georgia, 'even more people were killed' in South Ossetia after Shevardnadze's accession to power 'than during the earlier phase'.[28] A peacekeeping mission of the Organisation for Security and Cooperation in Europe (OSCE) has been deployed in South Ossetia since 1992. However, several rounds of talks between Georgian and South Ossetian representatives made little progress toward an agreement on South Ossetia's future status.

Just like the Armenia–Azerbaijan conflict over Nagorno-Karabakh, the South Ossetian territorial problem of Georgia still lingers on. Since a new (this time anti-Shevardnadze) coup in Georgia and election in January 2004 of president Mikhail Saakashvili, the South Ossetian situation has got a tendency of going from bad to worse.

Back in 1990, in another union republic, Moldavia (now Moldova), two separate minority groups – ethnic Slavs (Russians and Ukrainians) in the Transdniester region and Turkish Christian Gagauz – made an attempt to set up autonomous administrative entities *within* the republic. The process was triggered by concerns of those minorities (at the 1989 census, comprising some 35 per cent of the total population of the republic) over ethnic the Moldavian nationalism and possible unification of the republic with Romania. The concerns could probably be understood: in September 1989, the Moldavian parliament introduced Romanian as the 'official' language; in September 1990, the blue, yellow and red tricolour of Romania was adopted as Moldavia's official flag.

The Moldavian-dominated government denied, however, claims for a higher autonomous status of the Slavic and Gagauz minorities and, in accordance with the republican constitution, introduced a state of emergency in both regions. First, that happened on 26 October 1990, in the Gagauz-dominated Komratsky, Vulkaneshtsky and Chadir-Lukgsky districts (in the southern parts of Moldavia), and several locations of Bessarabsky district. A week later, on 2 November 1990, a state of emergency was declared in Slavic-dominated cities of Dubossary, Tiraspol and Bendery of the Transdniester region.

The measure was supported by sending some 50,000 armed ethnic Moldavian 'volunteers' to the Gagauz area. Violence was prevented only because of the dispatch of USSR federal troops to the region. Yet, the armed conflict broke out in the Transdniester region in December 1991 after a new attempt of the Moldavian government to gain control over the area. More than six months of warfare were accompanied by mutual accusations of the sides of receiving military and other assistance from Russia and Romania. By June 1992, some 700 people (mainly Slavs) were believed to have been killed and approximately 50,000 people forced to take refuge in neighbouring Ukraine. The warfare stopped after appointment of General Alexander Lebed' as the Commander of the former USSR 14th Army stationed in the region.[29]

II

Since adoption of the Law 'On a State of Emergency' of 1991, this special regime has been declared in Russia (or RSFSR) three times: in Chechnya in November 1991, Ossetia-Ingushetia in 1992–1995, and in Moscow in October 1993.

The first time it was introduced by President Yeltsin's Decree No.178 of 7 November 1991 under a declared goal to 'put an end to mass disturbances, accompanied by violence, [and] stop activities of illegal armed formations, in the interests of guaranteeing safety of citizens and protection of constitutional order of the republic'. A state of emergency with all its elements (like a curfew, ban on meetings, demonstrations, and strikes, confiscation of armed weapons, etc.) was to come into effect at 5 a.m. on 9 November and last for 30 days. In reality, it happened to be the shortest emergency on the territory of Russia, because the Russian Supreme Soviet refused to ratify it.[30] Putting aside a discussion about political circumstances of the introduction and termination of the emergency (lack of co-ordination between branches of government, different interpretation of events in Chechnya, etc.) and which decision was right, that was the only instance when the Russian Parliament effectively exercised a 'termination clause' of the legal mechanism of a state emergency. Yet, that would be fair to say that an abrupt termination of emergency in 1991, just two days after its introduction by the Russian President, caused a kind of a 'Chechen syndrome' and became one of the reasons of future reluctance of Russian federal authorities to use the 1991 law.

The longest state of emergency was in effect in parts of North Ossetia (official name of the republic is 'North Ossetia – Alania') and Ingushetia between November 1992 and February 1995).

A conflict between these two Russian republics of the Northern Caucasus was caused by territorial claims of Ingushetia upon Prigorodny district of North Ossetia. The conflict situation had deep roots, but was provoked by normative idealism of the first Russian lawmakers, their tendency to view the law as a panacea for social problems, and to make the law absolute without recognising the limits of any legal action.

On 26 April 1991, the RSFSR Supreme Soviet passed the Law '*On the Rehabilitation of the Repressed Peoples*'. The act promised not only '*political*', but '*territorial* rehabilitation' of the 'repressed peoples' too. It spoke about the re-establishment of 'historical borders'. Specifically, Article 6 of the law provided for 'the restoration of the ['repressed peoples" – *A.D.*] national borders existing before the frontiers were changed by an anti-Constitutional force'. The law raised a question of reconsidering existing 'inner borders', unleashed a wave of territorial claims of ethnic republics and administrative regions against each other, and – consequently – led to local conflicts. Behind a smoke screen of proud words about 'human rights', 'repentance' and the necessity to 'rehabilitate the repressed peoples', the law provided the regional elites (often of ethnic minorities) with a legal sanction for the redistribution of territories, power, and property in the federation and for boosting their political and economic influence.

Two major emergencies were triggered by that law: 'Chechen struggle for independence', which actually began in September 1991 and had its culmination in December 1994–July 1996 and since October 1999 in a form of two 'federal interventions',[31] and the Ossetian-Ingush conflict over Prigorodny district (*raion*) of North Ossetia. The federal interventions in Chechnya were exercised without a formal introduction of *any* special legal regime, thus avoiding the necessity to test President's power to declare a state of emergency or martial law by other branches of government and risk making such power an object of an (even limited) parliamentary control (art.102(b), (c) of the 1993 Constitution). Emergency *de jure* in North Ossettia and Ingushetia and *de facto* emergency in Chechnya were introduced under different Russian constitutions – of 1978 (amended) and 1993 – and illustrate the phenomenon when under a changing legal (constitutional) framework the same executive has to play differently.

The Chechen conflict has traditionally attracted much more attention of Western and Russian scholars and policy-makers.[32] Yet, as it was so vividly and dramatically demonstrated by the horrific tragedy in Beslan on 1–3 September 2004, the situation in North Ossetia and Ingushetia is far from being resolved, and remains a major 'hot spot' on the political map of Russia. For the purposes of this study, I will concentrate on the *de jure* state of emergency in the disputed parts of North Ossetia–Alania and Ingushetia of 1992–1995.

The Ingush (like Chechens, Kalmyks, Crimean Tatars, Germans and some other small ethnic groups) are known as a 'repressed people'. In 1941–1944, they were deported to Siberia, Central Asia or Kazakhstan for well-established collaboration of significant numbers of their population with Hitler's troops.[33] The deportations were not much different from the 'relocation' of the Japanese Americans from the Pacific Coast to inland territories, but certainly more cruel.[34]

The decree ordering the deportation, and abolishing the Chechen-Ingush Autonomous Soviet Socialist Republic (CIASSR), was dated 7 March 1944. It explained the action as follows:

> During the Great Patriotic War, and especially during the period when the German-Fascist army was operating in the Caucasus, many Chechens and Ingush betrayed their motherland, went over to the side of the fascist occupants, enlisted in detachments of saboteurs and spies sent by the Germans into the rear of the Red Army, followed German orders by forming armed bands to fight against the Soviet power, for several years took part in armed actions against the Soviet authorities, and for a long period of time without engaging in honest work have conducted bandit raids against the collective farms of neighbouring regions, robbing and killing Soviet people. Therefore, the Presidium of the Supreme Soviet orders: 1. Deportation to other regions of the USSR of all Chechens and Ingush living on or adjacent to the territory of the Chechen-Ingush ASSR, and liquidation of the Chechen-Ingush ASSR . . .[35]

Subsequently, some districts of the Chechen-Ingush ASSR were transferred under jurisdiction of the North Ossetian ASSR. Unlike Chechens and Ingush, their neighbours Ossetians (mainly Orthodox Christian and predominantly pro-Russian, having joined the Russian Empire voluntarily in 1774) didn't become victims of Stalin's deportations.

After reconstitution of CIASSR in 1957, not all of their former lands were returned under jurisdiction of the republic. Unlike the northern Naursky and Shelkovsky districts that became parts of Checheno-Ingushetia again, Prigorodny district (neighbouring Vladikavkaz, the capital of North Ossetia) stayed within North Ossetia, thus becoming a 'hot spot' between two republics, even though a large section of ethnic Russian Stavropol'sky *krai* was attached to CIASSR (as a form of 'compensation' for Progorodny district).

On 15 September 1991, an assembly of Ingush deputies passed a resolution calling for the formation of the 'Ingush Autonomous Republic within the RSFSR'. A referendum was conducted on 30 November to 1 December 1991 in three predominantly Ingush districts of CIASSR and approved the proposed separation from Chechnya. The Ingush decision was accepted by the Chechen leadership and confirmed by the Law *'On the Creation of the Ingush Republic in the Russian Federation'*, adopted the RF Supreme Soviet on 4 June 1992. This law failed, however, to fix the boundaries of the newly established Ingush Republic, providing instead in Article 5 that a commission of Russian federal government should consult with all parties concerned and propose a solution for the boundaries issue by 31 December 1993. The latest provision was absolutely justified in such a delicate matter, and it was similar to a provision of the 1991 Law *'On the Rehabilitation of the Repressed Peoples'* (speaking of a discretionary transitional period before implementation of Article 6 of the Law on 'the restoration of the boundaries of national territories').

Impatience of the Ingush side, and its attempt to forcefully occupy Prigorodny district led to armed clashes between Ossetians and Ingush in October 1992. Inter-ethnic fighting in Prigorodny district and Vladikavkaz resulted in heavy casualties, killing of at least 478 people (by the beginning of November), and caused a huge flow of refugees. According to official statistics, 16,700 Ingush had to leave their homes. The Ingush authorities insisted that a much larger number of Ingush had to become refugees; in different sources they operated figures between 35,000 and 60,000 people.[36]

On 2 November 1992, a state of emergency was introduced in North Ossetia and Ingushetia. Later the state of emergency zone was reduced to Vladikavkaz, Mozdoksky, Pravoberezhny and Prigorodny districts of Ossetia, and Nazranovsky and Djeirakhsky districts of Ingushetia.

The essence of the emergency regime was determined by the President's Decree No.1327 *'On Imposition of a State of Emergency on the Territory of North Ossetian ASSR and Ingush Republic'*.[37] The decree banned 'meetings, street processions, demonstrations, and other mass gatherings' (art.4(a)), as well as strikes (art.4(b)), and ordered confiscation of fire and cold weapons, ammunition, poisonous, explosive and radioactive materials (art.4(c)).[38] Curfew was declared soon after.

The emergency zone was governed by the Provisional Administration for North Ossetia and Ingushetia, which, in its turn, was in power:

- to introduce 'special regime' of exit, entry and movement within the emergency zone, including search of transportation vehicles (art.5(a));
- strengthen protection of public order and essential services (art.5(b));
- order suspension of activities (after previous warning) of public organisations and mass movements, 'hampering normalisation of situation' (art.5(c));
- order to check documents and, in exceptional cases, personal, home and transportation search (art.5(d));
- order to extradite violators of public order who are not local citizens from the emergency zone 'at their own expense' (art.5(e));
- impose censorship of printed editions, radio and TV programs (art.5(f)).

The state of emergency was repeatedly extended, usually for a two-month period. In 'technical legal' terms, however, it was not 'prolonged', but rather lifted and re-introduced. So, each time it was necessary for the President (or before the adoption of the new Russian Constitution in December 1993 – for the Russian Supreme Soviet) to issue a new decree on imposition (rather than on prolongation) of the state of emergency. That's an example of how it was actually exercised. On 30 May 1994, the President issued a new Decree No.1112 *'On Imposition of a State of Emergency on a Part of the Territory of the Republic of North Ossetia and Ingush Republic'*. In Article 1 of the decree, the state of emergency was lifted 'at 14:00, 31 May 1994'. In Article 2, it was introduced again coming into effect 'at 14:00, 31 May 1994, until 14:00, 31 July 1994'.

New decrees used to have their peculiarities. For instance, when extending the state of emergency from 30 January to 31 March 1993, the Supreme Soviet in its decree of 28 January also directed the interim administration in the area to ensure the public order during the Ingush presidential elections scheduled for 28 February. Strictly speaking, elections should not be held during a state of emergency, but the 'Russian parliament has agreed to the presidential elections being held rather than see the population take the matter into its own hands', Ann Sheehy correctly observed.[39] As a result of the election, a former Russian paratrooper general, and a hero of war in Afghanistan, Ruslan Aushev, was elected the President of Ingushetia.

Another 'extension' decree (issued by President Yeltsin, and approved by the Federation Council on 31 May 1994) not only prolonged the state of emergency (until 31 July 1994) but also extended its territorial effect to a number of villages in the Malgobeksky and Sunzhensky districts of Ingushetia. Reports of the extension of the state of emergency to those two districts, parts of which are claimed by Chechnya, aroused a hostile reaction on Chechnya's part, but Movladi Udugov, a spokesman for the separatist Chechen government, said on 31 May that Chechnya agreed that the villages affected are part of Ingushetia and the decree did not pose any immediate threat to Chechnya. He added, however, that Chechnya still thinks the state of emergency was 'unjustified'.[40]

On 1 August 1993, the same day when a state of emergency was prolonged again, Victor Petrovich Polyanichko, Head of the Provisional Administration for North Ossetia and Ingushetia, and Vice Prime Minister of the Russian Federation was assassinated. Footprints of the assassins' horses led to Ingushetia. In the next four years, the Procuracy collected about 100 volumes of materials related to this case, more than 3,000 people were interviewed as 'witnesses', but the murderers were never found.[41]

In December 1993, Yeltsin signed a decree giving Ingush refugees (who were displaced in the course of the violent ethnic conflict in 1992–93) the right to return to their former settlements in the neighbouring Ossetia. The measure proved to be still-born. On 2 August 1994, Russian TV news quoted Ingush president Ruslan Aushev as complaining that Yeltsin's decree of December 1993 had not been implemented. Aushev repeatedly asked the Acting Prosecutor-General, Alexei Ilyushenko, to place the resettlement of the refugees under control of the Prosecutor-General's office.

The Federation Council was very close to lifting the state of emergency in the fall of 1994. First, on 6 October, as a quite rare example of its 'independence', the upper chamber of the Russian parliament failed to approve Yeltsin's decree (issued on 4 October) that extended the state of emergency for another two months. *Interfax* news agency quoted Russian Deputy Prime Minister Sergei Shakhrai as expressing the hope that a compromise solution could be reached on 7 October, although he characterised the positions of the North Ossetian and Ingush deputies as 'poles apart'. Shakhrai was right; the President's decree was approved, but the Federation Council's reluctance to rubber-stamp it was an indication of a more general dissatisfaction of Russian federal and regional elites with the methods of handling the conflict.

The Chairman of the Human Rights Commission under the President's Administration, and State Duma deputy, Sergei Kovalev, inspected Ingushetia and North Ossetia–Alania and in early November 1994 addressed a memorandum to President Yeltsin on the situation in the region. In an interview with *Segodnya* a veteran human rights campaigner said that he found 'large-scale, gross violations of human rights' in the state-of-emergency zone. The main reason for the deteriorating situation in the region, in Kovalev's opinion, was a 'totally unconstructive position of the North Ossetian leadership'.

The Ingush, in turn, were radicalised 'partly due to the lack of progress on the return of refugees' to Prigorodny district. In a separate report titled

'Two Years After the War' (also highlighted by *Segodnya*), the Moscow-based human rights centre *Memorial* rejected claims that an organised repatriation of the Ingush refugees had begun, observing to the contrary that 'the federal authorities have been unable and unwilling to ensure in practice the observance of human rights'. Noting that the abuses have mainly victimised the Ingush, the report concluded that 'the blame lies with the Russian leadership and officials administering the state of emergency ... The federal organs could not or would not' restrain the perpetrators, *Memorial*'s report said.[42]

The reports of Kovalev and *Memorial* encouraged Ingush President Ruslan Aushev to intensify his criticism of federal efforts to solve the problem in the region. He addressed a closed session of the Federation Council dedicated to the situation in the North Ossetian and Ingush republics, and on 18 November 1994, made a complaint at a press conference that 'the Russian federal authorities follow a misconceived policy in the Caucasus' and that 'the main reason for the [North Ossetians'] anti-Ingush actions is the Russian authorities' failure to understand that this is a conflict for political control, not an interethnic one'. Aushev particularly criticised the November 6 raid of the Special Police Unit (OMON) on village of Altievo in Ingushetia where five Ingush were killed and six arrested. The state of emergency in the region was to expire on 2 December, and Aushev urged that it be maintained in Prigorodny district to ensure the return of Ingush refugees to four localities, as mandated but not implemented by Moscow. While renouncing claims to Vladikavkaz, Aushev insisted that Prigorodny district must be returned to Ingushetia through negotiations. Speaking on Russian Radio four days later, Aushev accused the Russian Federal Counterintelligence Service of giving President Boris Yeltsin misleading information on the basis of which decisions were made favouring North Ossetia.

Despite assurance on 27 November by Russia's Ministry of Internal Affairs that the situation in the North Ossetian–Ingush state of emergency area was 'tense', but 'under control' of the army and internal troops, the Ingush government expressed concern (in a statement on 28 November) that 'the tension may lead to a new large-scale conflict in North Caucasus'. In view of the expiration on 2 December of the state of emergency in the conflict area, the Ingush were concerned that the handful of repatriated Ingush in Prigorodny district would be left unprotected and that the repatriation process will stop before it has really begun.

The Ingush arguments were not left unnoticed. At a closed session on 6 December, Federation Council narrowly voted against approving Yeltsin's decree (issued on 2 December) that again extended (this time until 31 January 1995) the state of emergency in parts of North Ossetia and Ingushetia. Deputies argued that even though the state of emergency had been in force for two years, it proved to be ineffective and failed to contribute to solving the region's problems. Its invalidation would, however,

seal that failure by removing minimal security guarantees for the repatriation of the Ingush forcibly evicted from North Ossetia in November 1992.
Ingushetia accused the Moscow-instituted Provisional Administration in
the state of emergency area, and North Ossetia's pro-Moscow authorities,
of failing to implement the pilot programme, mandated by another presidential decree, to return 600 Ingush families to four villages in Prigorodny
district. Only 114 families had returned as of 5 December, *ITAR-TASS*
reported. And even those who had returned to their villages were experiencing harassment, allegedly intended to deter the mass of Ingush
refugees from coming back.

Following hot debates in the Federation Council, Yeltsin had to revise
his initial decree (of 2 December) and on 9 December persuaded the
upper chamber to approve it. The new text of the decree instructed
Russia's Security Council to consider proposals by the Federation Council
and by the North Ossetian and Ingush presidents on developing measures
to stabilise the region and to prepare conditions for lifting the state of
emergency. In addition, the Federation Council created a commission to
monitor the implementation of the presidential decree jointly with the
Security Council. On 9–10 December, Ingush President Ruslan Aushev
told *Interfax* that he still found the amendments inadequate. In his
opinion, the decree appeared to continue favouring North Ossetia, and it
didn't stipulate that the Ingush expelled from Prigorodny district must be
allowed to return to their homes.

The state of emergency was lifted in February 1995, less than two
months after the beginning of the 'federal intervention' to Chechnya. First,
on 31 January 1995, Yeltsin issued a new state-of-emergency extension
decree, but on 3 February the Federation Council failed to ratify it,
because it lacked quorum. Council Chairman Vladimir Shumeiko had to
remind the deputies of a 'constitutional provision', according to which a
state of emergency decree not approved in three days 'loses its force and
the population of the territory under question is informed of that through
mass media'. Shumeiko was confused. The 1993 Constitution doesn't
contain such provision.

Following the Council vote, Yeltsin reissued the decree on 5 February
and said it would be resubmitted to the upper chamber. But on 7 February, for the second time, the Federation Council failed to ratify a state of
emergency decree for Ingushetia and North Ossetia. This time not for a
technical reason ('lack of quorum'), but a principal one: only 76 of the
necessary 90 deputies supported the motion. The prospects for a compromise between the president and the Federation Council were uncertain.
As Peter Shyrshov, Chairman of the Federation Council's Defence Committee, told *AFP*, 'we are asking for an in-depth revision of the text, as the
war situation [in neighbouring Chechnya] demands strict and concrete
measures'. In such circumstances President Yeltsin decided not to 'revise'
the text of the decree again, but rather to lift the state of emergency

altogether. The decree of 16 February also provided for the creation of an *ad hoc* committee to oversee the repatriation of those Ingush citizens who became homeless during the fighting. The committee superseded the Temporary Administration headed by Vladimir Lozovoi, which had been repeatedly criticised as ineffective by Ingush President Ruslan Aushev.

Two-and-a-half years of the state of emergency in the region were able to prevent open fighting. In the first months after introduction of a state of emergency (November–December of 1992) only 26 persons were killed in the region comparing to 478 before 2 November 1992. In 1993, the number of victims was 124, including 40 Ossetians, 33 Ingush, 21 of 'other nationalities' (mainly Russian peacekeepers), and 30 of 'unknown nationalities'. In the first half of 1994, the number was reduced to 16. That was probably the most important result of the emergency regime.[43]

However, the state of emergency did not solve the problem itself, didn't bury roots of the conflict, and didn't bring refugees back home. In March 1996, the U.N. Committee Against Racial Discrimination made a review of the situation of ethnic minority rights in the Russian Federation and expressed a particular 'concern' for the Ingush refugees expelled from North Ossetia. As *Interfax* reported, the UN Committee requested Russia to ensure their rights, particularly the right of repatriation, under international pacts on the rights of ethnic minorities.[44]

A very unfortunate side-effect of the emergency regime in the region in 1992–1995 was a certain growth of 'anti-federal' (read: anti-Russian) sentiments among the Ingush. Federal intervention in Chechnya, whose people are closely related to the Ingush by language, religion and culture, alienated Ingush leadership along with the rest of the Ingush population. The position of Ingushetia in this question was not impartial at all. The Chechen militants enjoyed a strong support of the neighbouring republic.

First, in December 1994, the Ingush blocked the roads for federal troops marching to Chechnya, and they failed to enter Chechnya from the territory of Ingushetia. In March 1996, Ruslan Aushev decisively argued against plans of federal authorities – announced in Yeltsin's televised speech – to move some troops from Chechnya to the republics of Ingushetia and Dagestan in order to retain the option of either reintroducing troops into Chechnya or exercising its blockade. Aushev declared that his government opposed any relocation of Russian troops from neighbouring Chechnya to Ingushetia for, as he said, such a move would risk 'involving Ingushetia in combat actions' and would also expose it to 'looting by the Russian military'. President Aushev and Chairman of the Ingush People's Assembly (legislature) Ruslan Pliev also alleged that Ingushetia was accommodating, unassisted by Moscow, more than 100,000 Chechen refugees and some 50,000 Ingush refugees from North Ossetia – an additional reason why redeployment of federal troops in Ingushetia was impossible, in the opinion of the Ingush leadership, even for a few months. Moscow had to step back.[45]

Six months after the end of the state of emergency, on 18 August 1995, Ingush parliament passed a resolution demanding that Moscow introduce a 'direct federal rule' in North Ossetia's Prigorodny district. The idea was not new. It was first expressed about a year before, when in his letter of 1 September 1994 to the Russian President, Chairman of the Ingush People's Assembly Ruslan Pliev, asked Yeltsin to implement measures to stabilise the situation in the region. Specifically, Pliev requested to impose a direct federal rule on the disputed area, to make a legal assessment of the clashes two years ago in Prigorodny district and Vladikavkaz, and to send a permanent commission of the Russian Federal Assembly to the region to monitor the implementation of presidential decrees.[46]

In July 1997, President of Ingushetia Ruslan Aushev began a second round of his attempts to persuade federal authorities to impose a 'direct presidential rule' on North Ossetia's disputed Prigorodny district. In his words, it was necessary to 'defuse growing tensions in the region' and on the grounds that the North Ossetian leadership couldn't 'guarantee stability' in the area.

The problem, however, is that neither the Constitution of the Russian Federation, nor Russian legislation, provides for an imposition of such a legal regime as a 'direct presidential rule'. It's also hard to say (and hard to understand) what exactly Ingush authorities expected from such a regime. Aushev insisted on direct administration of the disputed area by the federal centre and deployment of 'peacekeeping forces formed of Russian internal troops' in the area failing to explain what should be the difference between a 'direct presidential rule' and a 'state of emergency'.

On the other side, North Ossetian President Aksarbek Galazov called Aushev's request an 'interference in North Ossetia's internal affairs' and an 'attempt to destabilise the situation' in the region. Deputy Chairman North Ossetia's legislature Ermak Dzansolov correctly noted that imposition of a federal presidential rule would violate both the Russian and the North Ossetian constitutions. *Nezavisimaya gazeta* quoted Galazov as affirming that all citizens of North Ossetia were equal before the law, and that alleged discrimination against the Ingush citizens of the republic was a reflection and consequnce of the catastrophic economic situation in the region.[47]

The Security Council of Russia, at its session on 21 July 1997, heard a testimony of both Presidents – Aushev and Galazov. The latter warned that 'if presidential rule is imposed in Prigorodny district, North Ossetia may quit the Russian Federation'. The next day the discussion continued among members of the Security Council. Aushev's idea of a 'direct presidential rule' was not supported. Among other alternative and conciliation measures for stabilisation of the situation in the region, the Security Council proposed restoration of Russian federal government's 'representation' (*predstavitel'stvo*), distinctive from more rigid and centralised 'administration' (*administratsia*) in North Ossetia's disputed Prigorodny district. Russian Nationalities Minister Vyacheslav Mikhailov was named as a possible candidate for that position.

At the end of July 1997, Secretary of the Security Council Ivan Rybkin visited the region. He was accompanied by Galazov, Aushev, and Russian Minister of Nationalities Vyacheslav Mikhailov. Rybkin could see that out of 16,700 Ingush who had to leave this region in 1992, only some 11,000 had actually returned home. He confirmed that the 200 billion roubles ($34.6 million) earmarked by the federal government for aid to refugees should be exempt from the budget sequester. (*Nezavisimaya gazeta* on July 26 quoted a local official as saying the North Ossetian leadership had received only 14 billion of the planned 200 billion roubles). According to press reports, the Security Council Secretary opposed a 'direct federal rule' for 'no army can decide this problem', but he neither agreed to nor rejected Aushev's suggestion that Russian federal Interior Ministry troops be deployed in Prigorodny district to prevent possible violence.

What was proposed instead was a creation of compact separated ethnic settlements in Prigorodny district and – respectively – exchange of houses between the Ingush and Ossetians. The position of the federal authorities was clear in this respect: the problem of return of Ingush refugees into their homes on the territory of Prigorodny district *can* be solved *without* pushing territorial claims of Ingushetia against North Ossetia.[48]

On 1 August 1997, Yeltsin issued a long-promised decree on nationality relations. It named former deputy chairman of the Federation Council, Ramazan Abdulatipov, as the seventh Russian deputy prime minister. Abdulatipov, an ethnic Avar from Dagestan and the author of a number of theoretical works on nationality problems, became responsible for 'ethnic relations, federal development and regions of Russia'. In an interview with *ITAR-TASS*, Abdulatipov characterised nationality relations within the Russian Federation as 'one of the most difficult and crisis-ridden spheres' in which 'very many mistakes were made and few constructive goals were achieved'.[49]

When announcing Abdulatipov's appointment, President Yeltsin excluded imposing presidential rule on Prigorodny district, saying 'this would not help to defuse tensions, and is contrary to the direction in which federalism in Russia should develop'.

Reluctance of the Russian Federation to deploy federal internal troops on the territory of the North Caucasian republics made other ethnic leaders to offer their alternative options. Some of such 'options' were pure speculations aimed at aggravating the situation in the region. First Deputy Prime Minister of separatist Chechnya Movladi Udugov, for instance, suggested, on 21 July 1997, creating a 'pan-Caucasian security organisation' modelled on the Organisation for Security and Cooperation in Europe that would serve as a forum for resolving regional conflicts. In fact, Udugov went even further and specifically commenting on the tensions between neighbouring Ingushetia and North Ossetia proposed the formation of a 'Caucasian peacekeeping battalion' that would be sent to Prigorodny district. He denied that such a security institution would have an anti-Russian orientation, arguing that Russia has a 'vested interest in the creation of such an organisation'. Ten days later (August 2) addressing North Ossetian parliamentarians, the Chairman of the Confederation of Peoples of the Caucasus Yusup Soslambekov expressed his concern at the escalation of tensions in Prigorodny district. Soslambekov said his organisation was willing to try to mediate between the conflict sides, and that it planed to establish its own peacekeeping force to help overcome inter-ethnic clashes in the North Caucasus.

Indeed, there is no vacuum in power politics. If the federal 'Centre' is unwilling or unable to preserve peace, order and stability in the 'subjects' of the Russian Federation, other (sometimes, hostile) forces will come out into the open – with not always predictable consequences.

Although Ingush President Aushev's proposal to declare a 'direct presidential rule' in Prigorodny district wasn't followed, it gave a boost to development of the Russian legislation. On 5 August 1997, in an interview with *Nezavisimaya gazeta* former head of Provisional Administration for North Ossetia and Ingushetia (December 1992–May 1993), and then President Yeltsin's Representative to the State Duma, Alexander Kotenkov, announced that a Law '*On Status of a Federal Territory*' had been drafted. In Kotenkov's words, the law would regulate the process when 'certain conflict zones, like Prigorodny district' could be declared a 'special federal zone' 'without changing legal status' of such region. Despite Kotenkov's announcement the bill wasn't introduced to the State Duma either in the fall session of 1997 or the spring session of 1998. A possible explanation to this delay is that the draft law either doesn't address the issue of a *force majeure* change of a territory's status at all, or fails the solve the dilemma: how a region can be declared a 'federal territory' (something similar to Aushev's 'direct presidential rule', 'president's rule' in states of India or provinces of Pakistan, 'federal intervention' in Latin American federations, etc.) 'without changing' its 'legal status'.[50]

Kotenkov's statement was strange indeed for the Russian Constitution is silent on a possibility of a transformation of any 'subject' of the Russian Federation into a 'special federal zone'. The Constitution divides all 89 federation units of Russia into six groups: 1) 'republics' (*respublica*), 2–3) national-territorial units: 'autonomous region' (*avtonomnaya oblast'*) and 'autonomous areas' (*avtonomny okrug*), and 4–6) administrative-territorial units: 'regions' (*oblast'*), 'territories' (*krai*) and two 'federal cities' (*goroda federal'nogo znacheniia*): Moscow and St. Petersburg. Such division makes Russia an 'asymmetric' federation. For instance, 'autonomous areas' are formally as equal (in their rights and responsibilities) as larger 'territories' or 'regions'. In reality, it's hard to speak about such equality because 'autonomous areas' are usually *constituent parts* of 'territories' and 'regions'. How can a 'territory' or 'region' exercise full jurisdiction on their territory if a part of it (an 'autonomous area') is presumably an 'equal' part of the Russian Federation as well? To get a better feeling of an 'asymmetric federation', American constitutionalists could consider a situation when State of Iowa and Johnson County – which is a part of Iowa – would be proclaimed 'equal' subjects of the USA.

The text of the Russian Constitution doesn't make the situation clearer. The only article dealing with this question is extremely vague. It only says that the 'relations of autonomous areas that form part of a territory or region may be governed by federal law and a treaty between the organs of state power of the autonomous area and, respectively, the organs of state power of the territory of region' (art.66(4)). Paradoxically, the Constitution itself has become one of the sources of chaos and confusion in federative relations in the country.

As to the 'status' of a subject of the Russian Federation, according to Article 66(1, and 2), it is defined by the Constitution of Russia and the constitutions of republics or by the Constitution of Russia and charters of all other types of subjects of the federation. Section 5 of the same article prescribes that 'the status of a subject of the Russian Federation may be changed by the mutual consent of the Russian Federation and the subject of the Russian Federation in accordance with a federal constitutional law'. But that concerns a possibility, for instance, of an upgrading of a status of a 'region' (*oblast'*) to an 'autonomous region' (*avtonomnaya oblast'*), or downgrading an 'autonomous area' (*avtonomny okrug*) to a 'region' (*oblast'*), or a merger of two neighbouring subjects of the Russian Federation to one, etc., and it doesn't presume a transformation of any of them to a non-existing 'special federal zone'.

Kotenkov's idea seems to be still-born. Since 1997, Russian lawmakers haven't adopted any new legislation introducing and regulating a new (the seventh one) type of a subject of the Russian Federation – 'special federal zone'. In 2002, the presidents of Ingushetia and North Ossetia signed a friendship agreement between the two regions trying to close the book on conflict in an effort brokered by President Vladimir Putin. Yet, the pact failed to outline any specific steps to resolve the territorial dispute.

All in all, during the Ingush-Ossetian conflict, President of Russia signed 37 decrees, including those imposing or 'extending' the state of emergency.

The actual inability of federal authorities to solve the conflict and stabilise the situation in the Northern Caucasus in general, and in the North Ossetian–Ingush region in particular, can be explained by three main factors:

1 passiveness, inertia and deficit of initiative of the federal centre;
2 absence of a single, complex, unified mechanism of solution of ethnic-territorial problems, based first of all on mutual rejection of territorial claims by both sides against each other; and

3   lack of political will of leaders of confronting republics to reach a compromise, and lack of understanding that, in principle, no conflict like this can be solved *completely* and *exclusively* in favour of just one of the opposing sides.

In such circumstances, introduction of a state of emergency and its operation in parts of North Ossetia and Ingushetia between November 1992 and February 1995 was moderately effective in stopping armed fighting and preventing the worst – an open warfare between two ethnic groups. However, it proved to be unsuccessful (although not necessarily doomed from the start) in solving the problem and eradicating the roots of the conflict.[51]

III

Out of all states of emergency that have ever been imposed on the territory of the former Soviet Union, observers can hardly identify a more dramatic and more significant by its consequences emergency regime than the one imposed by President Yeltsin on 4 October 1993 after brutal suppression of the first democratic Russian Parliament.[52] The event truly became *a defining episode* in contemporary Russian politics.[53] It cannot be ignored or overlooked in the context of the subject of the present study and deserves a special consideration.

Two acts of the first Russian parliament adopted in three-and-a-half years of its existence are of special importance for the purposes of this study. On 1 November 1991, on President Yeltsin's initiative the fifth Congress of People's Deputies (CPD) adopted Decrees '*On the Organisation of the Executive Power in the Period of Radical Economic Reform*' and '*On the Legal Safeguarding of the Economic Reform*' granting the President 'temporary' (for a one-year period) emergency powers in the legislative, administrative and economic spheres.[54]

The first decree allowed Yeltsin to decide independently questions 'concerning the reorganisation of executive power', including appointment of the heads of administration on regional and lower levels; significantly restricted executive independence of lower levels of administration in the country; and ordered a moratorium on elections and referendums. Using eagerness and willingness of the Russian parliament to move into a new market-economy era as fast as possible, Yeltsin asked for emergency powers to bring in reforms, and a majority of Russian deputies voted to let him have them – for one year.

The second decree granted the President the powers to rule by decree under a pretext of 'promoting economic reforms'. First, 'economic reform legislation' was declared to be superseding Russian and Union legislation which would be contrary to it. Second, the Supreme Soviet could consider 'economic reform legislation' *only* if it would be accompanied by an 'advisory opinion' of the President. Third, president's 'economic reform' decrees contradicting or violating Russian legislation had to be presented to the Supreme Soviet (or its Presidium), and if those bodies in a seven-day period didn't annul them, the executive decrees were to acquire legal power. Following the last provision of the decree, Yeltsin became the chief legislator of the Russian Federation and flooded the Supreme Soviet with his edicts on various subjects of economic law. In 1993 alone, Yeltsin, reportedly, issued some 2,300 decrees.[55]

By adopting the decree '*On the Legal Safeguarding of the Economic Reform*', the Russian Parliament demonstrated its initial support to a rigid monetary economic policy prescribed and approved by IMF and World Bank. In this respect, the Russian legislature certainly shared respons-ibility with the President for the beginning of experiments of 'Bolshevist monetarists' (Peter Stavrakis) and 'market Bolsheviks" (Peter Reddaway)[56] with the Russian economy. However, 'shock therapy' quite soon proved to be a 'shock without therapy'. A massive and rapid program of privatisation was aimed not at improvement of Russian economy, but rather had a purely political goal of creating of a class of 'oligarchs' and was subsequently defined by Marshall Goldman of Harvard University as 'piratisation of Russia'. In just four months, after evaluation of the first effect of the 'reforms' (a huge jump in prices after controls were lifted, and an acceleration in the fall in productive output), centrist MPs joined the leftists in calling for a slow-down and correction of the 'reforms'.[57] As a result, Yeltsin lost his parliamentary majority and from then on did his best to ignore Parliament and obstruct its work.

Ironically, it was in a speech at Westminster at the end of 1992, that Yeltsin first raised the threat of dissolving the Russian federal legislature, counterpart of the British Parliament. In March 1993, he went further, announcing a 'special form of government' (OPUS), a kind of an emer-gency regime, even though the Constitution didn't empower him to do it.[58] When adopting (on 24 April 1991) Laws '*On the President of the RSFSR*' and '*On the Election of the President of the RSFSR*' and amending the Constitution (on 24 May 1991) with Chapter 13-1 creating executive presi-dency,[59] legislators did not want it to be a licensed dictatorship. They had seen the value of the first democratic Parliament in Russia,[60] and did not want to abdicate powers of the legislature. When changing the Russian Constitution to create a presidency, parliamentarians were careful to set up a system of checks and balances. The President would not have the power to dissolve Parliament or, independently of the Parliament, declare a state of emergency. There would be a Constitutional Court to rule on the legality of his, and Parliament's, actions. Parliament would have the last word on the budget.

Providing the President with emergency powers to rule by decree in 1991 was an apparent mistake. The Chief Executive acquired a taste for, and got used to, governing outside constitutional limits and restraints.

When in March 1993, the ninth (emergency) CPD – by a 682 to 382 vote – annulled the President's emergency powers (which, again, were granted to him only *temporarily*) and fell 72 votes short of impeaching the President (617 votes instead of necessary 689), Yeltsin considered it 'a slap in his face' and decided to get rid of the both obstacles – the Parliament and the Constitution.[61]

There is an astonishing resemblance between granting emergency powers to the Russian president in 1991 'to reform economy' and a similar process in Colombia at the end of the 1960s.

The 1968 reform in Colombia greatly strengthened presidential powers *vis-à-vis* the Congress, especially in economic matters, a process that began with the 1886 Constitution and accelerated with the closing of the Congress in 1949. In 1968, the congress lost the power to initiate legislation dealing with social and economic development (except for limited 'pork barrel' funds) or with the modification or creation of new administrative structures. Although the president's powers under a state of siege were modified, a new power to legislate, following declaration of a 'state of national economic and social emergency', was created (in accordance to art.122). The resemblance will be even more visible, if we mention that, just like Yeltsin, President Lopez Michelsen (1974–1978), who enacted a major tax reform by decree after declaring a 'state of national economic and social emergency' in Colombia, became a president in 1974 following an overwhelming victory in the country's first competitive presidential elections in decades, and (again, like Yeltsin in the Russian Supreme Soviet) had a significant Liberal majority in the Congress.[62]

However, it's highly unlikely that Yeltsin's advisers consciously 'borrowed' the Colombian experience, or were even aware of it. Probably, it was a natural coincidence of effects of growing oligarchic and authoritarian tendencies on state power and government mechanisms in both countries.

At the Belgrade conference of the International Law Association (1980), Special Subcommittee of the ILA Human Rights Committee presented a report dedicated, in part, to 'the problems of the implementation of human rights which arise from resort to means such as proclamation of emergency'. Seven patterns of 'persistent derogations from basic human rights during a state of emergency' were studied in the report. Thirteen years after the Belgrade report, the very first of such patterns – 'the constitution is suspended; the duly elected parliament is dissolved; the country is governed by decrees promulgated by the ruling authority'[63] – would be repeated in Russia, when, on 21 September 1993, President issued Decree No.1400 under a paradoxical title '*On the Gradual Constitutional Reform in the Russian Federation*' (*O poetapnoy konstitutsionnoy reforme v Rossiyskoy Federatsii*).[64]

According to the Decree, the Congress and the Supreme Soviet were declared dissolved and their activities 'interrupted' (art.1); new parliamentary elections were declared to be held on 11–12 December 1993 (art.5), under rules which the executive laid down (art.4); representative bodies in Russian regions continued functioning (art.8).[65]

The last provision was aimed at guaranteeing neutrality of the representative bodies in the regions of Russia in Yeltsin's conflict with the federal parliament. It was a deceptive manoeuvre; as a result of issuance of Decree No.1723 *'On Main Principles of Organisation of State Power in Subjects of RF'* of 22 October, and Decree No.1760 *'On Reform of Local Self-Government in RF'* of 26 October, regional and local legislative bodies were dissolved too.[66]

When the Parliament declared Yeltsin's actions a coup, the executive ringed the parliamentary building (White House) with police cordons, cut off telephones, water, electricity, the heating, and the emergency systems, as well as the telephone line of Chairman of the Constitutional Court in the Court's building. On the streets of Moscow, the authorities began intercepting official cars providing services to the Parliament.

The necessity to dissolve the Parliament, as it was stated in Decree No.1400, was justified by the allegations that the Supreme Soviet lost its 'ability to be a representative body' and that 'the security of Russia and of her people' was 'a higher value than formal observation of discrepant norms', introduced by the Parliament. The problem with that explanation is that the Russian legislation adopted in 1991–1993 was signed into effect by the President himself. Sometimes he used his veto power. When not vetoing legislation, he accepted responsibility with the Parliament for all 'discrepant norms'. In the end, creation of presidency in Russia was also a 'norm' introduced by the Parliament. To what extent the Supreme Soviet 'represented' the Russian society, its wishes and interests, the Russian voters demonstrated in the next parliamentary elections of December 1993, when 85 per cent of them voted *against* pro-Yeltsin's 'party of power' (Egor Gaidar's 'Russia's Choice').

'Gradual Constitutional Reform' was aimed not only against the legislative branch of the Russian government. In Article 10 of his Decree No.1400, Yeltsin also 'advised' the Constitutional Court 'not to convene' until after the elections. The Constitutional Court didn't follow that 'advice' (which was a blunt violation of separation of powers and an infringement on the court's independence) and in an emergency session the same night,[67] voted nine to four that the President's action violated 11 articles of the Russian Constitution. The most important of those 11 counts was a violation of Article 121–6, one of key provisions of a chapter on presidency in the Russian Constitution. Originally, it was an article of the Law *'On the President of the RSFSR'* (of April 1991) which introduced presidency in Russia; later (in May 1991) the provision was included in the Constitution. According to the article, President couldn't use his powers 'to dismiss, or suspend the activities of, any lawfully elected agencies of state power'. Violation of the article was making President not just a subject to a long 'impeachment' procedure, as known in the U.S. and else-where.[68] Article 121–6 was a much more powerful constitutional check on authoritarian tendencies of the executive. In case of its violation, the President's powers were to be 'discontinued immediately'.

In accordance with the Constitution, the tenth CPD convened in the White House, and with its Resolutions No.5780-1 and 5781-1 discontinued the President's powers of Boris Yeltsin (at 10 p.m. on 21 September 1993) and named Vice President Alexander Rutskoi 'Acting President'.[69]

The 'Gradual Constitutional Reform' decree of 21 September 1993 didn't repeal the Constitution *in its entirety*, even though that would have been more logical (and more understandable in legal terms). The paradox of the situation was that Decree No.1400 was declared superior to the Constitution, but there was not any provision in the decree saying that the Constitution was abolished. The Constitution was allowed to function 'in that part where it doesn't contravene' Decree No.1400. As a result, in various decrees issued by Yeltsin in September–December of 1993 he appealed to *some* provisions of the Constitution and ignored or violated all the rest of them. Thus, when issuing Decree No.1400, Yeltsin violated a hierarchy of legal norms in any civilised legal system (Constitution– parliamentary legislation–sub-laws) subordinating the highest of them (Constitution) to sub-laws (like a presidential decree). From a legal point of view that also meant that the Constitution was not actually *suspended* and that it was *in effect*, albeit abused and violated. That poses a question who in those months was the *legitimate* President of Russia: the one in the Kremlin (Yeltsin), or the other one – first, in the White House and then in the KGB Lefortovo prison (Rutskoi)?

On 23 September, the President signed another decree pledging that the presidential elections would take place on 12 June 1994, and that the Federal Assembly must adopt an appropriate law to facilitate this not later than 1 February 1994.

The RF Ministry of Justice issued a special statement justifying the President's action to dissolve the federal legislature. The statement emphasised that although the President 'acted beyond the formal legal framework, he acted in accordance with the constitutional principles of government by the people, guarantee of the country's security and protec-tion of the rights and lawful interests of citizens ... Although, as a formal matter, he exceeded his powers, he used this violation, not to usurp power (the elections of the President are scheduled for 12 June 1994) but to protect the will of the people'.[70]

As we see, the authors of the statement acknowledged that Yeltsin 'acted beyond the ... legal framework', that he 'exceeded his powers' and that it was a 'violation' of Russian law. The only solid argument that they could find to counterbalance that acknowledgement of the president's illegal and illegitimate actions, besides a vague statement about some 'con-stitutional principles of government by the people' that Yeltsin allegedly followed, was to emphasise that new presidential elections were scheduled for 12 June 1994. The argument didn't hold water for it was another falsehood. New elections were not held until June 1996. As Sergei Filatov, Head of the President's Administration, later explained in his TV appearance, the decree was a 'concession' to the opposition, but since there was no more 'opposition' (indeed, some people were killed, many others thrown to prison), it was no longer necessary to keep that promise.

At 4 p.m. on 3 October 1993, Yeltsin signed Decree No.1575 '*On Introduction of a State of Emergency in Moscow*'.[71] Far from being perfect in terms of legislative technique overall, rarely have Yeltsin's decrees been so poorly drafted as Decree No.1575. Although the decree appealed to several provisions of the Act '*On a State of Emergency*' of 1991 and although the declared regime was called a 'state of emergency', it was introduced in violation of both the Constitution and the Russian 1991 Law.

The decree appealed to a number of provisions of the Russian Act of 1991 (art.22–24; allowing suspension of certain rights and freedoms), but it lacked an exhaustive list of such suspended rights, as prescribed by the same Act '*On a State of Emergency*' (art.10). The decree failed to give exact reasons that had made Yeltsin introduce a state of emergency, as prescribed by Article 4(a) of the 1991 law. The decree appealed to Article 24 of the law that named measures that might be undertaken under an emergency regime, even though, according to the Act, such measures could be made only when emergency is caused by natural disasters (and not by disturbances and political unrest, as was the case in October 1993). Yeltsin exceeded his powers and grossly violated the Russian legislation when he suspended norms of laws on the status of parliamentarians and lifted their immunity. The President didn't have a right to ban public organisations, seize their bank accounts, headquarters and property; it could be done only after giving them 'a preliminary warning'. Article 21 of the 1991 law allowed use of troops only with a consent of the Russian Supreme Soviet and exclusively when an emergency was caused by natural disasters ('military aid to civil ministries', 'military aid to the civil community', and 'military aid to the civil power', as it is known in Britain), and not to shoot protesters. In error, the Russian law of 1991 itself was called an act of the 'Russian Federation' whereas technically it was a RSFSR act. Finally, the emergency declaration was not approved by the Parliament (for it had been dissolved and soon would be physically destroyed), so what was introduced in Moscow was the state of emergency *de facto* – in the best traditions of authoritarian regimes in Africa, Asia and Latin America – not *de jure*, as it should be in law-governed states.

Tanks were called to shell the White House and set it on fire.[72] In the days after introduction of the state of emergency, hundreds of people were arrested; approximately 35,000 were detained for violation of curfew regulations (curfew was declared at 11 p.m. on 4 October); more than 54,000 were detained for 'administrative misdemeanours'; and 9,779 persons were accused of violating the internal passport system and deported from Moscow.[73] According to a Report of the Human Rights Commission, mass beatings of the detained were a common practice.[74]

Communist, nationalist and patriotic organisations, as well as the centrist People's Party of Free Russia, formally headed by Alexander Rutskoi, were banned. (From this time on, all political parties were forced to apply to the Russian Ministry of Justice to obtain a certificate stating that they had not been outlawed.) By Decree No.1616 of 19 October 1993, they were banned from participation in the forthcoming elections.[75]

On 7 October 1993, Yeltsin signed Decree No.1612 *'On the Constitutional Court of the Russian Federation'*[76] stripping the court of its key powers. The only fault of the court was that it obeyed the constitution, and 'ended up on the losing side when Yeltsin emerged victorious from the bloody events of October'.[77] It was only 18 months later as the new Constitutional Court of Russia resumed its normal work.

Again, an interesting parallel can be drawn between executive-judicial relations in Russia and Colombia in respect of emergency powers of the president. In 1974 the Supreme Court of Colombia ruled the declaration of the state of economic emergency was constitutional although it disallowed certain measures undertaken by the President. Gradually, step by step, a more activist judiciary began to curtail certain executive powers. So when the next President, Conservative Belisario Betancur (1982–1986), facing a Liberal majority in Congress, tried to enact a new tax reform in 1982 employing the same state of emergency powers, the Supreme Court (with several changes in its the membership) now declared it was not constitutional to do so. The main difference between Colombia and the Russian Federation here is that the President of Colombia obeyed the Court's decision, and the Russian President suspended the Court.

Censorship was introduced. *Nezavisimaya gazeta* (completely justifying its name as *nezavisimaya* or 'independent'), *Komsomolskaia pravda* and *Segodnya* were published with blank spaces on their pages indicating that certain articles were banned by the censors. Blank white spaces were telling more to readers than any article that could have been published there. Those newspapers were still relatively lucky. On 13 October, all the opposition dailies were banned. Criminal investigation was initiated against editors of 15 periodicals. In violation of the Law *'On Mass Media'* of 27 December 1991, editors-in-chief of two other newspapers – *Pravda* and *Sovetskaya Rossia* – were dismissed by the Ministry for Press and Information. The editors were also informed that if they were to be allowed to re-register their periodicals, they would have to change the names of the newspapers. Another newspaper – *Glasnost'* – was banned under a pretext that it had 'failed to undergo registration'. Not only communist and nationalist dailies were banned, but, for some reason, the moderate *Rabochaya tribuna* too. The parliament's press organs, the newspaper *Rossiyskaya gazeta*, and the journal *Narodniy deputat* were shut down back in September. *Rossiyskaya gazeta* resumed publication shortly, as a 'newspaper of . . . the Russian Council of Ministers'.

On 3 September 1995, the Procurator-General's Office closed its criminal investigation of the events of 3–4 October 1993. It was declared that both executive authorities and supporters of the Supreme Soviet were responsible for the armed clashes and bloodshed.

Still a mystery remains. According to the results of the ballistic expert, not a single person outside the White House was killed with the weapons found in the building. The expert failed to find any evidence showing that anybody outside the White House was killed with weapons found in the Parliament. Bullets didn't match; 'stockpiles of weapons' or 'impressive cache of arms'[78] inside the Parliament (about which Russian official and 'liberal' media and their Western counterparts were alleging those days) were never found. The conclusion of the ballistic expert emphasises an unsubstantiated character of statements like these: 'Sharp-shooting' [from the White House] 'inflicted damages on the federal troops'; 'snipers on the roof and the upper floors of the White House pinned down a column of government troops for hours'.[79] One can imagine what kind of repressions and judicial sanctions would have been used against the White House defenders if those kind of accusations were right. Then, whose forces were killing people?

Ten years after the massacre in Ostankino and the bloodbath at the White House and around it, the Russian press in a number of publications and TV reports tried to give an answer to some of those questions.[80] The publications brought to light some 'new' facts that have been repeatedly overlooked or denied by Western and Russian obedient press.

The first shooting on 3 October happened from the Mayor's Office and not from the White House. Among other people, the bullets from the Mayor's Office killed several servicemen of the 'Sofrinskaya' Brigade of the MVD Internal Troops that announced (at 3 p.m. on 3 October) that it switched sides and joined forces with anti-Yeltsin opposition. Information in Western editions about the 'felling of a member of the special forces by a sniper from the White House'[81] proved to be a part of Yeltsin propaganda. Sniper rifles were not used by the White House defenders. Lieutenant Gennady Sergeev of the *spetsnaz* 'Alpha' group was killed in front of the White House by a bullet that did not come from the White House.

According to the results of official investigation, alleged grenade-launcher shooting by demonstrators at the Ostankino TV Center never happened.[82] Private Sitnikov of the *spetsnaz* 'Vityaz' group was killed inside the TV Center by an explosion caused by munition of the 'Vityaz' themselves. The massacre at Ostankino lasted until the morning of 4 October and led to the killing of more than 40 civilians. One of them was a 26-year-old American lawyer, Terry Michael Duncan. He was evacuating the wounded when he was killed by a sniper. According to eyewitnesses,

Terry Duncan saved 12 lives and was murdered when he returned to help Paul Otto, a wounded photo correspondent of the *New York Times*.

Defenders of the White House represented nearly all strata of the Russian population. The first groups of supporters who came to the White House already in the evening of 21 September were representatives of Social Democrats and some ecological organisations. Nobody among the killed defenders of the White House had previous criminal convictions or a criminal record.

Answers to the final question – how many people became victims in those days of a 'civil war' in Moscow – vary from the 'official' number of 147 killed (half of whom were teenagers) and more then 700 wounded to estimated 'one thousand and a half'.[83] As to the precise number who were wounded and beaten, 'no one even tried to determine' it.[84]

In evaluation of an authoritative human rights organisation: 'The state of emergency ... was a major blow to human rights ... The state of emergency violated Russia's own domestic rules regarding states of emergency. It also violated the standards provided in Article 4' of ICCPR. 'Among the non-derogable rights that were violated was the right to life ... Moreover, the extent to which derogable rights, such as freedom of speech, were restricted also went beyond the boundaries of the covenant ... A wide range of measures taken during the state of emergency involved discrimination solely on the ground of race or colour – all violations of the covenant ... As the Russian human rights NGO *Memorial* has documented, the number of cases that have been pursued by the Procurator's Office is insignificant, particularly when compared to the scope of violations.'[85]

A Draft Constitution was quickly prepared to seize a moment and make Yeltsin's 'victory' even more monumental. The President offered a draft on 10 November, just a month before the referendum; it prohibited discussion of the draft in mass media, 'again, hardly a sound precedent of democratic practice', as British analysts wrote;[86] and reduced (for the very first time in Russian history since 1917) the minimum voter turnout needed for a valid parliamentary election from 50 to 25 per cent. The new Constitution, whose *actual* adoption by the Russian population is highly doubtful,[87] provided for one of the strongest presidencies in Europe, 'superpresidentialism' or 'a modern-day czar', and was described as placing Russia, once again, under something similar to an authoritarian rule.[88] Authors of one of the most complete studies of the first Russian Parliament were certainly right when writing about 'political myopia' of 'leaders of radical democrats': 'By destruction of that very institution that guaranteed a possibility of democratic reforms in Russia – sovereign parliament – and because of their decision to promote authoritarian mode of transformations, they lost all ways of influence on the policy of executive power. "Nomenclatura revenge" came not from where it was expected by radical democratic analysts: ... it was accomplished by the executive power structures.'[89]

As a 'victor's Constitution' (rather than a consensus – or social con-tract-based constitution), the 1993 Fundamental Law substituted the sepa-ration of powers and checks and balances with presidential supremacy and placed the Executive above other branches of government.[90] Among other things, the 1993 Constitution granted several areas of traditional court jurisdiction, like protection of civil rights and freedoms, to the President proclaiming him the 'guarantor of ... the rights and freedoms of the human being and citizen' (art.80(2)). 'Such delegation of authority to the Executive to protect constitutional rights 'not only violates separation of powers doctrine, but may give him or her a claim, albeit tenuous, to usurp the Court's jurisdiction, and suspend judicial review in a time of crisis'.[91]

This unhealthy concentration of authority in the hands of the Executive concerned emergency powers too. According to the original version of a draft Constitution introduced for a discussion at the Constitutional Assembly on 29 April 1993, a right to declare a state of emergency or martial law could be exercised by both President and Federation Council, the upper chamber of the Russian Parliament (art.96).[92] A similar provi-sion was contained in another draft of the Constitution prepared by the parliamentary Constitutional Commission.[93] The parliamentary draft pro-vided that a state of emergency could be introduced by both President (art.93(1)(m)) and of the RF Supreme Soviet (art.85(1)(c)). Unlike the Constitutional Assembly with its goal of preparing a draft of a superpresi-dential Constitution, the parliamentary Constitutional Commission in three years of its work crafted a draft with effective checks and balances between different branches of government. In the end, it was the Parlia-ment itself that introduced presidency in Russia. For instance, declaration of a 'state of war' was in the sphere of exclusive privileges of the President (art.93(1)(m)), but a right to extend or terminate a state of emergency belonged to the Supreme Soviet only (art.85(1)(c)). All the work was in vein. According to the new Russian Constitution of 1993, the Parliament was deprived of not only a right to introduce a state of emergency or martial law, but even the right to be consulted by the executive when declaring an emergency regime in the country. According to the Constitu-tion, the chambers can be only 'informed' (art.87(2), 88).

Power of the Federation Council to approve the President's decrees on introduction of martial law or a state of emergency (art.102(1)(b, c)) is far from being absolute too. At a close look, the Constitution doesn't say a word about an 'automatic' repeal of the President's decrees on martial law or a state of emergency if the Federation Council refuses to 'approve' any of them. In reality, only the RF President can impose an emergency regime (art.87(2), 88), and only the President can lift it. True, it would be a violation of the Russian constitution if the President refuses to lift a state of emergency in case of the Federation Council's refusal to 'approve' it. However, it happened so many times before when such violation was demanded by a 'political necessity'.[94] It's difficult to expect different behaviour from the President when the constitution doesn't contain any effective constraints of executive power (preventing him from violating the constitution itself), including the ultimate and most effective of such constraints, 'the extreme medicine' (Clinton Rossiter)[95] – impeachment.[96]

Dissolution of the Russian parliament and subsequent adoption of a semi-authoritarian Constitution marked an end to the first Russian republic and its attempts to establish a balanced system of government with a strong Executive, an effective Legislature, an independent judicial system, and responsible Cabinet of Ministers.[97]

Yet, as it was indicated in a recent opinion poll (held by Yury Levada's analytical centre among 1,600 respondents on 24–27 September 2004), 58 per cent of Russian citizens now believe that Yeltsin's decision to use force in his confrontation with the parliament was not justified (comparing to about 30 per cent of those who shared this opinion 11 years ago). Twenty-one per cent of those surveyed in 2004 say that the use of tanks was necessary, as compared to 51 per cent in 1993. Only 11 per cent of respondents believe that 'communist and extremist organisations' must be blamed for the confrontation.[98]

The results of the poll are definitely a sign of hope. Franklin D. Roosevelt was right: repetition does not transform a lie into a truth. Especially when it concerns a defining episode and a key event of contemporary Russian history such as the constitutional coup, violent dissolution of the first Russian parliament, and emergency regime in September–October 1993.

IV

A new Russian Constitution of 1993 provides for an adoption of a number of Federal Constitutional laws that would supersede some outdated acts. Article 88(2) of the Constitution specifically declared a necessity to adopt a new Federal constitutional law *'On a State of Emergency'* (*O cherzvychainom polozhenii*). The act was eventually adopted and signed by President Putin into effect on 30 May 2001 (No.3 – FKZ).

The first and the second State Dumas (elected in 1993 and 1995) made several attempts to pass that important piece of legislation (especially in the period of a state of emergency in North Ossetia and Ingushetia), but none of those attempts came to fruition.[99] In 2000–2001, the State Duma considered two bills on a state of emergency. One of then was introduced by President Yeltsin back in 1997. The other draft was an 'initiative bill' endorsed on 11 April 2000 by a group of liberal State Duma deputies: Edward Vorobyov, Victor Pokhmelkin, Sergei Stepashin and the late Sergei Yushenkov.

The initiative bill (consisting of six chapters and 36 articles) was obviously inferior to the President's bill and was seriously and deservedly criticised by other Duma deputies as well as by legal experts (from the State

Duma's Law Department, and the Institute of Legislation and Comparative Law) for its poor legal quality. Subsequently, the authors of the initiative bill agreed with the criticism and recalled their bill. So the work in the State Duma concentrated on improving the remaining presidential draft.

The bill was eventually passed by the State Duma on 26 April 2001. Federation Council considered the act on 16 May 2001. Despite its apparent significance to the country and its legal and political system as well as to rights and freedoms of its citizens, only three deputies of the upper chamber of the Russian Parliament actually raised any questions regarding some of the act's provisions.

Deputy Chairman of the Federation Council V.A. Varnavsky and V.P. Orlov, a Representative of Administration of Koryak autonomous region in the Federation Council, questioned a provision of Article 31 of the act. According to the provision, any citizen violating a curfew regime can be detained by the regime's administration for up to three days. The deputies argued that the norm does not correspond to Article 22(2) of the Russian Constitution proclaiming that 'arrest, detention and keeping in custody shall be allowed only by an order of a court of law' and guaranteeing that 'no person may be detained for more than 48 hours without an order of a court of law'.

Deputy Chairman of the Federation Council V.M. Platonov and Chairman of the Federation Council's Committee on Constitutional Legislation and Judicial and Legal Matters V.V. Leonov gave their clarification. Basically denying a direct effect of the Russian Constitution, they argued that constitutional provisions of Article 22(2) remain a 'dead letter' until adoption of a new RF Code of Criminal Procedure. The RF Code of Criminal Procedure was subsequently passed and came into force in July 2002.

One more question concerned a right of subjects of the Russian Federation to initiate an imposition of a state of emergency on their territory or give their consent to such an imposition. It's quite peculiar that the Chairman of Tatarstan State Council F.H. Mukhametshin didn't find any arguments for a direct criticism of the act and rather expressed his regret that he didn't get a 'credible answer' to his question during discussion of the act at the FC Committee on Constitutional Legislation and Judicial and Legal Matters. Speaking after him V.V. Leonov drew the attention of his fellow deputies to the fact that Mukhametshin's question was raised long after consideration and adoption of the bill at the State Duma. Leonov's position was shared by V.A. Ozerov, Chairman of Committee on Security and Defence, who informed the chamber that his committee had also considered the act on emergency powers, and unanimously voted to recommend its adoption by the Federation Council.

A visible support to the act by two high profile committees of the chamber predetermined impressive results of voting in the Federation

Council. The act was passed by 154 votes in favour to just one against and one abstention.

A new Federal Constitutional law *'On a State of Emergency'* maintains the main principles of the previous act of 1991 which – it's never too bad to repeat – was praised by the U.S. Lawyers' Committee for Human Rights as relying 'heavily on international human rights norms, and in particular on the International Covenant on Civil and Political Rights'.

The law (consisting of seven chapters and 43 articles) defines goals of a state of emergency, and conditions of its introduction. According to Article 2, a state of emergency is aimed at 'elimination of conditions that caused introduction of a state of emergency, maintenance of human rights and civil freedoms, defence of the constitutional regime of the Russian Federation'. Emergency can be introduced only under conditions posing an 'imminent threat to life and security of citizens or constitutional regime of the Russian Federation'. The Act divides such conditions to two groups. The first one includes attempts of a violent change of the constitutional regime in the country, armed mutiny, regional conflicts, etc. The second group embraces non-political emergency situations like natural disasters, technological catastrophes, or epidemic outbreaks (art.3).

In legal terms, it's a common error when Russian and foreign reporters use terms 'state of emergency' (*chrezvyhainoe polozhenie*) and 'emergency situation' (*chrezvyhainaia situatsia*) interchangeably. The Russian legislation makes a distinction between them. Unlike a 'state of emergency', which is declared for 'protection of human rights and civil freedoms, defence of the constitutional regime', etc., an 'emergency situation' occurs as a result of a natural or technological disaster or a catastrophe that 'can lead or has led to human casualties, a damage to human health and environment, significant material losses and interruption of functioning of essential spheres of life' (Federal law No.68-FZ of 21 December 1994, art.1; Resolution of the RF Government No.516 of 30 April 1997, art.1). Another federal law, more precisely identifies one of such technological disasters as a crash of a 'hydrotechnological construction' (Federal law No. 117-FZ of 21 July 1997, art.1).

Resolution of the RF Government No.1094 of 13 September 1997 introduced a classification of emergency situations depending on their magnitude (by a number of affected people, a scope of material loss or a size of affected territory). An emergency situation can get the highest ('federal') status if it:

a   led to 'sufferings' (*postradali*) of more than 500 people; or
b   caused interruption of functioning of essential spheres of life of more than 1,000 people; or
c   on the first day of an emergency situation, material losses exceeded 5 million minimum standard salaries (MROT); or
d   affected more than two regions of the Russian Federation (art.2).

A state of emergency is introduced by a President's decree on the whole territory of the Russian Federation for a period not longer than 30 days, or in certain localities for a period not longer than 60 days (art.9(1)), with a possibility of their extension (an unlimited number of times) by a new decree (art.9(2)).

For comparison, Article 201 of a similar American law (National Emergencies Act of 1976) empowers the U.S. President to introduce a national emergency for six months with a possibility of its extension an indefinite number of times (50 U.S. Code 1621). This special regime was introduced by President Bush on 14 September 2001 by his '*Declaration of National Emergency by Reason of Certain Terrorist Attacks*'. The declaration introduced a national emergency 'by reason of the terrorist attacks on the World Trade Center, New York, and the Pentagon, and the continuing and immediate threat of further attacks on the United States' (Proclamation 7463). The proclamation was accompanied by an executive order calling the ready reserve of the U.S. Armed Forces to active duty 'for not more than 24 consecutive months' (Executive Order 13223).[100]

The new Russian law doesn't oblige the President to hold consultations with subjects of the Russian Federation prior to issuing a decree on a state of emergency, but the decree must be approved by the Federation Council. The upper chamber of the Federal Assembly is to be convened 'as soon as possible, without a special call' (art.7(1)), within 72 hours since the decree's publication (*obnarodovanie*) (art.7(3)). If not approved within three days, the decree automatically loses its effect. As mentioned before, Bernard Siegan in his 'emergency clause' recommended that an emergency proclamation of the President shall require parliamentary confirmation 'within five days'.[101] Russian law-makers appeared to be even more decisive and limited the term of the decree's effect, without Federation Council's authorisation, by three days.

Drafters of the act can be praised for another major achievement. The act can be considered a major step towards creation of a legal institution of a 'federal intervention'. The author of this study began writing about the necessity of introducing this legal mechanism back in 1994–1995. That position was endorsed by the Council for Foreign and Defence Policy, an influential Russian think-tank, that published my report under its auspices.[102] Its shorter (yet, a full-page) version was also published by *Nezavisimaya gazeta*, one of the most well-informed Russian newspapers at that time.[103] A year later that approach was strongly supported by a deputy chairman of the Federation Council Ramazan Abdulatipov (also in a full-page article in *Nezavisimaya gazeta*).[104] Already in 1998, an absence of legal regulations of a federal intervention was recognised as one of major 'deficiencies' of Russian Constitutional Law. Seven years from the first publication dedicated to a federal intervention to an introduction of its legal mechanism in Russia in historical terms was not such a long period of time.[105]

Conclusion

I

The vast experience of decreeing states of emergency in various locations on the territory of Russia, and other Newly Independent States, including North Ossetia and Ingushetia or the Osh region in southern Kyrgyzstan (where a state of emergency was maintained for nearly five years – a 'record' for the former USSR),[1] indicates the existence of a serious danger to which both executive and legislative branches of government expose themselves when trying to solve social, interethnic, territorial and other problems chiefly by *exceptional* methods, without searching for *political* ways of settling them. Judging by post-Soviet experience, the longer an emergency (*de facto* or *de jure*) regime lasts, and the bigger emphasis on emergency methods is made, the less effective the state of emergency usually is, and the more counterproductive extraordinary measures become.

The mechanism of a state of emergency is a 'tactical', 'operational' weapon, rather than a 'strategic' one. In certain circumstances it can become an indispensable supplement to predominantly social, political, economic, financial and other 'normal' measures of crisis management, but it cannot and should not supersede or, moreover, substitute for them. A state of emergency is a 'fire' that constitutional governments use to fight another 'fire' – of unconstitutional actions threatening the state and society. The problem here is that the line between those two 'fires' is usually thin and dubious. The longer each of them lasts, the bigger damage they can create (including damage to the hands of a 'fireman'), the more casualties they produce and, to a large extent, they tend to backlash.

Governments and authorities in 'hot spots' of the world should always bear in mind that provoking the use of emergency powers, introduction of a state of emergency *de facto* rather then *de jure* remain one of the goals of secessionist, terrorist, 'revolutionary' and other antisocial groups, movements and forces. It shouldn't be a surprise that when the first federal intervention in Chechnya triggered a new round of discussions of legal regulations of a state of emergency and its practical implementation, two power structures proved to be the strongest supporters of introduction of a legal mechanism of a state of emergency in Chechnya: the State Duma and the Ministry of Defence.[2]

As is known, neither a state of emergency, nor martial law has ever been introduced in Chechnya. Two 'federal interventions' were exercised without imposing *any* special legal regime in Chechnya. Russian Presidents simply used their powers of the Commander-in-Chief to deploy troops to a rebellious republic. Obviously, a *legal* emergency regime would have imposed restrictions not only on those against whom such a regime was aimed (Chechen terrorists and separatists), but also on those who were ordered to implement it (armed forces and special police units). Introduction of a state of emergency in the most critical years of the federal interventions would also have stopped the campaign in the Russian liberal mass media (as well as in Western and Islamic countries) accusing the armed forces of acting outside *legal* restrictions in Chechnya.

Thus, a declaration of a state of emergency was in the interests of both people of Chechnya (apart from insurgents and terrorists) and federal armed forces and law-enforcement agencies. Absence of such declaration, shifting the emphasis from emergency *de jure* to emergency *de facto*, on the one hand, made the use of federal troops less legally defined and restricted and, on the other hand, made federal armed services responsible for certain grave mistakes of Moscow political leadership, especially in 1994–1996.

II

Foreign experts come to similar conclusions regarding correlation of terrorist activities and disproportionate use of emergency powers. Indeed, according to an observation of former officers of the Counterintelligence Directorate of the U.S. Air Force's Office of Special Investigations, 'forcing governmental overreaction (resort to martial law or other methods . . .) will continue to be a primary terrorist objective'.[3]

One of the statements in a Basque ETA training manual can be a perfect illustration to this conclusion: 'The enemy, altogether, is a thousand times stronger than we are. But each time we attack, at that very moment we are stronger than he is. The enemy, as a massive animal, stung by many bees, is infuriated to the point of uncontrolled rage, and strikes out blindly to the left and right on every side.' 'At this point', Basque terrorists say, 'we have achieved *one of our major objectives; forcing him to commit a thousand atrocities and brutal acts*. The majority of the victims are innocent. Then the people, to this point more or less passive and waiting, become indignant and in reaction turn to us. We could not hope for a better outcome'[4] (*italics added – A.D.*).

Lord Jellicoe made a similar judgement in analysing the application of the British Prevention of Terrorism (Temporary Provisions) Act of 1976.

In Jellicoe's opinion, extremists consider it highly important for them to make the government pass the 'toughest possible laws'. Their 'victory' lay in the circumstance that implementation of such legislation alienate that part of the society whose interests terrorists say they represent. If this alienation really comes about, extremists not only secure growing support from society but begin posing as lawful defenders of its interests.[5]

And if extremists really consider it highly important to make the government pass the 'toughest possible laws', the U.S. Government got in the same trap when adopting the PATRIOT Act (Uniting and Strengthening America by Providing Appropriate Tools Required to Intercept and Obstruct Terrorism Act, signed by President Bush into law on 26 October 2001), introducing military tribunals, etc.

Putin's government should try to avoid the same mistakes in the aftermath of the Beslan tragedy of 1–3 September 2004.

III

Coup d'etat and emergency rule in Russia in September–October 1993 is a classical example of a violation of a fundamental principle of governance defining the key power relations in a state – the system of separation of powers and society's allocation of authority to the legislature to enact laws. When one branch of government compromises this allocation, the result is, in essence, a new form of government with an entirely altered political power structure. Yelsin's coup and emergency regime can also be considered an evidence of a more general legal tendency that the executive branch is the most corruptible, and unless it is kept in check, the executive may, first, *create* an emergency situation (in Russia – with suicidal economic experiments disguised as 'reforms') and, second, *exploit* it (demonising opponents in the Parliament, using them as a scapegoat – 'Communist-fascist' scare – allegedly blocking 'reforms') as an opportunity for self-affirmation. The ultimate result is a *transformation and legitimisation* (through 'adoption' of a new Constitution) of naked political power into constitutional power to exercise its will.

Yet, a Rossiter's axiom seems to be relevant when analysing emergency regime in contemporary Russia: 'Even if a government can be constitutional without being democratic, it cannot be democratic without being constitutional'.[6]

IV

The transitional character of Russian constitutionalism, contradictory legacy of legal regulations of emergency powers, and of their use (especially in late 1980s–early 1990s) are the challenges that Russian President and policy-makers will have to meet when using a new Act '*On a State of Emergency*' of 2001.

Several issues need to be addressed and some observations and recommendations formulated at this moment.

The first of them concerns the 'trigger clause' of the mechanism of a state of emergency.

In the argument between two main points of view *pro* and *contra* advance legal regulation of those reasons and circumstances justifying introduction of a state of emergency (represented by some German jurists, like A. Hamann and H. Folz, on the one hand, and by French administrativist A. Matio and former USSR Minister of Justice S.G. Luschikov, on the other hand), the position of supporters of inclusion into a constitution and/or respective organic law of a detailed and complete ('*exhaustive*') list of these grounds seems to be more relevant. Absence in the texts of constitutions and legislative acts of a clearly defined and concrete list of such reasons and conditions, reliance on an 'opinion' of the head of state (or government) on presence of an 'emergency situation' or its imminent danger is more typical for some developing countries of Asia, Africa and Latin America. It creates wide possibilities for misuse by the Chief Executive of his discretionary powers, and might lead to gross abuses of personal freedoms and rights of autonomous units (in federations).

Drafters of the new Russian Act '*On a State of Emergency*' brought in compliance with major international documents the provision limiting declaration of a state of emergency to situations of 'actual or imminent danger'. Out of all acts regulating the institution of a state of emergency in Russia (and the USSR) in the 1990s, only the 1991 law contained such a provision. Most regrettably, the new Constitution of 1993 is silent about it too.

The European Court of Human Rights first laid down this principle in the *Lawless* case (1961) interpreting a 'public emergency' as: '*une situation de crise ou de danger exceptionnel et imminent*'. It's interesting that the English text of the judgement didn't contain the adjective 'imminent' and mentioned only 'exceptional situation'. The European Commission in the *Greek* case (1969) looked into that contradiction and confirmed that the formula from the French text (and not from the English version) was authentic. The first out of four characteristics of a 'public emergency', as described by the Commission, says that it must be 'actual or imminent'. Similarly, the 1984 Paris *Minimum Standards of Human Rights Norms in a State of Emergency* said that 'the expression 'public emergency' means an exceptional situation of crisis or public danger, actual or imminent ...' (sec.A, para.1(b)).[7]

If the point of the constitutional mechanism of a state of emergency is the swiftest possible return to 'constitutional normalcy', then the 'termination clause' seems key. Clinton Rossiter, for instance, believed that the best way to ensure termination of emergency powers is to require the most rigid time limit possible coupled with an explicit ban on executive power to unilaterally extend such a limit.[8] The author certainly agrees with another conclusion of Rossiter who advocated that the only way to truly guarantee compliance with a time limit is to leave at least some 'residual power' in the national legislature.[9]

It is noteworthy in this connection that if the 1990 USSR Act, '*On the Legal Regime of a State of Emergency*', allowed the state organs introducing a state of emergency to prolong it as many times as necessary when it was demanded by the 'circumstances', the 1993 Constitution represents a different approach: it does not require a time limit be declared at all. Although the Constitution doesn't allow dissolution of the State Duma during a state of emergency, it does not grant the Duma any authority to assert its power and stop unlawful seizure of emergency power by the President. How the President can 'legitimately' outplay the Parliament is to invoke his Articles 111(4) and 117(3) powers to dissolve the Duma (in case the Duma thrice rejects the candidates for the post of Prime Minister or twice within three months expresses no-confidence in the Government) and *then* declares a state of emergency *before* the Duma reconvenes.

Failing to provide sufficient declaration or termination provisions, the current Russian Constitution cannot be recognised as fully meeting the international law standards.

Parliamentary control is one of the weakest points of Russian constitutionalism in general and of the constitutional mechanism of a state of emergency in particular. However, it's a recognised fact that the Parliament shall play a crucial role at every stage of a state of emergency; 'in particular, the power and duty of the legislature to monitor with meticulous care the declaration and duration of a state of emergency is of pivotal significance for the maintenance of a rule of law during a serious public crisis'.[10] Two remarks need to be made here.

Parliamentary control in the sphere of emergency powers rests on the following principle: the Legislature should not curtail the power of the Executive to react promptly to an emergency situation, but the former can and must precisely regulate the amount of the Chief Executive's discretionary powers. An essential element of the parliamentary control is the Legislature's power to extend (or refuse to extend) a state of exception, thereby promptly and effectively controlling all admissible methods for the executive's emergency reaction to exceptional circumstances.

A similar postulate is laid down in the U.S. constitutional law: emergency powers should be very broad in scope, but the conditions for their exercise should be rigidly defined.[11] According to the decision in *Schechter Poultry Corporation v United States*, whatever emergency powers are to be given the President by the Congress ought to be circumscribed as to the specific circumstances in which they may be invoked, must include standards for their exercise and must, in any event, never amount to transfer of legislative powers to the executive or to abdication on the part of the Congress (295 U.S. 495, 529 (1935)).[12]

With respect to the power to introduce a state of emergency, the 1993 Russian Constitution appears to actually be a step backward not only from the Russian Law of 1991, but even from the Soviet Act of 1990. Article 88 of the Constitution grants the President the unilateral power to declare a state of emergency requiring only that he 'immediately informs' the chambers of the Federal Assembly. Likewise, Article 87 grants the President with the power to declare martial law requiring only that he 'immediately informs' the legislative bodies. Again, although this power is tempered by Article 109(5) which forbids dissolution of the State Duma (lower chamber) during martial law or a state of emergency, the Constitution fails to provide any effective checks and balances to the discretionary emergency powers of the President. Article 102(1b, c) only mentions the power of the Federation Council (upper chamber) to 'approve' the executive decrees introducing a state of emergency or martial law, but doesn't say a single word describing time limits of such 'approval'. Fortunately, this deficiency was corrected by the 2001 Act.

As it was analysed in Chapter 2 of this study, national legislation of the countries of the world regulates various models ranging between two extremes: complete or nearly complete disregard and abandonment of the principle of parliamentary control (with some decorative tricks) of the constitutions of Nepal of 1990 and Cyprus of 1975, on the one hand, and an over-regulated model of the Constitution of Brazil of 1988 not containing a '*force majeure*' clause at all, on the other hand. (In the first case, executive proclamations on a state of emergency are to be laid down before legislatures for approval within at least three months from the date of issuance; in the second case, the constitution requires completion of four different stages involving close collaboration of four constitutional organs and political actors – President, National Defence Council, National Congress and its upper chamber Council of the Republic – before the Chief Executive can actually introduce a state of emergency).

The model proposed by the 1991 Russian Act, '*On the State of Emergency*' (and mainly preserved in the new Russian Act of 2001) – demanding that the President must 'immediately' notify the Parliament of introduction of a state of emergency and that the latter must review the decree within 24 hours if in session, or within 72 hours if not in session (48 hours when 'martial law' is declared), – probably represents 'the golden mean' in the whole variety of existing options. On the one hand, it allows the President to introduce a state of emergency and undertake necessary measures if grave circumstances urgently demand them, but, on the other hand, it restricts authoritarian instincts of the executive tending to govern without checks and balances of other branches of government.

V

Another recommendation actually concerns the constitution itself. It's quite understandable why the 'President's constitution, proposed by the President and drafted by specialists completely sharing the idea of strong presidential power', as the Russian Constitution of 1993 was characterised by Lev Okun'kov,[13] former director of an influential Institute of Legislation and Comparative Law (an analytical and law-drafting institution of the Russian Government), overwhelmingly shifts the balance between chambers of the Federal Assembly in favour of a more predictable Federation Council. Yet, one may argue that in such vital questions for any state as questions of 'war and peace' (including introduction, extension and termination of a state of emergency or martial law) the role of the lower chamber of the Russian Parliament – elected directly by the population and to a much larger extent *representing* interests, views, and mood of the Russian people than the *'nomenklatura'*-based Federation Council – should be more vocal.

Although the 1993 Constitution contains a 'non-derogable clause' (art.56(3)) and lists 16 rights and freedoms which cannot be affected by a state of emergency and 'shall not be subject to restriction', the Constitution fails to establish any sort of 'proportionality clause' setting up the most minimal of restrictions on exercise of rights and freedoms and on altering governmental and constitutional structures under a state of emergency.

One of the most important safeguards for the protection of individual rights under a state of emergency, the principle of proportionality, is based on a more general legal theory of 'self-defence'. That theory requires the existence of an imminent danger and of a relationship between that danger and the measures taken to ensure protection against it. Such measures must be proportionate to the danger. In the words of Erica-Irene A. Daes, the principle implies 'that the extent of any limitation should be strictly proportionate to the need or the higher interest protected by the limitation'.[14]

The Siracusa Principles concretised the principle of proportionality as having three factors – namely, severity, duration and geographic scope[15] – envisaging that:

a   where ordinary measures would be adequate to deal with the public danger, the derogation measure cannot be considered strictly necessary;
b   the derogation measure must cease to operate when the intensity of the public danger that brought it into existence is no longer present; and
c   the zone of a state of emergency is limited by an area to which the public crisis is confined.

The 'forgetfulness' of the 1993 Constitution drafters to establish a 'proportionality clause' creates a danger that under certain circumstances Russia (or rather its Executive) can join the group of such countries like Uruguay, Syria, Colombia, Jordan, El Salvador, and Sri Lanka whose violations of the principle of proportionality in a public emergency were detected and severely criticised by the Human Rights Committee of the International Law Association.[16]

VI

Finally, it seems clear that the problem of emergency powers and a state of emergency, either taken in the Russian context (both pre- and post-Soviet) or in a broader sense, presents a crucial case of the general problem of constitutionalism.

It's an old truth that every state has a Constitution (a body of principles, institutions, laws, and customs that forms the framework of government), but not every state is truly 'constitutional'. These are emergencies, emergency powers, and states of emergency that put constitutionalism to the test. Indeed, there are grounds for presenting constitutionalism and emergency rule as antithetical in some ways. The former is premised upon the supremacy of law, the latter upon the logic of necessity and survival. The first of them stresses limitations; the second – unlimited authority. Constitutionalism enshrines personal rights, freedoms and liberties; emergencies, by their very nature, speak in the language of national interests and state necessities. Emergencies, in other words, tend to result in a concentration of power in the government, mainly in the executive branch, along with infringement of individual freedoms, which is precisely what constitutionalism is expected to prevent.

It's an ultimate dilemma of democracy – to reconcile 'constitutional government' and 'constitutional dictatorship'; 'effective, vigorous governmental action' and, yet, limited power of governmental bodies 'so as to forestall the rise of a despotic concentration of power'.[17] In this respect, there's hardly any country in the world, including Russia, with a perfect record. It won't be easy to find a solution to this problem, for, in Carl Friedrich's words, this 'task requires all the wisdom man can muster'.

Notes

Preface

1 The early decrees were usually adopted as joint decisions of All-Russian Central Executive Committee (ARCEC) and the Council of People's Commissars, or by ARCEC and the Council of Labour and Defence). Emergency measures for the 'salvation of the Bolshevik revolution' included creation of various extraordinary executive and extra-judicial agencies: the All-Russian Extraordinary Commission for Combating Counter-Revolution and Sabotage, a.k.a. Cheka, and 'revolutionary military tribunals'. See, e.g. Resolution of the All-Russian Central Executive Committee of 2 September 1918 '*Soviet Republic – a War Camp*' (*Sovetskaia respublika – voenniy lager'*) (*Pravda*, No.188, 4 September 1918); Resolution of the Council of People's Commissars of 5 September 1918 '*On the Red Terror*' (*O krasnom terrore*) (*Izvestiya*, No.195, 5 September 1918); Decree of the All-Russian Central Executive Committee and Council of Labour and Defence of 4 November 1920 '*On Locations Declared Under Martial Law*' (*O mestnostyakh, ob'yavlennykh na voennom polozhenii*) (*Izvestia*, No.257, 16 November 1920); two decrees of the All-Russian Central Executive Committee and Council of People's Commissars of 8 March 1923 and 10 May 1926 of the same title – '*On Emergency Measures for the Preservation of the Revolutionary Order*' (*O chrezvychainykh merakh okhrany revolutsionnogo poryadka*) (*Izvestia*, No.54, 10 March 1923; *Izvestia*, No.127, 4 June 1926). *For details* see N.F. Bugay, *Chrezvychaynye organy Sovetskoy vlasti: revkomy. 1918–1921 gg.* [Emergency Organs of the Soviet Power: Revolutionary Committees, 1918–1921] (Moscow: Nauka, 1990); Nikolay Kostin, *Sud nad terrorom* [Terror on Trial] (Moscow: Moscowskiy rabochiy, 1990).
2 See *Moscowskaya pravda*, 2 February 1990.
3 I. Baranovsky, 'General'naya repetitsiya' [The Last Rehearsal], *Moscowskie novosti*, No.1, 10 January 1993.
4 Daniel J. Gerstle, 'Nagorno-Karabakh's Deep Divide', *EurasiaNet.org*, 16 July 2004.
5 Carol Migdalovitz, *Armenia: Basic Facts* (CRS Report for Congress 94-604 F; Washington, D.C.: Congressional Research Service, The Library of Congress, 28 July 1994), p.2. Daniel Gerstle gives an even bigger number of victims of the Karabakh War: 25,000 people (Daniel J. Gerstle, *supra* note 4*).
6 Vladimir Ustinov, *Obvinyaetsya terrorism* [Terrorism as a Crime] (Moscow: 'OLMA-PRESS', 2002), p.135. The highest ransom was demanded for General Shpigun – US$15 million ('Chechensky kapkan' [Chechen Trap], *RenTV*, 30 September 2004).
7 They grew from 55.444 million roubles in 1999 to 105.393 – in 2000; 148.909 – in 2001; 190.444 – in 2002; 247.931 – in 2003; and 310.577 million – in 2004. (See a

chart in: Andrei Soldatov, 'Strana ne dlya zhizni' [A Country Not for Life], *Moscowskie novosti*, No.32, 27 August–2 September 2004).

8 'Apel'sinovy sok' [Orange Juice], *NTV*, 19 September 2004.

9 My incomplete list of states of emergency (in various forms) includes:

- September 1988 – Nagorno-Karabakh Autonomous Oblast (NKAO) and Agdam district of Azerbaijanian (a 'state of exception', *osoboe polozhenie*);
- January 1989 – NKAO (a 'special form of government', *osobaya forma upravlenia*);
- January 1990 – NKAO and surrounding districts of Azerbaijan, Gorissky district of Armenia and the USSR frontier zone on the Azerbaijani territory;
- February 1990 – Dushanbe, the Tajikistan capital;
- June 1990 – city of Osh and neighbouring Uzgensky, Sovietsky, Kara-Suysky, Aravansky and Anaysky districts of Uzbekistan;
- June 1990 – Frunze, the Kirgizia capital, and several other areas;
- June 1990 – city of Andizhan in Uzbekistan and five districts of Andizhansky Oblast on the border with Kirgizia: Jalalkuduksky, Kurgantepinsky, Markhamatsky, Pakhtaabadsky, and Khojaabadsky;
- August 1990 – Yerevan, the Armenia capital;
- October 1990 – areas of Gagauz settlements on the territory of Komratsky, Vulkaneshtsky and Chadir-Lukgsky districts (in the southern parts of Moldavia), and several locations of Bessarabsky district;
- November 1990 – cities of Dubossary, Tiraspol' and Bendery of the Russian-populated Transdniester region in Moldavia;
- December 1990 – city of Tskhinvali and Javsky district of South Ossetia;
- June 1991 – Makhachkala, the Dagestan capital;
- August 1991 – Moscow and 'some locations' in the USSR;
- September 1991 – city of Dushanbe (introduced by the Tajikistan Supreme Soviet, lifted a week later);
- September 1991 – Tbilisi, the Georgia capital (introduced by Georgian President Gamsakhurdia);
- November 1991 – Checheno-Ingushetia (introduced by Russian President Yeltsin; 'annulled' by Chechen President Dzhokhar Dudayev; after two days of debate, the Russian Supreme Soviet voted not to endorse Yeltsin's decree and resolved to try to settle the conflict by peaceful means);
- December 1991 – Megrinsky district of Armenia (neighbouring with Nakhichevan' Oblast of Azerbaijan);
- January 1992 – city of Khanckendi (Stepanakert), Shushinsky and 13 other districts of 'Nagorno-Karabakh Republic' (NKR) ('president's rule');
- January 1992 – cities of Tbilisi and Kutaisi and several districts of western Georgia;
- March 1992 – Moldova;
- May 1992 – Dagestani cities of Makhachkala and Kyzylyurt;
- June 1992 – North Ossetia;
- July 1992 – Mardakertsky district of Karabakh;
- August 1992 – NKR ('martial law', *voennoe polozhenie*);
- September 1992 – Kurgan-Tubinsky Oblast of Tajikistan;
- September 1992 – Nal'chik, the Kabardino-Balkaria capital;
- October 1992 – city of Dushanbe again;
- January 1993 – districts along the border of Tajikistan with Afghanistan;

- February 1993 – Armavirsky (former Oktemberyansky) district of Azerbaijan (on the border with Turkey);
- April 1993 – Azerbaijan (caused by a massive assault of the Armenian army);
- October 1993 – Moscow;
- January 1996 – 'Transdniester Republic' (in Moldova) (a state of 'economic emergency').

10 *Nezavisimaya gazeta*, 28 June 2001. By 1994, degradation of Russia's economy and its social sphere had reached such proportions that on average we got two serious accidents on gas and oil pipelines each day, once a week on transport, once a month in industrial enterprises, and major technological catastrophes twice a year. (Andrei Bayduzhiy, 'V Rossii nastupilo vremya katastrof' [The Time of Catastrophes Has Come to Russia], *Nezavisimaya gazeta*, 30 July 1994, pp.1–2). In the last ten years, the situation with technological accidents and catastrophes has become even worse making gruesome statistics in a book like Ryurik Povileiko's *Katastrofa!* [Catastrophe!] (Moscow: Nedra, 1990) not 'impressive' anymore. For more information see Boris Porfiriev, *Disaster Policy and Emergency Management in Russia* (Commack, NY: Nova Science Publishers, 1998).

11 Cited in Michael Linfield, *Freedom under Fire: U.S. Civil Liberties in Times of War* (Boston: South End Press, 1990), p.1.

12 President Lincoln's actions during the Civil War and President Roosevelt's measures during the Great Depression are graphic illustrations here.

13 On 5 July 1987, in a publication 'Reagan Advisors Ran Secret Government' *The Miami Herald* revealed that Lieutenant Colonel Oliver North and the Federal Emergency Management Agency (FEMA) had drafted a contingency plan providing for the suspension of the Constitution, the imposition of martial law, abolition of state and local legislatures and their replacement with military commanders, the round-up and detention in relocation camps of dissidents in the event of a national crisis. The plan, secretly obtained by *The Miami Herald*, provided for an executive order that President Reagan would sign but not make public until a crisis broke. Although the White House deny that the executive order was ever signed, according to Jules Lobel, 'some congressional sources believe that President Reagan did sign an executive order in 1984 and revised national military mobilisation measures to deal with civilians in a national crisis'. During the Iran-Contras hearings in the U.S. Congress in July of 1987, a question posed to Oliver North about the FEMA plan was referred to a 'closed session'. (See Jules Lobel, 'Emergency Power and the Decline of Liberalism', 98 *The Yale Law Journal* (1989), p.1385; Michael Linfield, *supra* note 11*, at 165–167).

14 William G. Saywell, 'Foreword', *Federalism-in-the-Making: Contemporary Canadian and German Constitutionalism, National and Transnational* (Dordrecht – Boston – London: Kluwer Academic Publishers, 1992. Edward McWhinney, Jerald Zaslove, and Werner Wolf, eds), p.ix.

15 It took about a year to convince the directorship of the institute to allow me to write my Candidate of Law (Ph.D. equivalent) thesis on emergency powers in Britain and India.

16 Nicole Questiaux, *Study of the Implications for Human Rights of Recent Developments Concerning Situations Known as States of Siege or Emergency*, E/CN.4/Sub.2/1982/15, 27 July 1982 (United Nations, Economic and Social Council), para.97, p.26. Russian translation of some excerpts from the study see *K zakonodatel'stvu o chrezvychainom polozhenii. Rabochie materialy* [On Legislation on a State of Emergency. Working Materials] (Moscow: International

Fund 'For Survival and Development of Humankind', Project Group on Human Rights, 1989. E.M. Ametistov, V.G. Golitsyn, S.A. Kovalev, *et al.*), pp.20–27.

17 V.M. Gessen, *Iskluchitel'noe polozhenie* [A State of Exception] (St. Petersburg: Pravo, 1908).

18 Alexander Domrin, *Konstitutsionniy mechanism chrezvychainogo polozhenia. Pravovoe regulirovanie i praktika primenenia v Velikobritanii i Indii* [Constitutional Mechanism of a State of Emergency: Legal Regulations and Practice of Implementation in Great Britain and India] (Moscow: Moscow Public Science Foundation, 1998). The book was preceded by 18 other publications by the author including two major reports for the Council for Foreign and Defence Policy: *Rezhim chrezvychainogo polozhenia. Opyt pravovogo regulirovania i praktika primenenia v zarubezhnykh stranakh* [States of Emergency: Transnational Law and Practice of Its Implementation] (Moscow: Council for Foreign and Defence Policy, [October] 1992); *Federal'noe vmeshatel'stvo v dela subyektov federatsii. Opyt pravovogo regulirovania i praktika primenenia v zarubezhnykh stranakh* [Federal Interventions Worldwide: Transnational Law and Practice of Its Implementation] (Moscow: Council for Foreign and Defence Policy, [February] 1995). In 1982, scholars of my department at the Institute of Soviet Legislation (now Institute of Legislation and Comparative Law under the Russian Government) prepared a major analytical report *Legislation of Bourgeois Countries on a State if Emergency*. Four years later it became available to the readers at the Institute of Scientific Information (INION) of the USSR Academy of Sciences (No.22288 of 29 August 1986). However, the study was never officially published: subject of the report was not recognised as having a 'topical interest' to the Soviet state and society of that period.

19 *Chrezvychainoe zakonodatel'stvo FRG* [Emergency Legislation of FRG] (Moskow: Yuridicheskaya literatura, 1968. V.M. Chkhikvadze, ed.)

20 For instance, in a recent thorough study *Freedom or Security: The Consequences for Democracies Using Emergency Powers to Fight Terror* (Westport, CT – London: Praeger, 2003) by Michael Freeman, Russia is mentioned only once: 'The conclusions of this study can be applied to cases like the United States or *even* Russia' (p.17; *italics added – A.D.*); in her fundamental 800-page book *The International Law of Human Rights and States of Exception with Special Reference to the Travaux Prepapatoires and Case-Law of the International Monitoring Organs* (The Hague – Boston – London: Martin Nijhoff Publishers, 1998) by Anna-Lena Svensson-McCarthy, the author periodically describes a special position of the Soviet delegations at multilateral international negotiations (pp.97–99, 204, 207, 210–211) and gives her (sometimes deserved, often unsubstantiated) criticism of the Soviet constitutional order (pp.97, 100), but never refers to emergency legislation and its use in Russia or the USSR (even in a chapter 'Public Emergencies Yesterday and Today').

21 Besides a book and numerous articles by this author, at least six doctorates (Candidate of Law) on various aspects of emergency powers have been defended in Russia in the last ten years (with four dissertations in 1998 only!): by Oleg Alexandrov (Moscow, 1994), Sergei Anikienko (Nizhny Novgorod, 2000), Igor' Goncharov (Moscow, 1998), Vladimir Lobzinev (Moscow, 1998), Sergei Pchelintsev (Moscow, 1998), Vladimir Ukhov (Moscow, 1998).

22 The most widely used source in this study – a 50-volume collection of *The Constitutions of the World* (Dobbs Ferry, NY: Oceana Publications, Inc., 1970–1997. Albert P. Blaustein & Gisbert H. Flanz, eds) – is abbreviated as follows: *Constitutions*. Besides original Russian constitutional texts, see *Basic Legal Documents of the Russian Federation* (New York – London/Rome:

Oceana Publications Inc., 1992. W.E. Butler, comp., trans. and ed.); *Constitutions* (USSR, Supplement, November 1990); *ibid.* (USSR, Supplement, The Russian Federation, May 1991); *ibid.* (USSR, Supplement 3, The Russian Federation, October 1991); *ibid.* (The Russian Federation, Supplement, Release 93-6, October 1993); *ibid.* (The Russian Federation, Supplement, Release 93-8, December 1993).

Introduction

1 *Konstitutsionnoe (gosudarstvennoe) pravo: Spravochnik* [Constitutional (State) Law: A Reference Manual] (Moscow: Yurist, 1995), p.173.
2 *Chrezvychainoe zakonodatel'stvo FRG* [Emergency Legislation of FRG], *supra* note 19* [Preface], p.7.
3 Clinton L. Rossiter, *Constitutional Dictatorship: Crisis Government in the Modern Democracies* (Princeton: Princeton University Press, 1948), pp.13, 301.
4 For details see, e.g. David Bonner, *Emergency Powers in Peacetime* (London: Sweet and Maxwell, 1985); J. Eaves, *Emergency Powers and the Parliamentary Watchdog: Parliament and the Executive in Great Britain, 1939–1951* (London: Hansard Society, 1957); K. Jeffery & P. Hennessy, *States of Emergency: British Governments and Strikebreaking Since 1919* (London, 1983); H. Levenson, 'A Survey of Emergency Powers in Britain', *Review of Contemporary Law*, No.2, 1981; Gillian Susan Morris, 'The Emergency Powers Act 1920', *Public Law*, Winter 1979; Gillian Susan Morris, 'The Police and Industrial Emergencies', 9 *The Industrial Law Journal* 1 (March 1980).
5 Benjamin Obi Nwabuese, *Constitutionalism in the Emergent States* (London: C. Hurst & Company, in association with Nwamife Publishers, Enugu, 1973. Foreword by S.A. de Smith), p.174.
6 Brian Loveman, *The Constitution of Tyranny: Regimes of Exception in Spanish America* (Pittsburgh & London: University of Pittsburgh Press, 1993), p.7.
7 See Louis Fisher, *Constitutional Conflicts Between Congress and the President* (Lawrence, Kansas: University Press of Kansas, 1995. 4th rev. edn), p.272. At least to some extent, this intensive use of emergency powers can be explained by the personality of President Franklin D. Roosevelt, who was named by Clinton Rossiter 'the most crisis-minded public figure in American history, a man who thrived on crises, emergencies, dangers, perils, and panics'. 'His long tenure of office was a continuos emergency', concluded Rossiter. (See Clinton L. Rossiter, *supra* note 3*, at 256). After spending a decade of staff work in the Office of Price Administration, the Navy, the Budget Bureau, and the White House, Richard E. Neustadt testified: 'What distinguishes' Presidents Roosevelt's and Truman's administrations 'can be put very briefly: emergencies in policy with politics as usual'. (See Richard E. Neustadt, *Presidential Power. The Politics of Leadership from FDR to Carter* (New York: Macmillan Publishing House; London: Collier Macmillan Publishers, 1980), p.5). Another American author wrote in his book of 1944 that 'the bank crash made [FDR] almost a dictator' (George Fort Milton, *The Use of Presidential Power* (Boston: Little, Brown and Company, 1944), p.319). *Also* see Leonard Bake, *Back to Back: The Duel Between FDR and the Supreme Court* (New York: The Macmillan Company, 1967).
8 Jonathan W. Daly, 'On the Significance of Emergency Legislation in Late Imperial Russia', 54 *Slavic Review*, 3 (Fall 1995), p.627. The article was subsequently used in Daly's remarkable monograph *Autocracy Under Siege: Security Police and Opposition in Russia, 1866–1905* (DeKalb: Northern Illinois University Press, 1998).
9 Certainly, outdated emergency legislation in Taiwan is just an illustration of a

more general troublesome legal situation in the country. Only one-fifth of the members of the Taiwan National Assembly are elected; most seats are held by Nationalists elected in 1947 for life, many of whom are in their 80s and 90s now. (See Tao-tai Hsia with Wendy Zeldin, 'Laws on Emergency Powers in Taiwan', in *Coping with Crises: How Governments Deal with Emergencies* (Lanham, New York, London: University Press of America, 1990. Shao-chuan Leng, ed.), pp.173–208.)

10 William J. Butler, John P. Humphrey, G.E. Bisson, *The Decline of Democracy in the Philippines: A Report of Missions* (Geneva: International Commission of Jurists, 1977), p.3.

11 *Ibid.*, pp.11, 45.

12 See 'The Republic of Bolivia: Chronology', in 2 *Constitutions* (Release 92-4, July 1992.), pp.4–5.

13 Jonathan Hartlyn, 'Presidentialism and Colombian Politics', in *The Failure of Presidential Democracy* (Baltimore and London: The Johns Hopkins University Press, 1994. Juan J. Linz and Arturo Valenzuela, eds), p.307. On states of emergency in two other Latin American states see, e.g. Mark J. Osiel, 'Dialogue with Dictators: Judicial Resistance in Argentina and Brazil', 20 *Law & Social Inquiry* (Journal of the American Bar Foundation) 2 (Spring 1995), pp.481–560.

14 Patricia Peppin, 'Emergency Legislation and Rights in Canada: The War Measures Act and Civil Liberties', 18 *Queens Law Journal* 1 (Spring 1993), p.130.

15 See the texts of presidential proclamations introducing and lifting national emergencies, in *The Gazette of India*, Extraordinary. No.97/26.10.1962; No.1/10.01.1968; No.213/03.12.1971; No.169/26.06.1975; No.177/29.06.1975; No.80/21.03.1977; No.95/27.03.1977. *Also* see, e.g. S.B. Nakade, *Emergency in Indian Constitution* (New Delhi: Cosmo Publishers, 1990); Meena Srivastava, *Constitutional Crisis in the States in India* (New Delhi: Concept Publ. Co., 1980); P.M. Verma, *Constitutional Validity of Emergency Laws* (Allahabad: the Indian National Renaissance Society, 1978); Alexander Domrin, 'Penjabski krizis i reforma instituta chrezvychainogo polozhenia v Indii' [The Crisis in Punjab and Reform of the Mechanism of a State of Emergency in India], *Yuzhnaya Azia. Istoria i sovremennost'* [South Asia: Yesterday and Today] (Moscow: Nauka, 1989); Alexander Domrin, 'Prezidentskoe pravlenie v shtatakh Indii: praktika primenenia' [President's Rule in the States of India: Experience of Its Implementation], *Konstitutsionnoe soveschanie*, No.2, October 1993; Alexander Domrin, 'Pravovye instituty chrezvychainogo rezhima v Indii' [Legal Regulations of Emergency Regimes in India], *Pravo i economika*. No.13–14, 1996.

16 *A Brief History of Emergency Powers in the United States. A Working Paper* (Washington: U.S. Government Printing Office, 1974. Prepared by Harold C. Relyea for the Special Committee on National Emergencies and Delegated Emergency Powers, U.S. Senate), p.v. *Also* see Robert Higgs, *Crisis and Leviathan: Critical Episodes in the Growth of American Government* (New York, Oxford: Oxford University Press, 1987. A Pacific Research Institute for Public Policy Book), p.251.

17 *Summary of Emergency Power Statutes. A Working Paper* (Washington: U.S. Government Printing Office, 1973. Prepared for the Special Committee on the Termination of the National Emergency, U.S. Senate), p.1.

18 See 'Nation Still Living Under Jaruzelski's Martial Law', 3 *RFE/RL Poland, Belarus, and Ukraine Report* 9 (13 March 2001).

19 *States of Emergency: Torture and Violations of the Right to Life under States of Emergency* (London: Amnesty International, July 1988), p.2.

20 See *Fifth Annual Report and List of States which have proclaimed, extended or*

terminated a state of emergency since 1 January 1985, presented by Mr. Leandro Despouy, Special Rapporteur appointed pursuant to Economic and Social Council 1985/37, UN doc. E/CN/.4/Sub.2/1992/23 (6 July 1992), p.3. My incomplete list of states of emergency (national and regional) that have been introduced (or prolonged) in the last 15 years, includes about 40 states: Afghanistan, Albania, Bangladesh, China, Columbia, Egypt, Guyana, Haiti, Iraq, Israel, Italy, Jordan, Madagascar, Mali, Myanma, Pakistan, Panama, Rwanda, Salvador, Senegal, South Africa, Sri Lanka, Sudan, Thailand, Turkey, USA, Venezuela, Zimbabwe. In some of them, like Algeria, Argentina, India (in a form of President's Rule in the States), Peru, Sri Lanka, republics of former Yugoslavia, and, of course, the Soviet Union and some of former Soviet republics (Armenia, Azerbaijan, Georgia, Moldova, Russia, Tajikistan) a state of emergency was imposed more than once.

21 See UN doc. CCRP/C/2/Rev.3 (12 May 1992), pp.43–87.

22 Nicole Questiaux proposed the following classification of emergency regimes: states of emergency not notified; *de facto* states of emergency (e.g. Uganda, 1971; Suriname, 1980; South Africa); permanent states of emergency (e.g. Cameroon, since 1969; Haiti, since 1971); complex states of emergency (e.g. Turkey; Brazil); institutionalisation of emergency regimes (e.g. Chile; Uruguay). (For details see Nicole Questiaux, *supra* 16* [Preface], paras.96–145, pp.26–32.)

23 Allan Rosas, 'Emergency Regimes: A Comparison', in *Broadening the Frontiers of Human Rights. Essays in Honour of Asbjorn Eide* (Oslo: Scandinavian University Press, 1993. Donna Gomien, ed.), p.165.

24 Yuri Tikhomirov, *Yuridicheskaya collizia* [Legal Collision] (Moscow: Manuscript, 1994), p.4.

25 This observation should not be overstated. A recent American study finds that the 'distribution of attitudes toward democracy within the Russian population is not so very different from many other countries in transition' (Timothy J. Colton, Michael McFaul, *Are Russians Undemocratic?* (Carnegie Endowment for International Peace, No.20, June 2001), p.21). Overall, the results of Colton-McFaul's study corroborate the conclusions of a group of Iowan scholars made several years ago (based on 600 completed interviews in 1990, 1,400 in 1991, 1,300 in 1992 and 1,750 in 1995) that Russian legal values are close or similar to those in other former Soviet republics or in the United States: 'The Russian mass public is not ... hostile to the rule of law ... We discover more support for legal procedure [in Russia] than might have been expected ... On the whole Russians show greater support for legality than do Lithuanians ... We find American and Russian publics to have a very similar proportion of those willing to jettison suspects' rights in the name of fighting crime' (William M. Reisinger, Arthur H. Miller, and Vicki L. Hesli, 'Russians and the Legal System: Mass Views and Behaviour in the 1990s', 13 *Journal of Communist Studies and Transition Politics* 3 (September 1997), pp.24, 25, 45).

26 More on 'civil society', its legal elements and peculiarities of its understanding in Russia see, e.g. Alexander Domrin, 'Ten Years Later: Society, "Civil Society", and the Russian State', 62 *The Russian Review* 2 (April 2003); Alexander Domrin, '"Grazhdanskoe obschestvo" v Rossii: zametki russkogo pravoveda' ['"Civil Society" in Russia: Notes of a Russian Legal Scholar'], *Novy zhurnal* (New York), No.233, December 2003; Alexander Domrin, '"Grazhdanskoe obschestvo" v Rossii: istoricheskaia neizbezhnost' ili novy vitok sotsial'nykh experimentov' ['"Civil Society" in Russia: An Historical Necessity or a New Round of Social Experiments'], *Predstavitel'naia vlast' – XXI vek: zakonodatel'stvo, kommentarii, problemy*, No.5, 2003; Alexander Domrin, 'Controls over Foreign Funding of NGOs: What Do They Have to Do

with Development of Civil Society in Russia', 2 *The Untimely Thoughts* No.101, 3 August 2004.

27 Richard Sakwa, *Putin: Russia's Choice* (London and New York: Routledge, 2004), p.37

28 Also see Alexander Domrin, 'The Sin of Party-Building in Russia', *Russia Watch: Analysis and Commentary* (John F. Kennedy School of Government, Harvard University). No.9, January 2003.

29 Richard Rose, 'Rethinking Civil Society: Postcommunism and the Problem of Trust', 5 *Journal of Democracy* 3 (July 1994), pp.25–26. Russia is not unique in this respect. Rose finds a 'similar level of distrust' in the Czech Republic, Slovakia, Hungary, and Poland (p.25).

30 See Nikolay Popov, 'Fantazii na temu demokratii' [Democratic Fantasies], *Novoe vremya*, No.34, 2001.

31 *Interfax*, 19 April 2000.

32 A later opinion poll, conducted by the All-Russian Centre for Public Opinion Studies (VTsIOM) in mid-January 2001, indicated similar results showing that 75 per cent of Russians believe that in historical terms the Yeltsin era did Russia more bad than good (with 15 per cent who don't think so). See *Strana.ru*, 1 February 2001.

33 *Polit.ru*, 21 April 2000; *Interfax*, 12 July 2001.

34 A recent survey of 400 journalists across Russia conducted by the Institute of Sociology of the Russian Academy of Sciences found that 30 per cent of them had inserted hidden advertising into stories 'regularly' or 'occasionally'. Overall, 67 per cent of journalists had done it 'more than once'. (See Galina Stolyarova, 'Poll Highlights Media's Weakness', *St. Petersburg Times*, 28 August 2001).

35 In this book, the term 'liberal' is, as a rule, used in its Russian confusing interpretation. In reality, many aspects of what is considered 'liberal' in Russia, including a flat 13 per cent income tax, are identical to fundamentalist right-wing Republican Party views in the U.S. or radical Conservative views in Great Britain).

36 *Obschaya gazeta*, No.31, 26 July 2001.

37 Yuri Levada, 'Sotsvopros' [A Social Question], *Novaya gazeta*, No.53, 30 July 2001.

38 *Interfax*, 28 June 2001; *Trud*, 6 January 2000.

39 Michael Hirsh and Frank Brown, 'Seeing Red: Spreading Democracy Is a Bush Theme. Back in Russia, Guess Who's Defending Democracy? The Communists', *Newsweek International*, 27 September 2004.

40 See charts in A.Yu. Reteyum, *Dvenadtsat' let iz zhizni strany* [Twelve Years in a Life of the Country] (Moscow: Khorion, 2004), pp.67–68.

41 For comparison, Belarus didn't implement this kind of 'reforms' and in ten years lost just 1 per cent of its industrial output; output of its light and food industries shrank by 17 and 19 per cent, respectively. See charts in: I.A. Gundarov, *Demografickeskaia katastrofa v Rossii: prichiny, mekhanizm, puti preodolenia* [Demographic Catastrophe in Russia: Reasons, Mechanism, Ways to Overcoming] (Moscow: URSS, 2001), pp.185–187.

42 The conclusion belongs to Murray Feshbach, a former branch chief of at the U.S. Bureau of the Census and a research professor of Georgetown University, now a Senior Scholar at the Wilson Center. (See *The Washington Post*, 12 July 1995).

43 Nicholas Eberstadt, 'Russia: Too Sick to Matter?', *Policy Review* (June-July 1999), p.6. *Quoted in:* Paul Klebnikov, *Krestny otets Kremlya Boris Berezovsky ili Istoria razgrablenia Rossii* [Kremlin's Godfather Boris Berezovsky, or History of Russia's Pillage] (Moscow: 'Detectiv-Press', 2002), p.106.

44 'Post Scriptum', *TV-Tsentr*, 25 September 2004.
45 See, e.g. 'Russian Demography. Death Wish: Russia Appears to Be Committing Suicide', *The Economist*, 2–8 October 2004. What *The Economist* calls 'suicide' was defined as 'genocide' by the Russian State Duma deputies formulating 'articles of impeachment' against Yeltsin in 1998.
46 *Sotsial'no-ekonomicheskie preobrazovania v Rossii: sovremennaia situatsia i novye podkhody* [Social and Economic Reforms in Russia: Current Situation and New Approaches] (Moscow: Institute of Economics of the Russian Academy of Sciences, 1994), p.10.
47 'Middle Class in Russia: Growing Pains', *RIA Novosti*, 24 September 2004.
48 *Finansovye izvestia*, 12 January 1995; *Sovetskaia Rossia*, 1 February 1994 (quoting *Wall Street Journal Central European Report* (Winter 1994), 31 January 1994; *Izvestia*, 19 January 1995.
49 Oleg Platonov, *Gosudarstvennaia izmena* [Treason] (M.: Algoritm, 2004), pp.485–486. A reporter of the *Guardian* in Russia (1991–1998) came to a conclusion 'how little U.S. academia had learned from its clumsy interventions in Russian economic policy in the early 1990s, when a flood of America-knows-best advisers introduced unscrupulous Russians to the Pandora's box of shareholder capitalism without taking any real interest in the checks and balances – trade union, subsidies, lobby groups, public transport, welfare – which enable the "free" market to work without complete brutality, even in the U.S.' (James Meek, 'Reasons to Be Miserable', 26 *London Review of Books* 13 (8 July 2004), p.5). Russia-watchers should agree with a scholar (from Johns Hopkins University's School of Advanced International Studies) that the failure of American 'reform strategy' 'has probably destroyed Russians' trust in the West for generations to come' and follow his advice: 'Those of us who care about the advance of democracy in the world should make it our foremost intellectual and practical task to find out why our reform strategy went wrong in so much of the former Soviet bloc' (Charles H. Fairbanks, Jr., 'The Feudalisation of the State', 10 *Journal of Democracy* 2 (April 1999), p.39).
50 UNDP Press Release 'Men Hardest Hit by Hurried Transition to Free Markets in Ex-Soviet Countries', in *Transition 1999. Human Development Report for Central and Eastern Europe and the CIS*, available at www.undp.org/rbec/pubs/hdr99/pr.htm.
51 The Beslan atrocity was rightly defined as 'Russia's 9–11': 'although Russia, unlike the U.S., has long been the target of Chechen-led terrorism, the methodical slaughter of Beslan schoolchildren has plumbed a new depth of moral depravity, not only in Russia's but the global terror experience' (see Vlad Sobell, *Russia After Beslan: Putin's Strengthening of Regional Oversight Is a Return to Russia's Political Tradition, Hopefully as a Prelude to Authentic Russian Democracy* (Daiwa Institute of Research Ltd.: 20 September 2004)). Reprinted in *Johnson's Russia List*, No.8377, 21 September 2004.
52 Mikhail Leontiev, 'V usloviyakh voennogo polozhenia. Politicheskie lidery dolzhny poyti na zhestkie mery dlya vosstanovlenia poryadka v Rossii' [Under Martial Law: Political Leaders Must Take Tough Measures to Restore Order in Russia], *Nezavisimaya gazeta*, 9 September 2004; Michael McFaul, 'State of Siege', *Washington Post*, 12 September 2004.
53 V.M. Gessen, *supra* note 17* [Preface], p.vii.

1 Legal origins and evolution of the 'emergency powers' concept

1 Carl J. Friedrich, *Constitutional Reason of State: The Survival of the Constitutional Order* (Providence, RI: Brown University Press, 1957), p.108.
2 Marcus Tullius Cicero, *O gosudarstve. O zakonakh* [On State. On Laws]

(Moscow: Nauka, 1966. I.N. Veselovsky, V.O. Gorenshtein and S.L. Utchenko, eds), p.135.

3 Cited in 1 *Istoria politicheskikh ucheniy: Uchebnik* [History of Political Theories] (Moscow: Visshaya shkola, 1971. K. Amokichev, ed. In 2 parts. 2nd edn), p.65.

4 See *Istoria politicheskikh i pravovykh ucheniy: Uchebnik* [*History of Political and Legal Theories*] (Moscow: Yuridicheskaya literatura, 1983. V.S. Nersesyants, ed.), p.76.

5 Carl J. Friedrich, *supra* note 1*, at 110.

6 Max Lerner, 'Introduction' to *The Prince and the Discourses* (New York: Modern Library, 1950. Christian E. Detmold trans.), p.xxv.

7 Boesche's remarkable study of the phenomenon of 'tyranny' in world history and in the works of European philosophers is especially impressive when he analyses Machiavelli's writings. (See Roger Boesche, *Theories of Tyranny from Plato to Arendt* (University Park, PA: The Pennsylvania State University Press, 1996), pp.111–165).

8 It's often overlooked that Machievelli started Chapter II 'Of Hereditary Monarchies' of *The Prince* with the words, 'I will not here speak of republics, having already treated of them fully in another place. *I will deal only with monarchies*, and will discuss how the various kinds described above can be governed and maintained' (Niccolo Machiavelli, 'The Prince', in *The Prince and the Discourses*, p.5) (*italics added – A.D.*).

9 *Compare*: 'And truly, of all the institutions of Rome, this one deserves to be counted amongst those to which she was most indebted for her greatness and dominion. For without some such an institution Rome would with difficulty have escaped the many extraordinary dangers that befell her ... And therefore all republics should have some institution similar to the dictatorship' (Niccolo Machiavelli, 'Discourses on the First Ten Books of Titus Livius', in *The Prince and the Discourses*, p.203).

10 Niccolo Machiavelli, *supra* note 6*, at 201. It's remarkable that this maxim of Machiavelli was used by Clinton L. Rossiter as an epigraph to his book on Constitutional Dictatorship. It's also noteworthy that in Arthur Selwyn Miller's conclusion, '"constitutional Machiavellism" has always been followed in the United States' (Arthur Selwyn Miller, *Democratic Dictatorship: The Emergent Constitution of Control* (Westport, CT, London: Greenwood Press, 1981. Contributions in American Studies, No. 54), p.xv).

11 See Thomas Hobbes, *Leviathan* (Cambridge – New York – Port Chester – Melbourne – Sydney: Cambridge University Press, 1991. Richard Tuck ed.), p.89.

12 John Locke, 'An Essay Concerning the True Original, Extent and End of Civil Government', in *Social Contract. Essays by Locke, Hume, and Rousseau* (Westport, CT: Greenwood Press, Publishers, 1980. Introduction by Sir Ernest Barker), pp.79–80, 95, 93.

13 Charles Louis Montesquieu, *The Spirit of Laws* (Berkeley – Los Angeles – London: University of California Press, 1977. A Compendium of the First English Edition. Edited, with an Introduction, Notes, and Appendixes, by David Wallace Carrithers), pp.223–224.

14 See Jean-Jacques Rousseau, 'The Social Contract', in *Social Contract. Essays by Locke, Hume, and Rousseau*, *supra* note 12*, at 290–291.

15 John Stuart Mill, *Considerations on Representative Government* (London: Longman, Gree, Longman, Roberts & Green, 1865. 3rd edn), pp.227, 261, 260.

16 2 William Blackstone, *Commentaries on the Laws of England* (1803. William Young Birch and Abraham Small, eds), pp.238–239, 257.

17 Cited in P.N. Ardashev, *Absolutnaia monarkhia na Zapade* [Absolutist Monarchy in the West] (St. Petersburg: Brokgauz-Efron, 1902), pp.8, 172–173.

18 2 Boris Chicherin, *Istoria politicheskikh ucheniy. Chast' 2. Novoe vremya.* [History of Political Theories. Part 2. New Times] (Moscow: Grachev and Co. Printing Office, 1872), p.113.

19 D.M. Petrushevsky, *Ocherki po istorii srednevekovogo obschestva i gosu- darstva* [Essays on the History of Medieval Society and State] (Moscow: Nauchnoe slovo, 1917. Rev. 4th edn), p.354.

20 Ivan Ilyin, *O monarkhii i respublike* [On Monarchy and Republic] (New York: Sodruzhestvo, 1979), pp.90–91. There is a certain correspondence of the given citation with the political philosophy of Thomas Hobbes.

21 See: Jacques-Yvan Morin, 'The Rule of Law and the *Rechtsstaat* Concept: a Comparison', in *Federalism-in-the-Making, supra* note 14* [Preface], at 62.

22 William Anson, *Angliyski parlament, ego konstitutsionnye zakony i obychai* [English Parliament, its Constitutional Laws and Traditions] (St. Petersburg: N.K. Martynov, 1908), p.306.

23 A.V. Dicey, *Introduction to the Study of the Law of the Constitution* (London: Macmillan and Co., Ltd., 1927. 8th edn), pp.179–201. Dicey's commentaries have always been well known in Russia. See, e.g. A.V. Dicey, *Osnovy gosu- darstvennogo prava Anglii* [Introduction to the Study of the Law of the Con- stitution] (St. Petersburg: L.F. Panteleev, 1891).

24 Cited in Joseph Robson Tanner, *Constitutional Documents of the Reign of James I, A.D. 1603–1625: with a Historical Commentary* (Cambridge: Cam- bridge University Press, 1960), pp.153–154.

25 E.C.S. Wade and A.W. Bradley, *Constitutional and Administrative Law* (London and New York: Longman, 1985. 10th edn by A.W. Bradley, 1st edn 1931), p.60.

26 See William Anson, *Angliyskaya korona, eyo konstitutsionnie zakoni i obychai* [English Crown, its Constitutional Laws and Traditions] (St. Petersburg: N.K. Martynov, 1914), p.307.

27 John Hampden was a colourful figure. Knight and rich landlord from Buck- inghampshire, jurist with Oxford and London education, and cousin of Sir Oliver Cromwell, he was one of the leaders of the parliamentary opposition (to King Charles I Stuart (1625–1649)) in the third Parliament of 1628–1629 which was famous for adoption of the *Petition of Rights* (and dissolved like its two predecessors).

28 4 William S. Holdsworth, *A History of English Law* (London: Methuen and Co. Ltd., 1924. 3rd edn In 7 vols.), p.104.

29 See David Lindsay Keir, *The Constitutional History of Modern Britain Since 1485* (London: Adam & Charles Black, 1969. 8th edn 1st edn, 1938), p.213.

30 12 G. Veber, *Vseobschaia istoria. Epokha neogranichennoy monarkhicheskoy vlasti v semnadtsatom i vosemnadtsatom stoletiyakh* [World History. The Era of Unlimited Monarchic Power of the Seventeenth and Eighteenth Centuries] (Moscow: V.V. Isleniev Printing Office, 1890), p.104.

31 *The Stuart Constitution 1603–1688. Documents and Commentary* (Cambridge: at the University Press, 1966. Edited and Introduced by J.P. Kenyon), p.88.

32 See 8 (2) *Halsbury's Law of England, Constitutional Law and Human Rights* (London: Butterworth & Co (Publishers) Ltd, 1996. 4th edn, reissue), para.820, note 2, p.478.

33 William Anson, *supra* note 26*, at 306.

34 *The Stuart Constitution 1603–1688, supra* note 31*, at 110.

35 See 17 (1) *The Digest. Annotated British, Commonwealth and European Cases. Custom and Usage. Deeds and other Instruments. Defence, Emergency and Controls Law* (London: Butterworth & Co (Publishers) Ltd, 1994. 2nd reissue), case 4560, p.449. See a brief, annotated version of the decision in: 11(1) *The Digest. Annotated British, Commonwealth and European Cases.*

Conflict of Laws. Constitutional Law (London: Butterworth & Co (Publishers) Ltd, 1994. 2nd reissue), pp.567–568. In Russian complete text of the judicial decision on *R v Hampden* is published in *Zakonodatel'stvo angliyskoy revolutsii 1640–1660 gg.* [Legislation of English Revolution 1640–1660] (Moscow-Leningrad: USSR Academy of Sciences, 1946. N.P. Dmitrevsky, ed.), p.7.

36 *The Stuart Constitution 1603–1688, supra* note 31*, at 113.

37 D. L. Keir, *supra* note 29*, at 171, 197.

38 See R.Yu. Vipper, *Uchebnik novoy istorii* [Textbook of New History] (Moscow: Gosudarstvennoe izdanie, n.y), p.63.

39 2 William S. Holdsworth, *A History of English Law* (London: Methuen and Co. Ltd., 1966. 4th edn), p.289.

40 That would be appropriate at this point to quote an opinion of a prominent British scholar, author of a fundamental 16-volume history of English law, Sir William S. Holdsworth, arguing against exaggeration of the 'importance in England of the conception of a fundamental law which even Parliament cannot change ... It is as well to remember that Magna Carta itself, though in form declaratory, was after all enacted law. When the king and Parliament talked of fundamental laws in the seventeenth century ... they were thinking of the rights which in their opinion the existing law gave to them. These rights they deemed to be fundamental in the sense that they were the basis of the constitution as they conceived it, not in the sense that King, Lords, and Commons could not change them. *It is only very exceptionally (e.g. in R v Hampden* (1637) 3 S.T. at 1235 and in *Godden v Hales* (1685) II S.T. 1165) *that we meet the idea of a law which Parliament cannot change, and then only in the arguments of the extreme prerogative lawyers. Even they avoid using it if they have any more solid reasons to advance*' (*Id.*, p.442) (*italics added – A.D.*).

41 Karl Marx, *The Eighteenth Brumaire of Louis Bonaparte* (New York: International Publishers, 1926. Eden & Cedar Paul trans.), pp.42–43. Also see Karl Marx, 'Vosemnadtsatoe brumera Lui Bonaparta' [The Eighteenth Brumaire of Louis Bonaparte], in 8 Karl Marx and Friedrich Engels, *Works* (Moscow: GIPL, 1957), p.135.

42 A.V. Dicey, *supra* note 23*, at 283–284. In the words of Justice Bradley, England's unwritten constitution rests in the understanding that its violation in any material respect 'would produce a revolution in an hour' (*Slaughter-House Cases*, 83 U.S. (16 Wall.) 36, 115 (1873) (Bradley, J., dissenting)). A contemporary scholar argues that 'Dicey, of course, was himself aware of the potential for contradiction' in the above-mentioned quotation. (See Nasser Hussain, *The Jurisprudence of Emergency: Colonialism and the Rule of Law* (Ann Arbor: The University of Michigan Press, 2003), p.21).

43 Louis Fisher, *Presidential War Power* (Lawrence, Kansas: University Press of Kansas, 1995), p.2.

44 The only exception to that principle was provided by Article VI: 'No State shall engage in any war without the consent of the United States, in Congress assembled, unless such state be actually invaded by enemies', or when there is an 'imminent' 'danger' of invasions 'by some nation of Indians'. (See 'The Articles of Confederation', in 1 George Ticknor Curtis, *Constitutional History of the United States from Their Declaration of Independence to the Close of their Civil Wars* (New York and London: Harper & Brothers Publishers, 1903. In 2 vols.), pp.716, 714–715.)

45 Louis Fisher, *supra* note 43*, at 2–3. Also see Gerhard Casper, *On Emergency Powers of the President: Every Inch a King?* (Chicago: University of Chicago Law School, 1973). Casper argued in this paper that there was consensus against granting the executive any emergency powers other than to repel sudden attacks.

46 *The Constitution of the United States of America. Analysis and Interpretation. Annotations of cases decided by the Supreme Court of the United States to June 29, 1992* (Washington: U.S. Government Printing Office, 1996. Prepared by the Congressional Research Service, Library of Congress. Johnny H. Killian, George A. Costello, eds), pp.8–9. *Also* see William B. Fisch, 'Emergency in the Constitutional Law of the United States', 38 *The American Journal of Comparative Law* (1990).

47 *The Federalist or, the New Constitution. Second Edition by Alexander Hamilton, James Madison and John Day* (Oxford: Basil Blackwell, 1987. Edited with an Introduction and Notes by Max Beloff), pp.358, 261, 260.

48 6 *The Writings of James Madison*, p.148. Cited in Louis Fisher, *supra* note 43*, at 9.

49 David Gray Adler, 'Foreign Policy and the Separation of Powers: The Influence of the Judiciary', in *Judging the Constitution: Critical Essays on Judicial Lawmaking* (1989. Michael W. McCann and Gerald I. Houseman, eds), p.158.

50 *The Federalist*, *supra* note 47*, at 245–246.

51 2 *The Records of the Federal Convention of 1787* (New Haven, CT.: Yale University Press, 1937. Max Farrand, ed. Revised edn In 4 vols.) *Also* see 'Framers' Debate on the War Power (August 17, 1787)', in Louis Fisher, *supra* note 43*, appendix A, pp.207–208.

52 *Talbot v* See*man*, 5 U.S. 1, 28 (1801). Cited in Louis Fisher, 'Historical Survey of the War Powers and the Use of Force', in *The U.S. Constitution and the Power to Go to War: Historical and Current Perspectives* (Westport, CT – London: Greenwood Press, 1994. Gary M. Stern and Morton H. Halperin, eds), p.15.

53 Louis Fisher, *supra* note 43*, at x.

54 Gerhard Casper, *supra* note 45*, at 10.

55 3 *The Oxford English Dictionary* (Oxford: at the Clarendon Press, 1961. In 13 vols.), p.119. '1821 Byron *Mar.Fal.* v.i.183: On great emergencies // The law must be remodell'd or amended' (*id.*) *The New Bantam English Dictionary* (New York – Toronto – London: Bantam Books, 1979. Edwin B. Williams, ed.), p.295. This is how the dictionary explains the meanings of these synonyms: 'An *emergency* names such a condition as demands immediate action; it is sudden, unforeseen and urgent. An *exigency*, too, is urgent, but it names a need rising out of a certain situation, rather than, like *emergency*, the situation itself. The *exigencies* of a journey require certain expenditures, adjustments, etc.; the loss, after one had started, of all the money one had provided for the journey in a strange land, would constitute an *emergency*' (*id.*).

56 *The Law Dictionary. Pronouncing Edition. A Dictionary of Legal Words and Phrases with Latin and French Maxims of the Law, Translated and Explained* (Cincinnati: Anderson Publishing Co., 1986. 6th edn, revised by Wesley Gilmer. 1st edn, 1888); J. Kendrick Kinney, *A Law Dictionary and Glossary* (Chicago: Callaghan & Co., 1893). The author found a similar silence of American law dictionaries regarding a definition of 'civil society': the term 'is practically unknown in American law' (Alexander Domrin, 'Ten Years Later: Society, 'Civil Society', and the Russian State', *supra* note 26* [Introduction], at 199).

57 Bouvier's *Law Dictionary* gives the term as a synonym of an 'accident' (from latin *Accidere*, – *ad*, to and *cadere*, to fall): 'An event which, under the circumstances, is unusual and unexpected. An event the real cause of which cannot be traced, or is at least not apparent' (1 John Bouvier, *Law Dictionary and Concise Encyclopaedia* (Kansas City, MO: Vernon Law Book Co., St. Paul, Minn.: West Publishing Co., 1914. In 3 vols. 8th edn, 3rd revision by Francis Rawle), pp.1008, 101). *The Cyclopedic Law Dictionary* gives it as 'any event or

occasional combination of circumstances which calls for immediate action or remedy; pressing necessity, exigency (21 Ill. App.274)' (Walter A. Shumaker and George Foster Longsdorf, *The Cyclopedic Law Dictionary* (Chicago: Callaghan & Co., 1940. 3rd edn by Frank D. Moore. 1st edn, 1922.), p.380).
Black's *Law Dictionary* and Ballentine's *Law Dictionary with Pronunciations* are the most complete: the former contains four main definitions for the term 'emergency' (generally repeating the same explanations as in other dictionaries) and its combinations: 'emergency doctrine', 'sudden emergency doctrine', and – separately – 'national emergency', and the latter – five of them: *'emergency'* ('confrontation by sudden peril', 'an unforeseen occurrence or condition calling for immediate action to avert imminent danger to life, health, or property') and *'sudden emergency'* ('an occurrence fraught with danger which is unexpected and occurs so abruptly as to be unnoticed before the peril is presented. *Booth v Price*, 183 Ark 975, 39 SW2d 717, 76 ALR 957'), 'emergency measures', 'sudden emergency doctrine', and 'financial emergency'. According to *'Emergency Doctrine'* (also known as the 'emergency', 'imminent peril', or 'sudden peril' doctrine), as the Black's *Law Dictionary* explains, 'when one is confronted with a sudden peril requiring instinctive action, he is not, in determining his course of action, held to the exercise of the same degree of care as when he has time for reflection'. (See Henry Campbell Black, *Definitions of the Terms and Phrases of American and English Jurisprudence, Ancient and Modern* (St. Paul, Minn.: West Publishing Co., 1979. 5th edn), p.469; James A. Ballentine, *Ballentine's Law Dictionary with Pronunciations* (Rochester, NY: Lawyers Cooperative Publishing, 1969. 3rd edn; William S. Anderson, ed. 1st edn, 1930), p.398).
58 H.C. Black, *supra* note 57*, at 923.
59 J.A. Ballentine, *supra* note 57*, at 398.
60 B.O. Nwabuese, *supra* note 5* [Introduction], at 180.
61 'Chrezvychainoe polozhenie. Yuristy obsuzhdayut: kakim dolzhen byt' zakon dlya extremal'noy situatsii' [A State of Emergency. Lawyers Discuss What Should Be the Law for an Extreme Situation], *Moscow News*, 25 July 1989, at 10. The roundtable at the *Moscow News* was quite memorable. Knowing about my research in foreign national security law and government powers in emergencies, Ernest Ametistov, a colleague at the Institute of State Development and Legislation (under the USSR Supreme Soviet) and future judge of the Russian Constitutional Court, invited me to participate in the roundtable. However, instead of me, the director of the institute decided to send heads of two departments of the institute who hadn't had any previous experience or publications in that area and who privately contacted me before the roundtable with a request to share my materials with them. Judging by a transcript of the roundtable, other participants were equally innocent in emergency powers studies. Otherwise, it's hard to explain a wrong statement of Mikhailovskaya or a suggestion of another participant (Lev Simkin) to use a state of emergency to fight a tiny nationalist organisation *Pamyat'*.
62 Norman Redlich, Bernard Schwartz, John Attanasio, *Constitutional Law* (New York: Matthew Bender, 1989), p.277.
63 H.C. Black, *supra* note 57*, at 923.
64 'What matters is whether or not the circumstances involved in a declared emergency situation justify any restrictions of human rights and freedoms and, if so, which restrictions' (Fried van Hoof, 'The Protection of Human Rights and the Impact of Emergency Situations under International Law with Special Reference to the Present Situation in Chile', in *International Protection of Human Rights* (Iowa City, IA: University of Iowa College of Law, 1991), p.24).

65 Mark M. Stavsky, 'The Doctrine of State Necessity in Pakistan', 16 *Cornell International Law Journal*, No.2, Summer 1983, p.343.
66 The full citation is quite remarkable: 'These United States have used war and the threat of war to stifle freedom while at the same time proclaiming freedom to be our national purpose. Often, the cry of freedom has been a cover for the use of force. The fiction that U.S. foreign policy has been based on the protection and expansion of freedom depends on our believing what has been said and ignoring what has been done ... The United States has always been disposed to war'. (Ramsey Clark, 'Notes on War and Freedom', in Michael Linfield, *supra* note 11* [Preface], at xv–xvi).
67 Allan Rosas, *supra* note 23* [Introduction], at 165.
68 See 9 V.I. Lenin, *Predislovie k broshure 'Dokladnaya zapiska direktora Departamenta politsii Lopukhina'* [Preface to a brochure 'Report of the Director of Police Department Lopukhin'] (Moscow: Politizdat, 1979), p.331.
69 Constitutional Supervision Committee (CSC), an embryonic form of the Constitutional Court, was created in December 1989. Foreign observers were right when concluding that the creation of the Committee marked 'a significant shift towards a law-governed society' (Julie Kim, *USSR: Major Legislation* (CRS Report for Congress, 8 September 1990), p.21) and 'forged the way for the establishment of the rule of law in the USSR' (Elizabeth Teague, 'Constitutional Watchdog Suspends Presidential Decree', 42 *Report on the USSR* (1990), pp.9–11). The Committee had not taken (and was not designed to take) upon itself the full functions of a Constitutional Court. (On a republican level, that happened only with a creation of the Russian Constitutional Court in 1991). But one should not forget that it took the US Supreme Court 17 years after its formation to assert the power of judicial review in the famous decision of *Marbury v Madison* in 1803.
70 'Do you remember what a noise was made this spring [of 1991 – *A.D.*] over the joint [police] and army patrol?', – Colonel Victor Alksnis, a leader of an influential in 1990–91 *Soyuz* (Union) political movement, asked an American interviewer. And continued: 'Now [in June 1991] that Sobchak has been elected mayor, his first order was to introduce joint patrols in Leningrad'. (See interviews with Alksnis and some other visible Russian politicians of that period in: Michael McFaul, Sergei Markov, *The Troubled Birth of Russian Democracy: Parties, Personalities, and Programs* (Stanford, CA: Hoover Institution Press, Stanford University, 1993), p.235.)
71 The term *fashizatsiya* (or 'fascisation' – from 'fascism') was especially often exploited in Soviet legal and political publications (and publications of the Communist International) between the mid-1920s and late 1930s (see, e.g. V. L-n, 'Vnutropoliticheskaia programma germanskoy burzhuazii i fashizatsiya gosudarstvennogo upravlenia' [Domestic Political Program of the German Bourgeoisie and Fascisation of State Administration], *Sovetskoe gosudarstvo i pravo*, 10 (1930), at 89–103; Hans Bekker, 'Konets polosy sotsial'nykh reform. (K fashizatsii Germanii)' [The End of the Period of Social Reforms. On Fascisation of Germany.], *Sovetskoe gosudarstvo*, 1–2 (1933), at 112–123; O. Grossman, 'Fashizatsiya Avstrii i problema "anshlusa"' [Fascisation of Austria and the Problem of 'Anschlusse'], *Kommunisticheskiy internatsional*, 15 (1933), at 22–30). Quite justified in many cases in the 1930s, a new wave of criticism of the 'fascisation' process in bourgeois countries (first of all, in the United States) was raised with the beginning of the Cold War (see, e.g. B.A. Shabad, 'Fashizatsiya gosudarstva SShA' [Fascisation of the State Mechanism of the USA], *Sovetskoe gosudarstvo i pravo*, 4 (1951), at 38–45; I.D. Levin, 'Fashizatsiya gosudarstvennogo stroya SShA' [Fascisation of the State System of the USA], *Sovetskoe gosudarstvo i pravo*, 4 (1951), at 69–79; R.D. Rakhunov,

'Fashizatsiya amerikanskogo ugolovnogo protsessa' [Fascisation of the Penal Process in the USA], *Sovetskoe gosudarstvo i pravo*, 9 (1951), at 65–69). The 'theoretical' basis for such criticism was laid down by a remarkable statement of Iosif V. Stalin, according to which capitalist countries cannot wage a war without putting chains on 'their' workers and 'their' colonies; 'from this necessity comes gradual fascisation of policy of bourgeois governments' (see 10 I.V. Stalin, *Sochinenia* [Works], p.282).

72 See *Burzhuaznye konstitutsii v period obschego krizisa capitalizma* [Bourgeois Constitutions in the Period of General Crisis of Capitalism] (Moscow: Nauka, 1966. I.D. Levin, B.S. Krylov, eds), p.61; Yu.I. Avdeev, V.N. Strunnikov, *Burzhuaznoe gosudarstvo v period 1918–1939 gg.* [The Bourgeois State in 1918–1939] (Moscow: IMO, 1962), p.62; A.A. Zhdanov, '"Chrezvychainoe polozhenie" po administrativnomu pravu imperialisticheskikh gosudarstv' ['A State of Emergency' in Administrative Law of Imperialist States], *Pravovedenie*, 1 (1965), at 42; Yu.I. Avdeev, 'Krizis burzhuazno-demokraticheskikh institutov (Chrezvychainoe polozhenie – instrument razrushenia burzhuaznoy demokratii)' [Crisis of Bourgeois Democratic Institutions (A State of Emergency Is an Instrument of Destruction of Bourgeois Democracy], *Sovetskoe gosudarstvo i pravo*, 9 (1969), at 128; *Gosudarstvennoe pravo burzhuaznykh stran i stran, osvobodivshikhsya ot kolonial'noy zavisimosti* [State Law of Bourgeois States and Countries Liberated of the Colonial Dependency] (Moscow: MSU, 1969), p.278.

73 V.N. Danilenko, *Deklaratsiya prav i real'nost'. K 200-letiyu Deklaratsii prav cheloveka i grazhdanina* [Declaration of Rights and Reality: 200th Anniversary of Adoption of the Declaration of the Rights of Man and the Citizen] (Moscow: Mezhdunarodnye otnoshenia, 1989), pp.109, 44, 55; *Chrezvychainoe zakonodatel'stvo FRG* [Emergency Legislation of FRG], *supra* note 19* [Preface], at 35, 21–22. In a typical twist of the *perestroika* period, Leonid B. Volkov, an author of the above-mentioned study, conveniently changed his views overnight and in 1990 was elected to the Russian parliament as a 'radical democrat' and staunch supporter of Boris Yeltsin. Similarly, back in 1971, a Sverdlovsk legal scholar insisted that law 'by its nature cannot be above the state' and that rule of law is a 'deceitful, false, scientifically untenable (*lzhivaya, fal'shivaya, nauchno nesosyatel'naya*) bourgeois theory' (see Sergei S. Alekseev, *Sotsial'naya tsennost' prava v sovetskom obschestve* [Social Value of Law in the Soviet Society] (Moscow: 1971), p.193). Nineteen years later he was elected chairman of the first Soviet constitutional watchdog – USSR Constitutional Supervision Committee – intended to maintain and protect that very 'deceitful, false, scientifically untenable bourgeois theory'. In 1993, Alekseev became Chairman of the 'Constitutional Assembly' (aimed at drafting Yeltsin's semi-authoritarian, superpresidential, 'imperial' constitution) and was characterised by a sympathetic western observer as a 'liberal lawyer' (see Leon Aron, *Yeltsin: A Revolutionary Life* (New York: St. Martin's Press, 2000), p.511.) Yuri Afanasiev, another 'radical democrat' and a co-chairman of the Inter-Regional Group of Deputies (1989–1990) was a former professional CPSU ideologue and head of the All-Union Young Pioneer organisation, 'which indoctrinated children from ten to fourteen before they joined the Komsomol', and later Rector of the Moscow Historical Archive Institute, a 'breeding ground for Party propagandists' (*ibid.*, p.313). (In the index of the book by Leon Aron, Yuri Afanasiev was confused with Victor Afanasiev, editor-in-chief of *Pravda*).

74 Cited in Robert S. Rankin, *When Civil Law Fails. Martial Law and Its Legal Basis in the United States* (Durham, NC: Duke University Press, 1939), p.v.

75 Allan Rosas, *supra* note 23* [Introduction], at 166.

76 Jaime Oraa, *Human Rights in States of Emergency in International Law*

(Oxford: Clarendon Press, 1992. Oxford Monographs in International Law. General Editor: Prof. Ian Brownlie.), p.1.
77 See *Habeas Corpus in Emergency Situations (Arts. 27(2), 25(1) and 7(6) American Convention on Human Rights)*, Advisory Opinion OC-8/87 of January 30, 1987, Series A, No.8.
78 See M. Ameller, *Parliamenty* [Parliaments] (Moscow: Progress, 1967), p.232; J. Vedel, *Administrativnoe pravo Frantsii* [Administrative Law in France] (Moscow: Progress, 1973), p.41.
79 Brian Loveman, *supra* note 6* [Introduction], at 7.
80 *A Brief History of Emergency Powers in the United States*, *supra* note 16* [Introduction], at v.
81 *Ibid.*
82 The National Emergencies Act, Pub. L. No.94-412, 90 Stat. 1255 (1976) (codified as amended at 50 U.S.C. para.1601–1651 (1976 & Supp.IV 1980). *Also* see *The National Emergencies Act (Public Law 94-412). Source Book: Legislative History, Texts, and Other Documents* (Washington: U.S. Government Printing Office, 1976. Prepared by Harold C. Relyea, *et al.* for the Committee on Government Operations and the Special Committee on National Emergencies and Delegated Emergency Powers, U.S. Senate).
83 The use of a concurrent resolution to control executive action was invalidated by the U.S. Supreme Court's decision in *INS v Chadha* in 1983. Two years later the Congress passed new legislation repealing the concurrent resolution procedure for national emergencies and replacing it with action by joint resolution, which satisfies *Chadha*'s requirements (99 Stat. 448, sec.801 (1985); 131 Cong. Rec. 14947–48 (1985). According to Louis Fisher, no concurrent resolution was ever introduced after President Carter declared a national emergency over the Iranian crisis in 1979. The Senate Foreign Relations Committee and the House Foreign Affairs Committee simply wrote letters to Carter stating that action on a resolution of disapproval was unnecessary (126 Cong. Rec. 11270–71, 11537 (1980)). As a result, 'the requirement for congressional consideration every six months was rendered a nullity through disuse ... The automatic ... review has remained a dead letter' (Louis Fisher, *supra* note 7* [Introduction], at 273).
84 The International Emergency Economic Powers Act, Pub. L. No.95-223, tit. II, 91 Stat. 1625, 1626–29 (codified at 50 U.S.C. §1701–1706 (Supp.IV 1980)).
85 For details see, e.g. 'The International Emergency Economic Powers Act: a Congressional Attempt to Control Presidential Emergency Power' 96 *Harvard Law Review* (1983), pp.1102–1120.
86 'The National Emergencies Act exempted certain provisions of law, including Section 5(b) of the Trading with the Enemy Act, originally enacted in 1917. Over the years this provision had been the basis for controlling domestic as well as international financial transactions. Its reach went far beyond trading with the enemy, providing a source of presidential authority in peacetime as well as wartime. For example, it was under Section 5(b) that President Roosevelt declared a national emergency in 1933 and announced a bank holiday to prevent hoarding of gold. Presidents Johnson and Nixon invoked this clause to justify other controversial actions' (Louis Fisher, *supra* note 7* [Introduction], at 273).
87 Niccolo Machiavelli, *supra* note 6*, at 203.
88 See *Politologia* [Political Science] (Moscow: Moscow University of Commerce, 1993. Yu.I. Averyanov, ed.), p.101.
89 Jorge I. Dominguez, *A Constitution for Cuba's Political Transition: The Utility of Retaining (and Amending) the 1992 Constitution* (Miami: Institute for Cuban and Cuban-American Studies, University of Miami, 2002), p.8.

90 In 1861, President Abraham Lincoln asked his famous rhetoric question whether a republic must 'of necessity, be too *strong* for the liberties of its own people, or too *weak* to maintain its own existence?' and seized the power he needed to quell the insurrection under the theory that it was justifiable and that if subject to prosecution he would be pardoned (6 *Messages and Papers of the Presidents* (1898. J. Richardson, ed.), p.20).

91 Jack C. Plano and Milton Greenberg, *The American Political Dictionary* (Fort Worth, Philadelphia *et al.*: Harcourt Brace College Publishers, 1993. 9th edn), pp.41–42. Also see 'National Emergencies and the President's Inherent Powers', 2 *Stanford Law Review* (February 1950), pp.303–320.

92 *McCulloch v Maryland*, 4 Wheaton 316 (1819) is considered one of 'landmark decisions' of the U.S. Supreme Court. Two important principles of American government were firmly established by this decision: the doctrine of 'implied powers', which has given the national government a vast source of power, and the principle of 'national supremacy', which denies to the states any right to interfere in the constitutional operations of the national government.

93 For details see James Garfield Randall, *Constitutional Problems under Lincoln* (Urbana: University of Illinois, 1964. Rev. edn 1st edn, 1951).

94 *Dames & Moore v Regan*, 453 U.S. (1981) at 678. The excerpt contains a quotation from another well-known U.S. Supreme Court decision in the area of foreign powers and national security: *Haig v Agee* 453 U.S. (1981) at 280, 291. In that case, the U.S. Supreme Court upheld the revocation of the passport of a former CIA employee Philip Agee (who published a book about dirty operations of the CIA overseas and revealed identities of CIA officers and agents in various countries of the world) by the Secretary of State Alexander Haig, acting under the authority of a regulation 'permitting such revocation when the Secretary determines that a citizen's activities abroad are causing, or likely to cause, serious damage to national security or foreign policy'. In other words, in *Haig v Agee* the U.S. Supreme Court held that 'Congress may deny the right to travel abroad in circumstances where the First Amendment might dictate a different result at home'. (For details see, e.g. Derreck A. Bell, Jr. *Constitutional Conflicts. Part 1* (Cincinnati: Anderson Publishing Co., 1997), pp.65, 320; Phillip R. Trimble, *International Law: United States Foreign Relations Law* (New York: Foundation Press, 2002), p.92).

95 In his autobiography, Theodore Roosevelt described his 'stewardship theory' of Presidential power, emphasising that 'the executive is subject only to the people, and, under the Constitution, bound to serve the people affirmatively in cases where the Constitution does not explicitly forbid him to render services'. (See Daniel A. Farber, William N. Eskridge, Jr., Philip P. Frickey, *Constitutional Law: Themes for the Constitution's Third Century* (St. Paul, MN: West Publishing House, 1998. American Casebook Series. 2nd edn), p.926).

96 *Ibid.*, pp.925–926.

97 Jack C. Plano and Milton Greenberg, *supra* note 91*, at 41.

98 Daniel P. Franklin, *Extraordinary Measures: the Exercise of Prerogative Powers in the United States* (Pittsburgh, PA: University of Pittsburgh Press, 1991), p.3.

99 Cromwell continued: 'Feigned necessities, imaginary necessities ... are the greatest cozenage men can put upon the providence of God ...' (4 Carlyle, *Cromwell's Letters and Speeches* 74 (1870), *quoted in* Mark M. Stavsky, *supra* note 65*, at 343; Jules Lobel, *supra* note 13* [Preface], at 1386).

100 See E.C.S. Wade and G. Godfrey Phillips, *Konstituttsionnoe pravo* [Constitutional Law] (Moscow: Inostrannaya literatura, 1950), p.431.

101 E.C.S. Wade and A.W. Bradley, *supra* note 25*, at 251.

102 Emergency Powers Act 1964, Ch. 38. Also see 8 (2) *Halsbury's Law of England, Constitutional Law and Human Rights*, *supra* note 32*, at 478.
103 E.C.S. Wade and A.W. Bradley, *supra* note 25*, at 251.
104 Milligan, an Indiana citizen, was tried and sentenced to death for disloyal activities during the Civil War by a military commission established by President Lincoln. After the Civil War ended, the Supreme Court unanimously held that the President had acted unconstitutionally in creating military commissions to try civilians where the civil courts were still functioning. For an analysis of the *Milligan Case* see, e.g. Robert S. Rankin, *supra* note 74*, at 53–64; Charles Fairman, *The Law of Martial Rule* (Chicago: Callaghan and Company, 1943. 2nd edn), pp.157–163. Professor Lobel of the University of Pittsburgh School of Law defined the approach of the Supreme Court in the *Milligan Case* as an 'absolutist' one (see Jules Lobel, *supra* note 13* [Preface], at 1385–1386).
105 Further in his judgment on *Home Building and Loan Association v Blaisdell* Chief Justice Charles Evans Hughes declared: 'Although an emergency does not create power it may furnish occasion for the exercise of power'. In his opinion, 'the constitutional question presented in the light of an emergency is whether the power possessed embraces the particular exercise of it in response to particular conditions' (290 U.S. 398, at 426 (1934)).
106 For a thorough analysis of the case of *Youngstown Sheet and Tube Co. v Sawyer* see, e.g. Alan I. Bigel, *The Supreme Court on Emergency Powers, Foreign Affairs and Protection of Civil Liberties, 1935–1975* (Lanham, New York, London: University Press of America, 1986), pp.126–150.
107 Cited in Michael Foley, *The Silence of Constitutions: Gaps, 'Abeyances' and Political Temperament in the Maintenance of Government* (London, New York: Routledge, 1989), p.46.
108 See 'Prezidentskoe pravlenie i pravo' [President's Rule and Law], *Glasnost'*, No.6, 1991.
109 Cited in Louis Fisher, Neal Devins, *Political Dynamics of Constitutional Law* (St. Paul, MN: West Publishing Co., 2001. American Casebook Series. 3rd edn), p.177. In another interview of 1952, Truman added: 'Nobody [Congress, the courts – *A.D.*] can take [inherent powers] from the President, because he is the Chief Executive of the Nation, and he has to be in a position to see that that the welfare of the people is met' (*ibid.*, p.178).
110 See, e.g. *The U.S. Constitution and the Constitutions of Asia* (Lanham, New York, London: University Press of America, 1988. Kenneth W. Thompson ed. Miller Center Bicentennial Series on Constitutionalism, vol. IV); *Constitutionalism and Rights: The Influence of the United States Constitution Abroad* (New York: Columbia University Press, 1990. L. Henkin and A.J. Rosenthal, eds)
111 I also find it quite indicative that the author of a book on the 'moral foundations' of U.S. constitutional democracy never mentioned 'inherent powers' in his study, thus denying them a right to be among such 'moral foundations'. (See James H. Rutherford, *The Moral Foundations of Unites States Constitutional Democracy* (Pittsburgh: Dorrance Publishing Co., 1992).

2 Elements of the constitutional mechanism of a state of emergency

1 *Study of the Rights of Everyone to Be Free from Arbitrary Arrest, Detention and Exile* (United Nations Department of Economic and Social Affairs, U.N. Doc. E/CN4/826 Rev.1 (5 Jan 1962)), p.257, para. 754. See another list in O'Donnell, 'States of Exception', *Int. CJ Review*, 21 (1978), p.54. For an overview of the studies of the German and French scholars see Yu.A. Avdeev, *supra* note 72* [Ch. 1]; A.A. Zhdanov, *supra*, note 72* [Ch. 1]; S.L. Zivs, *Krizis burzhuaznoy*

zakonnosti v sovremennykh imperialisticheskikh gosudarstvakh [Crisis of Bourgeois Legality in Modern Imperialist States] (Moscow: USSR Academy of Sciences, 1958), p.91; *Chrezvychainoe zakonodatel'stvo FRG* [Emergency Legislation of FRG], *supra* note 19* [Preface], at 15–17.

2 Zubair Alam, *Emergency Powers and Indian Democracy (1971–1984)* (New Delhi: S.K. Publishers, 1987), p.3.

3 See V.N. Durdenevsky, U.F. Ludshuveit, *Konstitutsii Vostoka* [Constitutions of the Orient] (Leningrad: Gosudarstvennoe izdatel'stvo, 1926), p.49. *Poland in a World in Change: Constitutions, Presidents, and Politics* (Lanham, New York, London: University Press of America; The Miller Center, University of Virginia, 1992. Kenneth W. Thompson, ed.), p.224. 'The Constitution of the Turkish Federated State of Cyprus', in 5 *Constitutions* (April 1978), p.51. Also see 'Konstitutsionniy zakon 19 fevralya 1947 g. o strukture i kompetentsii vysshikh organov Pol'skoy Respubliki' [Constitutional Law of 19 February 1947 'On Structure and Competence of Supreme Bodies of the Polish Republic'], *Sovetskoe gosudarstvo i pravo*, 4 (1947), at 80–82; *Konstitutsia i osnovnye zakonodatel'nye akty Pol'skoy Narodnoy Respubliki* [Constitution and Main Legislative Acts of the Polish People's Republic] (Moscow: Inostrannaya literatura, 1953. D.S. Karev, ed.).

4 See Carl J. Friedrich, *Constitutional Government and Democracy. Theory and Practice in Europe and America* (Waltham – Toronto – London: Blaisdell Publishing Company, 1968. 4th edn), pp.557–581.

5 Ivan Solonevich, *Narodnaya Monarchia* [People's Monarchy] (San Francisco: Chapter of Russian People's Monarchy Movement in California, 1979), p.78; M. Ameller, *supra* note 78* [Ch. 1], at 232.

6 See, e.g. N.A. Sakharov, *Institut prezidentstva v sovremennom mire* [Institute of the President in the World Today] (Moscow: Yuridicheskaya literatura, 1994), pp.30–32.

7 See, e.g. *The Breakdown of Democratic Regimes* (Baltimore: Johns Hopkins University Press, 1978. Juan J. Linz and Alfred Stepan, eds); *Parliamentary Versus Presidential Government* (Oxford: Oxford University Press, 1992. Arendt Lijphart, ed.); *The Failure of Presidential Democracy*, *supra* note 13* [Introduction]; Alexander Domrin, 'Institut prezidentstva' [The Presidency], *Predstavitel'naya vlast' – XXI vek: zakonodatel'stvo, kommentarii, problemy* [Representative Power – Century 21: Legislation, Commentaries, Problems], 1 (2002).

8 See, e.g. Mathew Soberg Shugart and John M.Carey, *Presidents and Assemblies: Constitutional Design and Electoral Dynamics* (Cambridge: Cambridge University Press, 1992); *Presidentialism and Democracy in America* (Cambridge: Cambridge University Press, 1997. Scott Mainwaring and Mathew Soberg Shugart, eds), especially, Julio Faundez, 'In Defense of Presidentialism: The Case of Chile, 1932–1970', in *id.*, pp.300–320.

9 In the words of an American scholar, 'the extreme crisis of government which have recently afflicted' Russia, Poland and Brazil 'should serve as a warning to present and future constitutional architects' (Mark P. Jones, *Electoral Laws and the Survival of Presidential Democracies* (Notre Dame, IN – London: University of Notre Dame Press, 1995), p.163).

10 See 2 *Parliaments of the World: A Comparative Reference Compendium* (Inter-Parliamentary Union: Gower Publishing Company Ltd. (England), 1986. 2nd edn), pp.1273–1301.

11 'The French Constitution (Adopted by the Referendum of 28 September 1958 and Promulgated on 4 October 1958 (As Amended on 18 May 1960, 28 October 1962, 30 December 1963 and 29 October 1974)) in, 7 *Constitutions* (June 1988), p.27.

12 'The Constitution of the Gabonese Republic' in, 7 *Constitutions* (Release 93–4, June 1988), p.15, 20.

13 For details see, e.g. Martin Harrison, 'The French Experience of Exceptional Powers: 1961', 25 *The Journal of Politics* 1 (February 1963), pp.139–158; Martin Harrison, 'Government and Press in France During the Algerian War', 58 *The American Political Science Review* 2 (June 1964), pp.273–285.

14 Jonathan Hartlyn, *supra* note 13* [Introduction], at 305.

15 Constitutional Law *'On Structure and Competence of Supreme Bodies of the Polish Republic'* of 19 February 1947 *supra* note 3*.

16 'The Constitution of the Federal Republic of Yugoslavia' in, Supplement *Constitutions* (Release 94-2, March 1994), p.29. Original text of the Constitution see *Politika* (Belgrade), 28 April 1992.

17 'Constitution of the Republic of Slovenia', in 17 *Constitutions* (Release 92-6, October 1992), p.18.

18 'Constitution of the Argentine Nation', in 1 *Constitutions* (Release 95-3, May 1995), pp.32, 44, 50–51.

19 'The Spanish Constitution' in, 18 *Constitutions* (March 1991), pp.67–68.

20 *Minimum Standards of Human Rights Norms in a State of Exception. Report of the Committee*, International Committee on the Enforcement of Human Rights Law, International Law Association Paris Conference (1984), p.5. Also see Richard B. Lillich, 'The Paris Minimum Standards of Human Rights Norms in a State of Emergency', 79 *The American Journal of International Law* 4 (October 1985), pp.1072–1081.

21 'Constitution of the Republic of Paraguay', in 15 *Constitutions* (Release 93-2, April 1993), p.57.

22 Bernard H. Siegan, *Drafting a Consitution for a Nation of Republic Emerging into Freedom* (Fairfax, VA: George Mason University Press, 1994. 2nd edn), p.87.

23 'The Constitution of the Kingdom of Nepal, 2047 (1990)', in 13 *Constitutions* (Release 94-4, June 1994), p.104.

24 'The Constitution of the Turkish Federated State of Cyprus', 5 *Constitutions*, p.51.

25 'Constitution of the Portuguese Republic', in 15 *Constitutions*, October 1991, p.45.

26 'Constitution of the Republic of Suriname', in 18 *Constitutions*, Release 91-6, November 1991, p.45.

27 'The Constitution of the Federative Republic of Brazil' in, 3 *Constitutions* (Booklet 2, Release 96-7, November 1996), p.111.

28 See *Poland in a World in Change supra* note 3*, at 241. Also see Wyktor Osiatynski, 'A Brief History of the Constitution', 6 *East European Constitutional Review*, 2–3 (Spring/Summer 1997), at 66–76; Leszek Lech Garlicki, 'The Presidency in the New Polish Constitution', 6 *East European Constitutional Review*, 2–3 (Spring/Summer 1997), at 81–89.

29 *V.N. Shukla's Constitution of India* (Lucknow: Eastern Book Company, 1990. Mahendra P. Singh, ed. 8th edition), p.287; *Constitution of the Islamic Republic of Pakistan, 1973* (Lahore: Nadeem Law Book House, 1993. With Commentary by Syed Shabbar Raza Rizvi), p.280.

30 For details see, e.g. Andre Alen and Rusen Ergec, *Federal Belgium After the Fourth State Reform of 1993* (Brussels: Ministry of Foreign Affairs, External Trade and Development Cooperation, 1994), pp.24–39.

31 *Dekret-zakon ob osobom polozhenii v Bel'gii* [Law-decree on a State of Exception in Belgium] (11 February 1982) (unpublished manuscript, on file with the Institute of Legislation and Comparative Law, Moscow).

32 'The Coordinated Constitution of Belgium of 17 February 1994', in 2 *Constitu-*

tions (Release 94-8, November 1994), p.42. Russian translation of the Constitution of Belgium of 1831 see 1 *Sovremenniye konstitutsii. Sbornik deistvuyuschikh konstitutsionnikh aktov. Konstituttsionniye monarkhii* [Modern Constitutions. A collection of Acting Constitutional Laws. Constitutional Monarchies] (St. Petersburg: Pravo, 1905. V.M. Gessen and B.E. Nolde, trans. and eds), pp.138, 129.

33 'The Constitution of the Federative Republic of Brazil', *supra* note 27*, at 109, 111.

34 'Constitutional Law of the People's Republic of Angola of 11 November 1975 (as revised and altered by the Central Committee of the MPLA-Worker's Party on 11 August 1980)', in 1 *Constitutions* (Release 92–7, November 1992), p.11. Also see *Konstitutsia Narodnoy Respubliki Angola* [Constitution of the People's Republic of Angola] (Moscow: Yuridicheskaya literatura, 1978), p.14; *Konstitutsia Narodnoy Respubliki Kongo* [Constitution of the People's Republic of the Congo] (Moscow: Yuridicheskaya literatura, 1983), pp.19, 15; *Konstitutsia Narodnoy Respubliki Mozambik* [Constitution of the People's Republic of Mozambique] (Moscow: Yuridicheskaya literatura, 1978), p.11; 'The Constitution of the Somali Democratic Republic', in 17 *Constitutions* (November 1981), p.2.

35 'The Constitution of the Somali Democratic Republic', 17 *Constitutions* (November 1981), p.19; *Konstitutsia Narodnoy Respubliki Kongo* [Constitution of the People's Republic of Congo], *supra* note 34*, at 26.

36 'The Constitution of the People's Republic of China' in, 4 *Constitutions* (Release 92-5, September 1992), at 47, 50, 54, 53. Also see 1 *Konstitutsii sotsialisticheskikh gosudarstv* [Constitutions of Socialist States] (Moscow: Yuridicheskaya literatura, 1987. B.A. Strashun, B.N. Topornin and G. H.Shakhnazarov, eds In 2 vols.), pp.291, 296.

37 'The Constitution of the Kingdom of Nepal, 2047 (1990)', 13 *Constitutions*, p.104.

38 'The Constitution of the Federative Republic of Brazil', 3 *Constitutions*, p.109; 'The Constitution of Republic of Bolivia', in 2 *Constitutions*, p.32.

39 See, e.g. *SSSR i mezhdunarodnoye sotrudnichestvo v oblasti prav cheloveka. Dokumenty i materialy* [USSR and International Cooperation in the Sphere of Human Rights. Documents and Materials] (Moscow: Mezhdunarodnye otnoshenia, 1989), pp.303–304, 164, 267–268.

40 Erica-Irene A. Daes, *The Individual's Duties to the Community and the Limitations on Human Rights and Freedoms under art.29 of the Universal Declaration of Human Rights*, UN Doc E/CN 4/Sub 2/432/ Rev 2 (1983), p.192.

41 Nicole Questiaux, *supra* note 16* [Preface], para.55(4), p.16.

42 'The Siracusa Principles on the Limitation and Derogation Provisions in the International Covenant on Civil and Political Rights', 7 *Human Rights Quarterly. A Comparative and International Journal of the Social Sciences, Humanities, and Law*, 1 (February 1985), at 7–8. 'Sirakuzskie printsipy tolkovania ogranicheniy i otstupleniy ot polozheniy Mezhdunarodnogo pakta o grazhdanskikh i politicheskikh pravakh' [The Siracusa Principles on the Limitation and Derogation Provisions in the International Covenant on Civil and Political Rights], *Vestnik Moscowskogo universiteta*, 4 (1992), at 62.

43 Daniel O'Donnell, 'Commentary by the Rapporteur on Derogation', 7 *Human Rights Quarterly* 1 (February 1985), at 23–24.

44 'The Siracusa Principles', *supra* note 42*, at 8.

45 1980 Report of the U.N. Special Rapporteur on Chile, U.N. Doc. A/35/522, para.31.

46 Daniel O'Donnell, *supra* note 43*, at 24.

47 'The Siracusa Principles', *supra* note 42*, at 8.

48 The *Lawless* case (Merits), E.Ct.H.R.Jt. of 1.7.1961, Series A, no.3. The decision was also published in 3 *Journal of the International Commission of Jurists* 2 (Winter 1961), at 112–117. The case of *Lawless v Ireland* (1961) is thoroughly analysed in a publication by the Director of the Department on Human Rights of the Council of Europe: A.H. Robertson, 'The European Convention on Human Rights', in *The International Protection of Human Rights* (New York, Washington: Frederick A. Praeger, Publishers, 1967. Evan Luard, ed.), pp.106, 115–116, 122–123.

49 See the *Greek* case, 12 *Yearbook of the European Convention on Human Rights, 1969* (The Hague: Martinus Nijhoff, 1972), at 72. A whole issue of the 1969 Yearbook was dedicated exclusively to the *Greek* case.

50 *Report on the Situation of Human Rights of a Segment of the Nicaraguan Population of Miskito Origin* (Washington: Organisation of American States, Inter-American Commission on Human Rights, OAS/Ser.L/V/II.62, doc.10, rev.3, 29 November 1983), pp.121–122.

51 For the texts of the Copenhagen and Moscow Documents, see 29 *International Legal Materials*, 5 (1990), p.1306, and 30 *ibid.*, 6 (1991), p.1671.

52 Sub-Commission on the Prevention of Discrimination and Protection of Minorities, Forty-third session, Summary Record of the 22nd meeting (21 August 1991), UN doc. E/CN.4/Sub.2/1991/SR.22, pp.2–3.

53 See S.V. Ryabov, *Pravovoe polozhenie i fakticheskaya rol' prezidenta v gosudarstvakh Latinskoy Ameriki* [Legal Status and Actual Role of the President in the Countries of Latin America] (Moscow: Nauka, 1976), p.188.

54 Cited in Ergun Ozbudun and Mehmet Turhan, *Emergency Powers* (Strasbourg: Council of Europe Publishing, 1995. European Commission for Democracy through Law Report), p.15.

55 'Constitution of Bolivia', in 2 *Constitutions*, p.42.

56 Jonathan Hartlyn, *supra* note 13* [Introduction], at 307, 310.

57 If the country is *at war* indeed, the order appointing the War Delegation to replace the *Riksdag* is issued by the members of the Foreign Affairs Advisory Council. The Act stipulates that the Prime Minister of the country is to be 'consulted' before such order is issued, but doesn't make this consultation obligatory – only if it's 'possible'. The Government can issue such decree too, 'if war conditions prevent the Council from convening'. According to additional provisions, if the country is *exposed to the danger of war*, the order shall be issued by the members of the Foreign Affairs Advisory Council and the Prime Minister jointly. This order shall be effected 'only if the Prime Minister and six members of the Council are in agreement thereon' (art.2(2)).

58 'Constitutional Documents of Sweden', in 18 *Constitutions* (June 1985), pp.157, 111–113. Also see *Shvetsia. Konstitutsia i zakonodatelnye akty* [Sweden. Constitution and Legislative Acts] (Moscow: Progress, 1983. M.A. Mogunova, ed.), pp.55–58, 137; M.A. Mogunova, *Skandinavskie strany: tsentral'nye organy vlasti* [Scandinavian Countries: Central Organs of Power] (Moscow: Yuridicheskaya literatura, 1975), pp.75–76, 105, 108.

59 'The Basic Law of the Federal Republic of Germany' in, 7 *Constitutions* (Release 94-6, August 1994), at 127, 164–166. Also see Knut Ipsen, 'States of Emergency', in *Rights, Institutions and Impact of International Law according to the German Basic Law* (Baden-Baden: Nomos Verlagsgesellschaft, 1987. Christian Starck, ed.), pp.131–158; Eckart Klein, 'The States of Emergency according to the Basic Law of the Federal Republic of Germany', in *Reports on German Public Law* (Montreal: C.F. Muller, 1990. Bernhardt/Beyerlin, eds XIII International Congress of Comparative Law), pp.63–80.

60 'Konstitutsia Narodnoy Respubliki Albania' [Constitution of the Peoples' Republic of Albania, 1946], *Sovetskoe gosudarstvo i pravo*, 6 (1947), p.59.

61 'Konstitutsia Narodnoy Respubliki Albania. (4 iulia 1950 g.)' [Constitution of the Peoples' Republic of Albania. (4 July 1950)], *Sovetskoe gosudarstvo i pravo*, 1 (1951), pp.64, 63.

62 The original text of the Constitution of the People's Republic of Hungary (PRH), adopted by PRH State Assembly on 18 August 1949, didn't contain this or any other provisions regulating the mechanism of a state of emergency. See 'Konstitutsia Vengerskoy Narodnoy Respubliki. (Zakon No. 20 18 avgusta 1949 g.)' [Constitution of the Peoples' Republic of Hungary. (Law No. 20 of 18 August 1949)], *Sovetskoe gosudarstvo i pravo*, 10 (1949), pp.66–75.

63 1 *Konstitutsii sotsialisticheskikh gosudarstv* [Constitutions of Socialist States], *supra* note 36*, at 17, 171, 173.

64 *Konstitutsii gosudarstv Yugo-Vostochnoy Azii i Tikhogo okeana* [Constitutions of South-East Asia and the Pacific] (Moscow: Inostrannaya literatura, 1960), p.492.

65 Rossiter wrote in 1948: 'The modern version of Mr. Lincoln's question – "Can a democracy fight a successful total war and still be a democracy when the war is over?" – will be answered affirmatively by the incontestable facts of history' (Clinton L. Rossiter, *supra* note 3* [Introduction], at 3).

66 *Portugalia. Konstitutsia i zakonodatelnye akty* [Portugal. Constitution and Legislative Acts] (Moscow: Progress, 1979), p.39.

67 'Constitution of the Republic of Costa Rica', 5 *Constitutions* (Release 95-3, May 95), p.106.

68 John Rawls, *A Theory of Justice* (Cambridge, Mass: The Belknap Press of Harvard University Press, 1971), p.244; Rex Martin, *Rawls and Rights* (Lawrence, Kansas: University Press of Kansas, 1985); Robert Paul Wolff, *Understanding Rawls. A Reconstruction and Critique of 'A Theory of Justice'* (Princeton: Princeton University Press, 1977).

69 E.C.S. Wade and A.W. Bradley, *supra* note 25* [Ch. 1], at 547.

70 W.E. Butler, 'Civil Rights in Russia: Legal Standards in Gestation', in *Civil Rights in Imperial Russia* (Oxford: Clarendon Press, 1989. Olga Crisp and Linda Edmondson, eds), p.12.

71 J.E.S. Fawcett, 'Human Rights and Domestic Jurisdiction', in *The International Protection of Human Rights* (New York, Washington: Frederick A. Praeger Publishers, 1967), p.297.

72 See the remarks by Mr. Prado Vallejo, a member of the UN Human Rights Committee, in CCPR/C/SR. 351 (1982), p.8, para.32. See *also* the remarks of the Attorney-General of Ireland in the *Lawless case* (Counter-Memorial of the Government of Ireland), Ser. B: Pleadings, p.224.

73 Jaime Oraa, *supra* note 76* [Ch. 1], at 1.

74 See *Prava cheloveka. Sbornik mezhdunarodnykh dogovorov* [Human Rights. A Collection of International Treaties] (New York: United Nations, 1989); *Prava cheloveka. Sbornik mezhdunarodnykh dokumentov* [Human Rights. A Collection of International Documents] (Moscow: MSU, 1986).

75 F. Van Hoof, *supra* note 64* [Ch. 1], at 22.

76 Nicole Questiaux, *supra* note 16* [Preface], paras. 40–68, pp.15–19. Some 20 years before Questiaux formulated her 'Six Principles', the International Jurist Commission had worked out its 'Four Principles' in the report 'The Dynamic Aspects of the Rule of Law in the Modern Age' (1965). See Nirmal Chandra Chatterjee and P. Parameswara Rao, *Emergency and Law. With Special Reference to India* (London: Asia Publishing House, 1966), pp.122–123.

77 'Constitution of the Republic of Slovenia', in 17 *Constitutions*, p.3.

3 Legal regulation of emergency powers in Imperial Russia

1 21 V.I. Lenin, 'Tri zaprosa' [Three Questions. (December 1911)], *Polnoe sobranie sochineniy* [Complete Works] (Moscow: GIPL, 1961. 5th edn), p.114.

2 Richard Pipes, *Russia under the Old Regime* (London: Weidenfeld and Nicolson, 1974), p.305.

3 Again, in the words of Pipes, 'the significance of this legislation [emergency law of 1881 – *A.D.*] can perhaps be best summarised' in the words of A.A. Lopukhin, according to whom, 'in matters affecting state security there no longer were any objective criteria of guilt: guilt was determined by the subjective impression of police officials' (*ibid.*, p.307). Also see A.A. Lopukhin, *Nastoyaschee i buduschee russkoy politsii* [Russian Police Today and Tomorrow] (Moscow: V.M. Sablin, 1907); A.A. Lopukhin, *Otryvki iz vospominaniy* [Excerpts from Memoirs] (Moscow-Petrograd: Gosizdat, 1923. Foreword by M.N. Pokrovsky).

4 Through a Menshevik journalist Vladimir Burtsev, in 1908 Lopukhin betrayed a famous police secret agent Evno Azef. In 1912, Lopukhin was amnestied, returned to Moscow, and was promoted to a position of Vice Director of Siberia Trade Bank. In 1923 emigrated, and died in 1928 when on a board of directors of an international commerce bank in Paris. See details of the case in: Boris Nikolaevsky, *Istoria odnogo predatelya. Terroristy i politicheskaya politsia* [A Story of a Traitor: Terrorists and Political Police] (Moscow: Vysshaya shkola, 1999. First published in 1932); Anatoly Kukanov, 'A.A. Lopukhin – zhertva obstoyatel'stv ili soznatel'ny dissident' [A.A. Lopukhin – a Victim of Circumstances or a Conscientious Dissident], *Zhandarmy Rossii (Politichesky rozysk v Rossii XV-XX vek* [Russia's Gendarmerie: Political Search in Russia 15–20th centuries] (St. Petersburgh: 'Neva'/Moscow: 'OLMA-PRESS', 2002. 'Archive/Newest Studies' series), pp.437–446; K.N. Morozov, *Partiia sotsialistov-revoliutsionerov v 1907–1914 gg.* [Party of Socialist Revolutionaries in 1907–1914] (Rosspen, Moscow, 1998); Anna Geifman, *Entangled in Terror; The Azef Affair and the Russian Revolution* (Wilmington: Scholarly Resources Inc., 2000).

5 Lieven made very persuasive comparisons of some statements by Lopukhin to other sources showing that critical 'revelations' by the latter were hardly reliable and seemed to be more slanderous (D.C.B. Lieven, 'The Security Police, Civil Rights, and the Fate of the Russian Empire, 1855–1917', in *Civil Rights in Imperial Russia*, *supra* note 70* [Ch. 2], at 246). It's also indicative that Boris Savinkov, one of the most popular Russian terrorists, considered Lopukhin 'trustworthy', because he 'broke up with his [social] environment' (see Jean Longe, Georgy Zilber, *Terroristy i Okhranka* [Terrorists and *Okhranka*] (Moscow: Sovetskaya Rossia, 1991. First published in 1924), p.67).

6 Jonathan W. Daly, 'On the Significance of Emergency Legislation in Late Imperial Russia', *supra* note 8* [Introduction], at 603.

7 *Polnoe sobranie zakonov Rossiiskoi imperii* [Complete Collection of Laws of the Russian Empire] [hereafter: PSZ], series 2, vol.52, part 2, No.57748.

8 1 F. Mering, *Istoria germanskoy sotsial-demokratii* [History of German Social Democracy] (Moscow-Petrograd: GosIzdat, 1923. I. Stepanov, ed.), p.134.

9 2 *Gosudarstvenniy stroy i politicheskie partii v Zapadnoy Evrope i Severo-Amerikanskikh Soedinennykh Shtatakh* [State System and Political Parties in Western Europe and the United States of America] (St. Petersburg: N. Glagolev, n.y. E. Smirnov, ed.), p.189.

10 Brian Loveman, *supra* note 6* [Introduction], at 7.

11 For details see, e.g. Nasser Hussain, *supra* note 42* [Ch. 1].

12 More on Nikolay Mikhailovich Korkunov, his writings and legal views see

George L. Yaney, 'Bureaucracy and Freedom: N.M. Korkunov's Theory of the State', 71 *The American Historical Review* 2 (January 1966), pp.468–486.

13 N.M. Korkunov, *Sravnitelniy ocherk gosudarstvennogo prava inostrannykh derzhav. Chast' pervaya. Gosudarstvo i ego elementy* [Comparative Study of State Law of Foreign Countries. Part One. State and Its Elements] (St. Petersburg: M. Merkushev Printing Office, 1906), pp.148–149. Another famous book by N.M. Korkunov, *Obschaya teoria prava*, has recently been translated and published in the U.S. in the 'Law Classic' series: *General Theory of Law* by N.M. Korkunov (Beard Books, 2000).

14 For more on Vladimir Matveevich Gessen see Nina Berberova, *Lyudi i lozhi. Russkie masony 20 stoletia* [People and Lodges. Russian Masons of the twentieth century] (Khar'kov-Moscow: Progress-Traditsia, 1997), p.147; Oleg Platonov, *Ternoviy venets Rossii. Taynaia istoria masonstva 1731–1996* [Secret History of Masonry 1731–1996] (Moscow: Rodnik, 1996. 2nd edn), p.347.

15 V.M. Gessen, *supra* note 17* [Preface], at 109. Also see V.M. Gessen, *Lektsii po politseiskomu pravu* [Lectures on Police Law] (St. Petersburg: Sever, 1908. Students' Edition 1907–1908), p.97.

16 Cited in V.F. Deryuzhinsky, *Habeas Corpus Act i ego priostanovka po angliyskomu pravu. Ocherk osnovnikh garantiy lichnoy svobodi v Anglii i ikh vremennogo ogranicheniya* [Habeas Corpus Act and Its Suspension in English Law. Study of Main Guarantees of Personal Freedom and Their Temporary Limitation in England] (Yuriev (Derpt): G. Lakman Printing Office, 1895), pp.148–149. Also see V.F. Deryuzhinsky, *Politseiskoe pravo* [Police Law] (St. Petersburg: Senate typography, 1908. 2nd edition), pp.248–249.

17 Demonisation of the Russian history by both Communist and some Western authors is amazing indeed. Coverage of the reign of Ivan IV, or Ivan the Terrible (1547–1584) is one of numerous examples. Even his nickname 'the Terrible', 'le Terrible', 'der Schrekliche' is not just a wrong translation of 'Grozny' (which actually means 'the Stern'), but a pejorative term that was introduced to European historiography by Ivan IV's (or rather Russia's) opponents in France, Lithuania and Poland (see R.Yu. Vipper, *Ivan Grozny* [Ivan the Terrible] (Moscow: URAO, 1998. First published in 1922), pp.202–211). In reality, Ivan IV – one of the most educated European monarchs of the Middle Ages, known in his inner circle as an 'English tsar' who tried to marry a British Queen, owner of the largest library in Europe, who, like Thomas Jefferson in the U.S., doubled the territory of the country – can be called 'Terrible' only in that sense that his despotism is terribly exaggerated. In count of the leading Russian scholar on Ivan IV, as a result of 'mass terror' during 37 years of his rule, from 3,000–4,000 people of an approximately ten million Russian population were destroyed (see R.G. Skrynnikov, *Ivan Grozniy* [Ivan the Terrible] (Moscow, 1975), p.191). For comparison, in the same sixteenth century in England (with a smaller population than in Russia), 72,000 tramps and beggars (former peasants who lost their land) were executed during the reign of Henry VIII (I.N. Osinovskiy, *Thomas Moore* (Moscow, 1974), p.62). In the Netherlands, during the reign of Kings Karl V & Philip II the 'number of victims [of Inquisition – *A.D.*] ... reached 100,000' (I.G. Grigulevich, *Istoria Inkvizitsii* [History of Inquisition] (Moscow, 1971), p.271). On 23 August 1572, another contemporary of Ivan IV, French King Karl IX personally participated in the slaughter of more than 3,000 Huguenots (the Massacre of St. Bartholomew's Day) whose only 'crime' and 'sin' was that they belonged not to Catholicism, but to Protestantism. In other words, during one night in France approximately the same number of people were destroyed as during 27 years of Ivan IV's reign. But, as known, the Massacre of St. Bartholomew's Day continued and after two weeks of manslaughter about 30,000 Protestants were murdered

(S.G. Lozinskiy, *Istoria Papstva* [History of the Papacy] (Moscow, 1986), pp.264–265). In 1542, only in Geneva 500 'witches' were burned (E.B. Chernyak, *Sudyi i zagovorschiki* [Judges and Plotters] (Moscow: Mysl', 1984), p.185). All in all, in the estimation of Vadim Kozhinov, in the sixteenth century 'in the main countries of Western Europe (Spain, France, the Netherlands, England) ... at least 300,000–400,000 people were executed' (V.V. Kozhinov, *Istoria Rusi i russkogo slova. Sovremenniy vzglyad* [History of Rus' and the Russian Language. A Modern View] (Moscow: Charley, 1997), p.29), unless we trust a new 2004 study of Vatican scholars downsizing the Inquisition. That doesn't mean that we should admire and glorify Ivan IV for the fact that under his reign 'only' 3,000–4,000 people were executed. But there was nothing 'uniquely Russian' in Ivan IV's terror. On the contrary, even now Henry VIII, Philip II or Karl IX are highly respected kings in their countries, whereas in Russia Ivan IV has been damned for centuries. Vadim Kozhinov reminded his readers that when in 1862 a monument commemorating 1,000 years of Russian history was erected in Novgorod, there was no room for Ivan IV among 109 figures of Russian tsars, military commanders, and heroes. Needless to say the Russians have never built a monument to Ivan IV personally (*ibid.*, pp.32–33).

18 2 Anatole Leroy-Beaulieu, *The Empire of the Tsars and the Russians* (New York and London: G.P. Putnam's Sons, 1894. In 3 vols.), p.395.

19 Albert F. Heard, 'Russia of To-Day', 74 *Harper's New Monthly Magazine* 442 (March 1887), pp.579–589; Albert F. Heard, 'Law and Justice in Russia', 76 *Harper's New Monthly Magazine* 456 (May 1888), pp.920–932.

20 Albert F. Heard, 'Law and Justice in Russia', *supra* note 19*, at 930. Heard also reminded his American readers that capital punishment was abolished in Russia by Elizabeth in 1753 and that even though the laws of Finland recognised death penalty 'not an execution has taken place since its cession to Russia in 1809' (*id*).

21 *Svod zakonov Rossiyskoy imperii* [Code of Laws of the Russian Empire] [hereafter: SZ], vol.16, part 1, art.4.

22 Marc Szeftel, 'Personal Inviolability in the Legislation of the Russian Absolute Monarchy', 17 *The American Slavic and East European Review* (1958), p.2. Surprisingly, even though Marc Szeftel, Professor Emeritus of the University of Washington, included four works by Richard Pipes (*Russia under the Old Regime* among them) into a 45-page list of sources of his fundamental study of the first Russian Constitution, he not only never gave a single citation from any publication by Pipes, but even didn't mention his name anywhere in the book, including its last subchapter dedicated exclusively to an overview of main studies in the U.S. and other countries of the world of the last period of history of the Russian Empire. See Marc Szeftel, *The Russian Constitution of April 23, 1906. Political Institutions of the Duma Monarchy* (Bruxelles: Les Editions de la Librairie Encyclopedique, 1976).

23 William E. Butler, *Russian Law* (Oxford University Press, 1999), pp.28–29. 'Even to the revolutionary, the legal profession in Russia has its attraction as a channel for effectuating political and social change' (William E. Butler, *Soviet Law* (London: Butterworths, 1983), p.22). As known, Vladimir Lenin took courses at the Law School of Kazan' University and was a *magna cum laude* graduate from the Law School of St. Petersburg University. Despite the fact that his brother was executed as a terrorist, Lenin didn't have a problem with being admitted to the bar and practising law.

24 4 William Blackstone, *supra* note 18 [Ch. 1], at 18.

25 Leon Radzinowicz, A History of English Criminal Law and Its Administration from 1750. The Movement for Reform 1750–1833 (New York: The Macmillan Company, 1948), p.4.

26 The authorities could hardly find somebody who would agree to execute the Decembrists who were to be hanged ('to die by the rope') or simply know how to do it. Eventually, when the would-be executioner was found, he appeared to be so inexperienced that three out of five ropes tore and three victims fell down on the ground.

27 See Peter H. Juviler, *Revolutionary Law and Order: Politics and Social Change in the USSR* (The Free Press: A Division of Macmillan Publ. Co., Inc., New York; Collier Macmillan Publishers, London, 1976), p.25.

28 See Will Adams, 'Capital Punishment in Soviet Criminal Legislation, 1922–1965: A Code Content Analysis and Graphic Representation', in *On the Road to Communism: Essays on Soviet Domestic and Foreign Politics* (Lawrence: University Press of Kansas, 1972. Roger E. Kanet and Ivan Volgyes, eds), pp.79–121.

29 See S. Usherovich, *Smertnye kazni v tsarskoi Rossii* [Death Penalty in Tsarist Russia] (Moscow, 1933). Also see Donald Rawson, 'The Death Penalty in Late Tsarist Russia: An Investigation of Judicial Procedures', *Russian History* 11 (Spring 1984), at 44–45; S.S. Ostroumov, 'Repressii tsarskogo pravitel'stva protiv revolutsionnogo dvizhenia v Rossii v period imperializma (ugolovno-statisticheskoe issledovanie)' [Repressions of Tsarist Government Against Revolutionary Movement in Russia in the Period of Imperialism: Criminal Statistical Study], *Vestnik Moscowskogo universiteta*, 3 (1976), pp.35–41. Also see Alexander S. Mikhlin, *Death Penalty in Russia* (London: Simmonds & Hill Publishing Ltd.; Kluwer Law International, 1999. Translation with a Foreword by W.E. Butler), pp.8–17.

30 One of those 14 terrorists sentenced to death for his participation in assassination attempt on Alexander III was Alexander I. Ulyanov, older brother of Vladimir I. Ulyanov-Lenin, a founder of the Soviet state. (See, e.g. M.N. Gernet, 'Narodovol'tsy na eshafote' [Execution of Members of the People's Will], 2 *Pravo i zhizn'* (July 1922), pp.78–84).

31 This figure doesn't include the number of those who were killed in riots and disturbances. In 1861, the year of serfdom abolishment, there were 1,889 cases of protests in the Russian countryside. In 937 of them (49 per cent) the army was called 'to assist civil authorities'. However, the use of weapons was extremely rare – in three cases only. (See R.V. Narbutov, 'Pravovoe regulirovanie ispol'zovania vooruzhennykh sil dlya obespechenia obschestvennogo poryadka i bezopastnosti v dorevolutsionnoy Rossii [Legal Regulation of Use of the Army for Maintenance of the Public Order and Security in Pre-Revolutionary Russia]), *Sovetskoe gosudarstvo i pravo*, 12 (1991), p.141). The latest study by Peter Koshel' contains a full list of executions between 1878 and 1890: 1878 – 1, 1879 – 16, 1880 – 5, 1881 – 5, 1882 – 4, 1883 – 1, 1884 – 4, 1885 – 1, 1886 – 5, 1887 – 5, 1888 – 0, 1889 – 3, 1890 – 2. In 1901–1905 this number was equal to 93, 20 of them – for military crimes. (See P.A. Koshel', *Istoria nakazaniy v Rossii. Istoria rossiyskogo terrorizma* [History of Punishments in Russia. History of Russian Terrorism] (Moscow: Golos, 1995), p.82).

32 E.B. Chernyak, *supra* note 16*, at 191. In England the last witch trial was reportedly held in 1944. Old Bailey Court in London used 'anti-witchcraft' act of 1795 (!) against a famous medium Helen Dunken and sentenced her to nine months imprisonment. (See 'Reabilitatsia ved'my' [Rehabilitation of a Witch], *Moscowskiy komsomolets*, 5 February 1998, at 3).

33 E.B. Chernyak, *supra* note 17*, at 200.

34 See, for instance, Henry Lissagaray, *History of the Paris Commune of 1871* (New Park Publications, 1976. Translated from the French by Eleanor Marx, 1886. First published, 1876). An interesting Russian connection deserves mentioning here. In 1847, a Russian writer Alexander Herzen emigrated from

164   *Notes*

Russia, which, in his opinion, was the 'concentration of the evil', and whose biggest crime was the execution of five Decembrists. In about a year, right before Herzen's eyes 11,000 participants of the Paris rebellion were executed. Poor writer nearly went insane and wrote to his friends in Russia: 'I wish God let the Russians take Paris over, it's high time to finish this stupid Europe! ... I am ashamed of France ... But what is the most terrifying is that not a single Frenchman is ashamed of what's going on ...'. (Cited in V.V. Kozhinov, *supra* note 17*, at 35).

35 See, for instance: *Revolution and Reaction: The Paris Commune of 1871* (Amherst, MA, 1973. Hicks, J. and Tucker, R., eds); Robert Tombs, *The War Against Paris, 1871* (Cambridge: Cambridge University Press, 1981). Also see the Paris Commune 1871 Internet memorial on the web site of the University of New South Wales (Sydney): http://www.arts.unsw.edu.au/pariscommune/index.html.

36 Robin Milner-Gulland, *The Russians* (Malden, Mass.: Blackwell Publishers, 1997), p.228.

37 Among other Russian and foreign scholars, this view is shared by Jonathan W. Daly, arguing that 'Alexander's reform placed Russia firmly on the road toward the rule of law, meaning, inter alia, the absolute supremacy or predominance of regular law as opposed to the influence of arbitrary power, ... or even of wide discretionary authority on the part of the government' (Jonathan W. Daly, 'On the Significance of Emergency Legislation in Late Imperial Russia', *supra* note 8* [Introduction], at 604, quoting A.V. Dicey, *supra* note 23* [Ch. 1], at 202).

38 P.A. Zaionchkovskiy, *Krizis samoderzhavia na rubezhe 1870–1880-x godov* [Crisis of Autocracy at the End of the 1870s – in the Beginning of the 1880s] (Moscow: MGU, 1964), pp.91–98, 113, 124.

39 Deborah Hardy was certainly right when saying that the Zasulich's case was 'unique' and that it 'set a new course for the Russian revolutionary terrorists' (see Deborah Hardy, *Land and Freedom: The Origins of Russian Terrorism, 1876–1879* (New York; West Port, CT; London: Greenwood Press, 1987. 'Contributions to the Study of World History' series, no.7, p.59). In March 1878, Zasulich was acquitted in a jury trial. The acquittal of Zasulich is an indication that in the 1870s rights of the jury were firmly protected. There was no reason for the jury members in Russia to be afraid of tsarist persecution for their decision to acquit a terrorist. The country had made a significant progress in its transition to the rule of law. Ironically, it was the same way that led Russia to a national disaster of 1917. (See speeches of Zasulich's attorney P.A. Alexandrov and Judge A.F. Koni in: *Sud prisyazhnykh v Rossii: Gromkie ugolovnye protsessy 1864–1917 gg.* [Jury Trials in Russia: Loud Criminal Processes, 1864–1917] (Leningrad: Lenizdat, 1991. S.M. Kazantsev, comp.), pp.281–316).

40 1 *Za sto let (1800–1896): Sbornik po istorii politicheskikh i obschestvennykh dvizheniy v Rossii* [A Hundred Years (1800–1896): A Collection of Articles on History of Political and Social Movements in Russia] (London: Russian Free Press Fund, 1897. Vladimir Burtsev, comp. In 2 vols.), pp.151–154.

41 More on the Supreme Executive Commission for the Preservation of the State Order and Public Tranquillity and the system of political security and investigation in Russia see, e.g.: Z.I. Peregudova, Politicheskiy sysk Rossii 1880–1917 [Political Investigation in Russia: 1880–1917] (Moscow: ROSSPEN, 2000); P.A. Zaionchkovskiy, *supra* note 38*, at 148–229.

42 On Alexander II and his time, see a remarkable study by a famous Russian historian of the nineteenth century Sergey S. Tatischev (1902): S.S. Tatischev, *Imperator Aleksandr Vtoroy. Ego zhizn' i tsartsvovanie* [Emperor Alexander II: His Life and Reign] (Moscow: Charley, 1996. In 2 vols). Also see L.M.

Lyashenko, *Tsar'-osvoboditel'. Zhizn' i deyania Aleksandra II* [Tsar-Liberator. Life and Work of Alexander II] (Moscow: Vlados, 1994).

43 As a classic example of double standards of Russian revolutionaries, consider this: when in July 1881, four months after assassination of the Russian tsar, the U.S. President James A. Garfield was murdered, the Executive Committee of the 'People's Will' issued a public statement, saying: 'We express our deep condolences to the American people and consider our duty on behalf of Russian revolutionaries to protest against violent actions like a life attempt of Gito' (See G.E. Mironov, *Istoria gosudarstva Rossiyskogo. Istoriko-biographicheskie ocherki* [History of the Russian State: Historical and Biographical Essays] (Moscow: Knizhnaya palata, 1995), p.487).

44 N.I. Lazarevsky, *Lektsii po russkomu gosudarstvennomu pravu* [Lectures on Russian State Law. Vol.1. Constitutional Law] (St. Petersburg: Slovo, 1910), pp.102–103.

45 SZ, vol.1, part 1, article 53. In his attempt to reveal another devilish uniqueness and Byzantine slyness of the Russian state and law, Richard Pipes discovered a kind of a conspiracy even in the fact *how* the Ordinance was published. 'In a manner *characteristic of Russian legislative practices*, – Pipes wrote, – in the official Collection of Statutes and Ordinances this momentous piece of legislation is casually sandwiched between a directive approving minor alterations in the charter of the Russian Fire Insurance Company and one concerning the administration of a technical institute in the provincial town of Cherepovtsy' (Richard Pipes, *supra* note 2*, at 305. *Italics added – A.D.*). Actually, that is quite typical for all (or nearly all) countries of the world when a position of a new piece of legislation in a collection of statutes is predetermined either by the date when this law was adopted and its registration number (in legal periodicals and annual collections: Public Law in the U.S., Public General Acts in Great Britain, etc.) or by the alphabetical order (in most selections of the legislation). It's a common practice for any country of the world and there is nothing 'characteristic of Russian legislative practices' in it.

46 For instance, one such *ukaz* (issued on 2 April 1879, after another regicide attempt) granted the Governors-General the right to transfer to martial courts any persons whose actions were deemed potentially 'harmful to public order and tranquillity', to arrest or banish any person, to close any periodical publication, and, as if that were insufficient, 'to take *any* measures … deemed necessary for the preservation of tranquillity'⁴⁶ (*italics added – A.D.*). The positions of three new ('temporary') Governors-General (in St. Petersburg, Khar'kov, and Odessa) were created and added to the existing three (in Moscow, Kiev and Warsaw). Each of them was empowered to subject to his authority the three to five provinces constituting a local military district which, taken together, comprehended 21 of the 50 provinces of European Russia, plus the ten of the Polish Kingdom. (See P.A. Zaionchkovskiy, *supra* note 38*, at 87).

47 *Obzor deiatel'nosti Departamenta politsii za tsarstvovanie v Boze pochivshego Gosudaria imperatora Aleksandra III (1 marta 1881 – 20 oktiabrya 1894 gg.)* [A Review of Activities of the Police Department under the late Emperor Alexander III (1 March 1881–20 October 1894)] (State Archive of the Russian Federation [hereafter: GARF], f.102, op.253, d. 98, l. 5.

48 See *Organi i voiska MVD Rossii. Kratkiy istorichesky ocherk* [Organs and Troops of the Ministry of Internal Affairs. A Brief Historical Essay] (Moscow: MVD Rossii, 1996. V.F. Nekrasov, A.V. Borisov, M.G. Detkov, *et al.*), pp.27–28; Mark Szeftel, 'Personal Inviolability in the Legislation of the Russian Absolute Monarchy', *supra* note 22*, at 1–24.

49 *V.N. Shukla's Constitution of India*, *supra* note 29* [Ch. 2], at 816–817.

50 *Sobranie uzakoneniy i rasporiazheniy pravitel'stva, izdavaemye pri Pravitel'stvuiuschem Senate* [Collection of By-Laws and Resolutions of the Government, issued under the Governing Senate], no.94, 9 September 1881, art.616, 1554–1555.
51 Jonathan W. Daly, 'On the Significance of Emergency Legislation in Late Imperial Russia', *supra* note 8* [Introduction], at 623, quoting '*Spiski mestnostei, nakhodiaschikhsia na voennom polozhenii i na polozhenii chrezvychainoi okhrany*' [A List of Localities Declared under Martial Law or Extraordinary Security], GARF, f.102, op.302, d.4, ll. Also see *Pravo*, 12 March 1906, no.10, cols.909–916.
52 See M.N. Gernet, 5 *Istoria tsarskoy tur'my* [History of Tsarist Prison] (Moscow, GIYuL, 1956. In 5 vols.), p.90.
53 See Neil B. Weissman, *Reform in Tsarist Russia: The State Bureaucracy and Local Government, 1900–1914* (New Brunswick: Rutgers University Press, 1981), pp.10–11.
54 D.C.B. Lieven, *supra* note 5*, at 240.
55 Jonathan W. Daly, *Autocracy Under Siege: Security Police and Opposition in Russia, 1866–1905, supra* note 8* [Introduction], at 9.
56 See 'Pis'mo B.V. Savinkova to V.N. Figner' [B.V. Savinkov's Letter to V.N. Figner], in 18 *Minuvshee. Istoricheskiy Al'manakh* [The Past. Historical Almanac] (Moscow–St. Petersburg: Atheneum-Phoenix, 1995. R.A. Gorodnitskiy & G.S. Kahn, publ.), p.195.
57 Vera Figner, *Zapechatlenniy trud* [Preserved Labour] (Moscow, 1921), p.174.
58 See A.A. Levandovsky, 'Smertel'ny schet (Ubiystvo Alexandra II)' [Deadly Count: Assassination of Alexander II)', in *Tsareubiystva: Gibel' zemnykh bogov* [Regicide: Murder of Earthly Gods] (Moscow: Kron-Press, 1998), p.414.
59 See Vladlen Izmozik, 'Politichesky rozysk vedyot Tretye Otdelenie (1826–1880 gody)' [Political Search is Exercised by the Third Department (1826–1880)], *Zhandarmy Rossii (Politichesky rozysk v Rossii XV-XX vek* [Russia's Gendarmerie: Political Search in Russia 15–20th Centuries] (St. Petersburg: 'Neva'/Moscow: 'OLMA-PRESS', 2002. 'Archive/Newest Studies' series), p.253.
60 3–4 Aleksandr I. Solzhenitsyn, *The Gulag Archipelago 1918–1956* (Harper & Row, Publishers: New York, 1975. In 4 vols.), p.10. Also see P.S. Squire, *The Third Department: The Political Police in Russia of Nicholas I* (Cambridge, 1968); S. Monas, *The Third Section: Police and Society in Russia under Nicholas I* (Harvard, 1961).
61 V.E. Petrischev, *Zametki o terrorizme* [Notes on Terrorism] (Moscow: Editorial URSS, 2001), p.192.
62 See George Leggett, *The Cheka: Lenin's Political Police. The All-Russian Extraordinary Commission for Combating Counter-Revolution and Sabotage (December 1917 to February 1922)* (Oxford: Claredon Press, 1981), pp.22–27, 372–373. The situation was quite typical. In 1902–1913, Iosif Stalin, for instance, was arrested and sentenced to exile six times, but evaded penalty four times.
63 See Anna Geifman, *Thou Shalt Kill: Revolutionary Terrorism in Russia, 1894–1917* (Princeton University Press, 1993), pp.21–22. The book was also translated into Russian and published under a title: *Revolutsionniy terror v Rossii 1894–1917* [Revolutionary Terror in Russia, 1894–1917] (Moscow: Kron-Press, 1997). In her remarkable study Geifman uses an interesting tactical approach. First agreeing with certain views and cliches expressed by more 'authoritative' authors, she seems to be unwilling to openly argue against them, but gives such facts and arguments that draw a completely different picture. For instance, she rushes to say that one of such 'authorities' Walter Laqueur is 'entirely justified in cautioning against sweeping definitions that claim ... that

all 'terrorists are criminals, moral imbeciles, mentally deranged people or sadists (or sado-masochists)' (p.167), but then dedicates a whole chapter of her book (Chapter 5 'The "Seamy Side" of the Revolution') proving quite the opposite. Consider the following observations: 'a number of [revolutionaries] were recognised by contemporary medical experts as 'unconditional degenerates' (p.167); 'the personality of Kamo presents a striking example whose derangement became a catalyst for violent behavior that ... happened to take revolutionary form' (p.167); 'the emotional problems experienced by the terrorists covered the entire range of mental illness' (p.168); 'a significant per centage of active Russian terrorists ... made one or more attempts on their own lives' (p.168); 'psychological instability [of the revolutionaries] ... became increasingly common' (p.169); 'a large number of assassins and expropriators experienced (and were frequently treated for) emotional breakdowns of varying severity' (p.169); 'many terrorists were described by their fellow radicals as 'turbulent and unbalanced', 'hysterical', or 'suicidal', and some were openly recognised as 'completely abnormal' (p.170); 'numerous cases of revolutionary violence involving behavior classifiable only as sadistic' (p.171); 'sometimes physical illness or disfigurements produced an escalating self-loathing projected by the afflicted individual onto others, resulting in increasing frustration ultimately expressed in violent acts that were later rationalised as political actions. Sexual abnormalities [like an incident involving a young hermaphrodite whose gender ambiguity was discovered following his arrest for the political murder of a police official – *A.D.*] undoubtedly played a role in driving certain individuals to bloodshed as well' (p.172). It is hard to accuse Geifman of being biased or opinionated. There are numerous similar examples that were left out of her book. Dzerzhinsky himself was described by his contemporaries as an 'almost epileptically nervous' person who was possessed by two childhood dreams: to become a Roman Catholic priest, and to find a magic cap that would make him invisible and give him power, as he said, 'to slay all the Russians' (See V. Mitskevich-Kapsukas, 'Iz vospominaniy F. E. Dzerzhinskogo' [F.E. Dzerzhisky Remembered], *Proletarskaia revolyutsia*, IX (September 1926), p.55). In his adult life Dzerzhinsky was able to partially accomplish only the latter dream. A publication of a contemporary Russian scholar contains an impressive list of active revolutionaries who ended their lives in a suicide or a mental institution (see A.I. Suvorov, 'Politichesky terrorizm v Rossii XIX – nachala XX vekov. Istoki, struktura, osobennosti' [Political Terrorism in Russia in the 19th–the Beginning of the 20th Centuries: Reasons, Structure, Peculiarities], *Sotsiologicheskie issledovania*, No.7, 2002, pp.54–61).

64 Lennard F. Gerson, *The Secret Police in Lenin's Russia* (Philadelphia: Temple University Press, 1976), p.15.

65 3–4 Aleksandr I. Solzhenitsyn, *supra* note 60*, at 11.

66 As another example, it can be mentioned that the daily norm for the Decembrist prisoners sent to Nerchink in Siberia after their soup-opera 'revolution' in 1825 was 118 pounds of ore to be mined and loaded every day. When a Russian writer and poet Varlam Shalamov trudged the same weary route as the Decembrists a hundred years later, the norm had gone up 240 times, to nearly 29,000 pounds. (See Jo Durden-Smith, 'Beware of "Nice" Foreigners', *St. Petersburg Times*, 7–13 October 1996).

67 S.A. Stepanov, *Zagadki ubiystva Stolypina* [Mysteries of Stolypin's Assassination] (Moscow: Progress-Academia, 1995), p.34; P.A. Koshel', *supra* note 31*, at 82. Gernet's estimation of 5,000 to 7,500 executions in 1907–1909 is the largest one, with the biggest (50 per cent) discrepancy. (See M.N. Gernet, *supra* note 51*, at 90).

68 See Donald Rawson, *supra* note 29*, at 37, table 1.

69 See G.E. Mironov, *supra* note 43*, at 726.
70 '30 oktyabrya – Den' politicheskikh zaklyuchennykh' [October 30: Political Prisoners Day], *Rossiiskiye vesti*, 30 October 1997. Also see J. Arch Getty, Gabor T. Rittersporn, and Victor N. Zemskov, 'Victims of the Soviet Penal System in the Pre-War Years: A First Approach on the Basis of Archival Evidence', 98 *American Historical Review* 4 (October 1993), pp.1017–1049.
71 Deborah Hardy, *supra* note 39*, at 48. Also see *Istoria terrorizma v Rossii* [History of Terrorism in Russia] (Rostov-na-Donu: Feniks, 1996. O.V. Budnitsky, ed. 2nd edn).
72 For a complete list see N.N. Ansimov, 'Okhrannye otdelenia i mestnaya vlast' tsarskoy Rossii v nachale 20 v.' [Security Police and Local Government in Tsarist Russia in the Beginning of the twentieth century], *Sovetskoe gosudarstvo i pravo* 5 (1991), p.122.
73 S.A. Stepanov, *supra* note 67*, at 34. An expert of Jerusalem University Leonid Priceman gave a slightly smaller number of the terrorists' victims in Russia between 1905 and May 1909: 2,691 persons killed and 3,029 wounded. (Leonid Priceman, 'Yad terrora' [Poison of Terror], *Nezavisimoe voennoe obozrenie*, 22 August 1996, p.5).
74 Vadim Kozhinov, *supra* note 17*, at 128. As a result of her calculations Anna Geifman came to the same conclusion: 'Close to 17,000 individuals became victims of revolutionary terrorism' (Anna Geifman, *supra* note 63*, at 20–21). At least two non-Russian scholars reveal a detail that other authors prefer not to touch upon: by 1900, almost 30 per cent of those arrested for political crimes were Jews; while in 1903 only 7 million (or 2.3 per cent) of the total population of the Russian Empire were Jewish, they comprised approximately 50 per cent of the revolutionary parties' membership (Leonard Schapiro, *Russian Studies* (New York, 1988), p.266; Anna Geifman, *supra* note 63*, at 32). 'Anyone who espoused patriotic, nationalist, or progovernment views could be labelled a member of the Black Hundreds (*Chernosotenets*), against whom violent acts were justified' (Anna Geifman, *supra* note 63*, at 34).
75 During one of previous attempts on Stolypin's life, his dacha was bombed, 29 persons murdered and 27 crippled, including Stolypin's 15-year-old daughter and his two-year-old son. See M.P. Bock, *P.A. Stolypin. Vospominaniya o Moyem Otse* [P.A. Stolypin. Memories about My Father] (New York: Liberty Publishing House, 1990); S.A. Stepanov, *supra* note 67*; Alexander Bokhanov, *Nickolay II* [Nicholas II] (Moscow: Molodaya gvardia, ZhZL, Russkoe slovo, 1997), pp.266–268. Also see a new study: V.M. Zhukhrai, *Terror. Genii i zhertvy* [Terror: Geniuses and Victims] (Moscow: 'AST Press Kniga', 2002), pp.177–217.
76 The texts of the Constitutions are given in a number of collections. See, e.g. 1 *Sovremenniye konstitutsii. Sbornik deistvuyuschikh konstitutsionnykh aktov. Konstitutsionniye monarkhii*, *supra* note 31* [Ch. 2]; *Konstitutsii i zakonodatel'nie akty burzhuaznykh gosudarstv XVII-XIX vv. (Anglia, SShA, Frantsia, Italia, Germania)* [Constitutions and Legislative Acts of Bourgeois Countries of the 17th–19th Centuries (England, USA, France, Italy, Germany)] (Moscow: Gosyurizdat, 1957. P.N.Galanza, ed.). Constitutional provisions regulating the institute of emergency decrees in German state and some other countries of the world are also given in A.M. Magaziner, *Chrezvychaino-ukaznoe pravo v Rossii* (St. 87 Osn. Zak.) [Law of Emergency Decrees in Russia (art.87 of the Basic Laws] (St. Petersburg: M.M. Stasulevich, 1911), Appendix II, pp.153–172.
77 SZ, vol.1, part 1, at 5–26.
78 'Stenograficheskiy otchet' [Stenographic Report], *Gosudarstvennaya Duma. Vtoroy sozyv 1907 g.*, vol. I, p.513. Cited in Samuel Kucherov, *Courts, Lawyers and Trials Under the Last Russian Tsars* (Greenwood Press, Publishers. Westport, CT, 1974), p.207.

79 Jonathan W. Daly, 'On the Significance of Emergency Legislation in Late Imperial Russia', *supra* note 8* [Introduction], at 621–622.

80 Richard Pipes, *supra* note 2*, at 331.

81 That concerned 'revolutionary literature' too. For instance, a book by Peter Alexeevich Kropotkin (1842–1921), a famous Russian anarchist and decisive enemy of 'tsarism', was first published in London in 1902, but officially reprinted in Russia already in 1906 (St. Petersburg: Znanie) and 1907 (St. Petersburg: Yasnaya Polyana). See P.A. Kropotkin, *Zapiski revolutsionera* [Notes of a Revolutionary] (Moscow: Moscowskiy rabochiy, 1988).

82 William E. Butler, *Russian Law*, *supra* note 23*, at 29; William E. Butler, *Soviet Law*, *supra* note 23*, at 22. The text of the Criminal Code of 22 March 1903 see *Rossiyskoe zakonodatel'stvo 10–20 vekov. Tom 9. Zakonodatel'stvo epokhi burzhuazno-demokraticheskikh revolyutsiy* [Russian Law of the Tenth–Twentieth Centuries. Vol.9. Law of the Period of Bourgeois-Democratic Revolutions] (Moscow: Yuridicheskaya literatura, 1994. O.I. Chistyakov, ed.), pp.271–320.

83 The text of the Basic State Laws of 23 April 1906 see *id.*, at 42–52.

84 D.C.B. Lieven, *supra* note 5*, at 239.

85 A.I. Spiridovich, *Zapiski zhandarma* [Notes of a Gendarme] (Khar'kov, 1928), pp.75–76.

86 Jonathan W. Daly, *Autocracy Under Siege: Security Police and Opposition in Russia, 1866–1905*, *supra* note 8* [Introduction], at 39.

87 Marc Szeftel, *The Russian Constitution of April 23, 1906. Political Institutions of the Duma Monarchy*, *supra* note 22*, at 150.

88 'The International Emergency Economic Powers Act: a Congressional Attempt to Control Presidential Emergency Power', *supra* note 87* [Ch. 1], at 1120.

89 1980 Report of the U.N. Special Rapporteur on Chile, U.N. Doc. A/35/522, para.31; 'The Siracusa Principles', *supra* note 41* [Ch. 2], at 8.

90 Cited D.C.B. Lieven, *supra* note 5*, at 240.

91 *Id.*, at 251.

92 Mikhail Menshikov, *Natsional'naya imperia* [National Empire] (Moscow: Imperial Tradition, 2004), pp.394–404.

93 31 V.I. Lenin, *Polnoe sobranie sochineniy* [Complete Works], at 106.

4 Emergency powers and states of emergency in Soviet and contemporary Russian law

1 Decree of the Presidium of the USSR Supreme Soviet of 22 June 1941 *'On a State of Martial Law'* (*O voennom polozhenii*) (*Vedomosti Verkhovnogo Soveta SSSR*, No.29, 1941); Resolution of the USSR Council of People's Commissars of 1 July 1941 *'On Additional Powers of the USSR People's Commissars During the War Period'* (*O rasshirenii prav narodnykh komissarov SSSR v usloviyakh voennogo vremeni*). Also see 3 *Reshenia partii i pravitel'stva po khoziaystvennym delam* [Decisions of the Party and Government on Economic Issues] (Moscow: Gospolitizdat, 1968), pp.40–41.

2 See, e.g. Resolution of the USSR State Committee on Defence of 19 October 1941 *'On Introduction of a State of Siege in the City of Moscow'* (*O vvedenii osadnogo polozhenia v g. Moscwe*), in *Kommunisticheskaia partia v period Velikoy Otechestvennoy voiny (iun' 1941 g. – 1945 g.). Dokumenty i materialy* [Communist Party in the Period of Great Patriotic War (June 1941–1945). Documents and Materials] (Moscow: Gospolitizdat, 1961), pp.97–98.

3 As a result of the 1988 constitutional amendments, the revised and expanded martial law powers were found in art.119(14). After the 1989–1990 amendments, those powers migrated to the new art.127(3)(16), becoming a

'presidential power'. For a translation, see Gordon B. Smith, *Soviet Politics* (NY: St. Martin's, 1992. 2nd edn), pp.370–72.

4 *Vedomosti Verkhovnogo Soveta SSSR*, No.49, 1988, item 727.
5 For a commentary on 'temporary presidential rule', see Elizabeth Fuller and Stephen Foye, 'Special Status, State of Emergency and President's Rule', 3 *Report on the USSR* (Radio Liberty/Radio Free Europe, Munich), No.5, 1991, pp.33–35. For a broader Soviet commentary on the new executive presidency, see B.M. Lazarev, 'Ob izmeneniakh v pravovom statuse Prezidenta SSSR' [On Changes in Legal Status of the USSR President], *Sovetskoe gosudarstvo i pravo*, No.8, 1991, pp.32–44.
6 *Vedomosti S'ezda narodnykh deputatov SSSR i Verkhovnogo Soveta SSSR*, No.15, 1990, item 250.
7 See V.N. Grigor'ev, 'Pravovoy rezhim chrezvychainogo polozhenia' [Legal Regime of a State of Emergency], *Pravovedenie*, 2 (1991), p.87.
8 Paul Goble, 'Draconian State of Emergency Law', *Report on the USSR* (Radio Liberty/Radio Free Europe, Munich), 4 May 1990.
9 For opposing views on the 'putsch' see, e.g. Mikhail S. Gorbachev, *Avgustovsky putsch. Prichiny i sledstvia* [August Putsch: Reasons and Consequences] (Moscow: Novosti, 1991); *Uroki avgusta 1991 goda. Narod i vlast'* [Lessons of August of 1991: People and Power] (Moscow: Yuridicheskaia literatura, 1994); Alexander Lebed', 'Spektakl' nazyvalsya putsch' [The Farce Was Called Putsch], *Literaturnaia Rossia*, No.34–36, 1993; Oleg Shenin, Vladimir Kryuchkov, Valentin Varennikov, *Process po delu GKChP* [The Case of GKChP] (Makhachkala: 'Golos Pravdy', 1995).
10 *Vedomosti S'ezda Narodnykh Deputatov RSFSR*, No.22, 1991, item 773.
11 *Human Rights and Legal Reform in the Russian Federation* (New York: Lawyers Committee for Human Rights, March 1993), pp.80–81.
12 'The Constitution of the Russian Federation' (adopted by referendum on 12 December 1993), 16 *Constitutions* (Release 94-3, May 1994), p.14.
13 Clinton L. Rossiter, *supra* note 3* [Introduction], at 299.
14 Carl J. Friedrich, *supra* note 1* [Ch. 1], at 117–118.
15 Nicole Questiaux, *supra* 16* [Preface], at 24.
16 See S. Jayakumar, 'Emergency Powers in Malaysia: Development of the Law 1957–1977', *The Malayan Law Journal*, January 1978, p.xxiv.
17 The U.S. Supreme Court's refusal to hold unconstitutional – in *Hirabayashi v United States* (320 U.S. 81 (1943)), *Korematsu v United States* (323 U.S. 213 (1944)), *Duncan v Kahanamoku* (327 U.S. 304 (1946)) – the government's internment of 119,803 Japanese-Americans (70,000 of whom were full-fledged U.S. citizens) during World War II is one of the most graphic illustrations of this observation. Rossiter prophetically observed: 'The next time it may be a slightly larger minority group. Whatever it was for its citizens of English, German, Jewish, or Chinese descent, the government of the American Republic was a naked dictatorship for its 70,000 Japanese-American citizens of the Pacific Coast' (Clinton L. Rossiter, *supra* note 3* [Introduction], at 283). For details see, e.g. Jacobus tenBroek, Edward N. Barnhart and Floyd W. Matson, *Prejudice, War and the Constitution: Causes and Consequences of the Evacuation of the Japanese Americans in World War II* (Berkeley & Los Angeles: University of California Press, 1970).
18 *Vedomosti S'ezda narodnykh deputatov RSFSR i Verkhovnogo Soveta RSFSR*, No.2, 1990, item 22.
19 NKAO is a predominantly Armenian enclave within the borders of Azerbaijan. In February 1988, the NKAO Supreme Soviet called for its transfer to jurisdiction of Armenia under a slogan of the 'right to self-determination' of ethnic (Christian) Armenians in NKAO. Gorbachev and the governments of

the USSR and Azerbaijan based their opposition to internal border changes and the annexation NKAO by Armenia on Article 78 of the USSR Constitution which stated that 'the territory of a union republic cannot be changed without its consent'.

20 *Vedomosti Verkhovnogo Soveta SSSR*, No.47, 1988, item 711; No.3, 1989, item 14.

21 See *Sovetskaya Kirgizia*, 8 June 1990. Also see S.D. Khazanov, 'Pravomernoe ogranichenie administrativno-pravovogo statusa grazhdan v usloviyakh chrezvychainogo polozhenia' [Legitimate Restrictions of the Legal Administrative Status of Citizens under a State of Emergency], *Pravovedenie*, No.5, 1991, p.63.

22 *Vedomosti Verkhovnogo Soveta SSSR*, No.3, 1990, item 40.

23 In her report to Congress C. Migdalovitz gave too excessive numbers of victims: 150 dead and 'thousands' wounded (Carol Migdalovitz, *Armenia-Azerbaijan Conflict* (CRS Report for Congress IB92109; Washington, D.C.: Congressional Research Service, The Library of Congress, updated 16 June 1994), p.3). By mistake, Migdalovitz called a state of exception (*osoboe polozhenie*) imposed in Karabakh 'martial law', but she was absolutely right in her conclusion that it was 'Michail Gorbachev's policy' that 'unleashed long-suppressed hostility between Armenia and Azerbaijan, and between each republic and Moscow' (p.3).

24 El'chibey's government ended in chaos, when in June of 1993 he fled to a remote village in the mountains and was stripped of presidential powers by the parliament. On 29 August 1993, more than 90 per cent of the electorate reportedly turned out for a national referendum, overwhelmingly expressing a lack of confidence in El'chibey's rule.

25 Hugh Pope and Guy Chazan, 'Georgia Sets Path of Confrontation. New President Saakashvili Angers Russia, Courts U.S. With Caucasus Ambitions', *Wall Street Journal*, 6 August 2004.

26 Members of the current government of President Mikhail Saakashvili continue referring to South Ossetia as the 'Tskhinvali region': 'Georgian Prime Minister Zurab Zhvania rejected any attempts to interfere with the Georgian–South Ossetian relations from the outside. "It's nobody's business what military units Georgia will deploy to the Tskhinvali region"'. (See, 'Georgia to Deal with Rebellious Autonomy Alone?', *RIA Novosti*, 2 June 2004).

27 The Emergency Proclamation was published in *Molodezh' Gruzii*, No.49, 14 December 1990.

28 *Georgia on Our Minds* (Report of a Fact-Finding Mission to the Republic of Georgia, July 1994, under the auspices of the Psychologists Against Nuclear Arms for Peace and Ecological Balance and the Transnational Foundation for Peace and Future Research), p.17. For the background of the Georgian–South Osettian conflict, see, e.g. Ronald Grigor Suny, *The Making of the Georgian Nation* (Bloomington, IN: Indiana University Press, 1988).

29 See, e.g. Gennady Zhavoronkov, 'Kishinev-Komrat: chetyre dnya protivostoyania' [Cisinau-Komrat: Four Days of Resistance], *Moscowskie novosti*, No.44, 4 November 1990.

30 *Vedomosti S'ezda narodnykh deputatov RSFSR i Verkhovnogo Soveta RSFSR*, No.46, 1991, items 1546, 1550.

31 As a populist tool in President Yeltsin's re-election campaign, the Russian government signed a 'peace treaty' with the Chechen separatists which was defined by the former Minister of the Interior Anatoly S. Kulikov as a 'national betrayal' and a capitulation to 'forces that are seeking the systematic elimination of the Russian state' (see 'Vsyo postroeno na lzhi i dvusmyslennosti' [Everything Is Built on Lies and Ambiguity], *Sovetskaya Rossia*,

5 October 1996). Subsequent events, including Chechen invasion of Dagestan and deadly bombings of apartment buildings in Moscow, Volgodonsk and Buynaksk in 1999 proved that Kulikov was right. Previously classified documents of that period, including a transcript of a secret meeting on 16 June 1995 between a future president of Chechnya Aslan Maskhadov and Minister Kulikov (with participation of an OCSE representative) were published in a book by a former Chairman of the State Duma Committee on Nationalities: Vladimir Zorin, *Chechnya: Kremnisty put' k miru. Dnevnik ne dlya sebya* [Chechnya: A Thorny Road to Peace. A Diary Not for Myself] (Moscow: 'Violanta', 1997), pp.304–377.

32 For a legal and constitutional analysis of attempts of Russian federal authorities to solve the Chechen crisis see, e.g. Elena Mizulina, 'Chechensky crisis i konstitutsionnoe pravosudie' [Chechen Crisis and Constitutional Justice], *Svobodnaya mysl'*, No.12, 1995, pp.20–30; A.I. Dolgova, O.E. Evlanova, 'Nekotorye pravovye problemy otsenok sobytiy v Chechenskoy Respublike' [Some Legal Problems of Evaluation of Events in the Chechen Republic], *Organizovanny terrorizm i organizovannaia prestupnost'* [Organised Terrorism and Organised Crime] (Moscow: Russian Association of Criminology, 2002. O.I. Makarova, etc., eds), pp.86–102. Also see Russian Constitutional Court's decision No.10-p of 31 July 1995 regarding constitutionality of Yeltsin's secret unpublished decrees No.2137 of 30 November 1994 and No.2166 of 9 December 1994 and Resolution of the Russian government No.1360 of 9 December 1994 on 'restoration of constitutional law and order' in Chechnya: *Vestnik Konstitutsionnogo suda*, No.4–5, 1995. See commentaries of the decrees in a book by a prominent member of the Italian Communist Party: Antonio Rubbi, *Yeltsiniada. Pervoe desyatiletie postsovetskoy Rossii* [Yeltsinism: The First Decade of Post-Soviet Russia. Original title of the book: *La Russia di Eltsin*] (Moscow: Mezhdunarodnye otnoshenia, 2004), pp.287–290.

33 While denouncing indiscriminate use of Stalin's 'justice' against the Chechens and Ingush, it's hard to deny disproportionate collaboration of representatives of those ethnic groups with Nazi invaders. Only 11,000 Ingush fought against Germany in the Red Army (Alexander Belousov, 'Ingushskaya divizia' [The Ingush Division], *Argumenty i fakty*, No.17, April 2004, p.24). 2,300 Chechens and Ingush in the Soviet armed forces were killed or lost in action in 1941–1945 comparing to 13,000 Soviet soldiers from Buryats, a twice smaller ethnic group than Chechens and Ingush combined, or 10,700 Ossetians, a 50 per cent smaller people (*Rossia i SSSR v voynakh XX veka: Statisticheskoe issledovanie* [Russia and USSR in Wars of the Twentieth Century: A Statistical Study] (Moscow: 2001), p.238). In January 1942, draft-dodging among Chechens and Ingush was equal to 50 per cent; in 1943 it reached 62 per cent. At the same time, the largest pro-Nazi subversive group in Checheno-Ingushetia – 'National Socialist Party of Caucasian Brothers' – reportedly exceeded 5,000 members. Another major saboteur group, 'Special Party of Caucasian Brothers' had a programme goal of 'establishing in the Caucasus a free brotherly Federated republic of states of brotherly peoples of the Caucasus under mandate of the German Empire'. In order to facilitate Nazi invasion to the Caucasus, Checheno-Ingushetia witnessed a number of mutinies in the fall of 1942. In 1941–1944, Soviet law enforcement agencies destroyed 197 gangs in the CIASSR; 657 of their members were killed, 2,762 were taken prisoners, and 1,113 surrendered, thus making 4,532 a total number of defeated gangsters. (See, e.g. Igor' Pykhalov, ''Kavkazskie orly' tretiego reikha' ['Caucasian Eagles' of the Third Reich], *Spetsnaz Rossii*, No.10, October 2001). The most complete 600-pages study *Pod znamenami vraga.*

Antisovetskie formirovania v sostave germanskikh vooruzhennykh sil 1941–1945 gg. [Under Enemy's Banners: Anti-Soviet Formations in German Armed Forces (1941–1945)] (Moscow, 'EKSMO', 2004) by S.I. Drobyazko contains numerous quotations from official Nazi documents praising 'mountaineers', Crimean Tatars, Kolmyks and some other 'repressed peoples' who proved to be 'excellent' in their fight against the Soviet army.

34 Archival evidence doesn't corroborate a myth about Chechens, Ingush and other 'repressed peoples' as the main victims of Stalin's system of repression. See, e.g. a remarkable study by J. Arch Getty, Gabor T. Rittersporn, and Victor N. Zemskov with their conclusion: 'In comparison with their weight in the general population, Russians, Belorussians, Turkmen, Germans and Poles were over-represented in the camps ... On the other hand, Ukrainians, Jews, Central Asians (except Turkmen) and people from the Caucasus were less represented in the GULAG system than in the population of the country; as national groups they suffered proportionately less' (*supra* note 70* [Ch. 3], at 1027–1028).

35 In an 'official' two-volume history of the CIASSR from ancient times through the 1970s (published in Grozny in 1972), one can find just one paragraph (of four lines) dedicated to this event: 'In 1944 as a result of violation of Lenin's principles of national and state building and socialist legality Chechen-Ingush ASSR was liquidated. The 20th Congress of the CPSU corrected these violations'. (See *Ocherki istorii Checheno-Ingushskoy ASSR s drevneishikh vremen do nashikh dney. Tom II. 1917–1970 gody.* [History of the Chechen-Ingush ASSR from Ancient Times until Our Days. Vol.1: 1917–1970] (Grozny: Checheno-Ingushskoye knizhnoye izdatel'stvo, 1972. In two vols., p.260).

36 Contemporary foreign reporters tend to use the numbers that were alleged by the Ingush side. Lately, Associated Press has reminded the Western audience of 50,000 ethnic Ingush who had to flee their homes in North Ossetia (see, e.g. Burt Herman, 'Russia School Siege Stokes Ethnic Tensions', *AP*, 7 September 2004).

37 Text of the decree see in: *Raion chrezvychainogo polozhenia (Severnaya Osetia i Ingushetia)* [The Zone of a State of Emergency (North Ossetia & Ingushetia] (Vladikavkaz, 1994), pp.1–4. Also see President's Decree No.1346 '*On Provisional Administration on the Territory of North Ossetian SSR and Ingush Republic*' of 11 November 1992; President's Decree No.1350 '*On Temporary Boundaries of a State of Emergency Zone*' of 12 November 1992.

38 The last provision was especially topical. Ethnic groups and tribes of Northern Caucasus have been traditionally armed; in dire straits – heavily armed. How much weapons are stored in the region we can judge by the results of a programme for the voluntary surrender of arms sponsored by law enforcement officials in Dagestan, another republic of Northern Caucasus. In just two months (1 October 2003 to 1 December 2003), local citizens surrendered more than a ton of explosives (including large quantities of hexogen and ammonite), 57 artillery rounds and missiles, three guided anti-tank rockets, 6,807 grenades, 1,256 detonators, 1,151,033 bullets, 962 rifles and pistols, 291 grenade launchers, and three flame-throwers. A leading American expert on the Caucasus and conflict in Chechnya Robert Bruce Ware correctly observed that the 'surrender programme recovered only a small fraction of the weapons, ammunition, and explosives circulating in Dagestan, since most of those wishing to dispose of these items would be better compensated on the black market'. (Peter Lavelle, 'Q&A: R.B. Ware – Chechnya's Future', 2 *The Untimely Thoughts* 117 (7 September 2004)).

39 Ann Sheehy, 'State of Emergency Extended in North Ossetia and Ingushetia', *RFE/RL Daily Report*, 29 January 1993.

40 Ann Sheehy, 'State of Emergency Extended in North Ossetia/Ingushetia', *RFE/RL Daily Report*, 1 June 1994.

41 Natalia Pulina, 'Ukaz prezidenta po Prigorodnomu raionu budet 37-m' [President Has Signed the 37th Decree on Prigorodny district], *Nezavisimaya gazeta*, 5 August 1997. More on Victor Polyanichko and his work in another emergency zone – in Azerbaijan in 1991 see Aleksandr Shagiakhmetov, 'Pogib na postu' [He Was Murdered When Being on Duty], *Zavtra*, No.30, August 1997.

42 See, e.g. *Segodnya*, 9 November 1994.

43 See the table in *Raion chrezvychainogo polozhenia*, *supra* note 37*, at 63–64. Radio Free Europe/Radio Liberty gives a bigger number of victims of the 'fighting in November 1992': '500–600 people'. Reuter, on the contrary, gives a much smaller number: 'about 200 people'. (See 'Ingush President Warns Tensions Are Rising', 1 *RFE/RL Newsline*, No.73, 15 July 1997; Timothy Heritage, 'Russian defence minister seeks Yeltsin's help', *Reuter*, 20 July 1997). Both figures are incorrect.

44 See, e.g. *Interfax*, 27 March 1996.

45 See, e.g. *Interfax*, 29–30 March 1996.

46 Pliev also asked Yeltsin to reject any attempt to link the repatriation of Ingush refugees to the situation in Chechnya. (Also see 'Ingush Want Direct Moscow Rule in Disputed Region', *Monitor: A Daily Briefing on the Post-Soviet States*, 21 August 1995; Liz Fuller, 'Ingush Congress Calls for Federal Rule', *RFE/RL Daily Report*, 2 September 1994).

47 See, e.g. *Nezavisimaya gazeta*, 23 July 1997.

48 See, e.g. Natalia Pulina, 'Ivan Rybkin protiv prezidentskogo pravleniya' [Ivan Rybkin Is Against President's Rule], *Nezavisimaya gazeta*, 29 July 1997; Natalia Pulina, *supra* note 41*; Victoria Grankina, 'Peregovory imeut perspectivu' [Negotiations Have a Good Perspective], *Nezavisimaya gazeta*, 5 August 1997.

49 See, e.g. *Nezavisimaya gazeta*, 2 August 1997.

50 Victoria Grankina, *supra* note 48*.

51 The North Caucasus is not the only region prone to the conflicts provoked by the 1991 Law 'On the Rehabilitation of the Repressed Peoples'. At the end of July 1997, *Nezavisimaya gazeta* published a lead article titled 'New Zones for Territorial Redistribution Emerge in Russia. Ignoring the Sad Experience of the North Caucasus Can Cause Destabilisation in the Volga Region'. The newspaper learnt about a recent secret visit of Saratov Governor Ayatskov to a territory of the Staropoltavsky district (*raion*) in the neighbouring Volgograd (former Stalingrad) region (*oblast*), where he met with local citizens. None of the Volgograd authorities were informed of the visit or invited to attend the meeting. The reason was that the Saratov delegation came to call on local people in Volgograd region to create a German autonomous area in their territory, which would then become a part of the Saratov region. The topic was very sensitive. The Germans began settling down in the Volga region in the sixteenth century; their autonomy existed in the Russian Empire and then USSR until 1941, when it was liquidated by a Stalin's decree. Some 700,000 to 800,000 Germans were deported to Siberia and Kazakhstan, thus, joining a list of 'repressed peoples'. Since *perestroika* days, most of ethnic German population has moved to Germany, and their share in a total population of the Volgograd oblast has shrank to less than eight per cent. The interest of Saratov governor had nothing to do with 'historical justice' or 'historical rehabilitation of the repressed people'. Apparently it lied in the economic sphere – in oil and gas resources on the territory of the Staropoltavsky district. According to the newspaper's analysts, oil mining

annually brings about 35 billion roubles (over US$6 million) in taxes to the district's budget (*Nezavisimaya gazeta*, 25 July 1997).

52 Democratic character of the first Russian parliament is beyond any doubt. According to the Central Election Commission, on 4 March 1990, 6,705 candidates ran for 1,068 seats in the Congress of People's Deputy (CPD) – an average of more than six per district. About 300 electoral districts had a race between more than four candidates; 24 electoral districts – more than 20! (See, e.g. *Human Rights and Legal Reform in the Russian Federation*, *supra* note 11*, at 44–45).

53 David Johnson, a leading American expert in Russian affairs and Research Director of the influential Washington-based Centre for Defense Information honestly admitted: 'I confess to remaining deeply disturbed by the enthusiastic demonisation of the opposition to Boris Yeltsin in the 1992–93 period, culminating in the military assault on the Russian Parliament. Western journalists, Western academics, and Western government officials (with rare exception) all contributed to the undermining of democratic institutions and practices as they encouraged Yeltsin's authoritarian tendencies and the adoption of policies that had little public support. *We, and Russia, continue to live with the consequences of that crucial period*' (see *Johnson's Russia List*, 1 May 1997) (*italics added – A.D.*). Seven years later, amid numerous accusations of Putin in his attempts to 'take Russia a step closer to authoritarian regime' and to 'undermine' Yeltsin-style 'democracy in Russia' and non-existing 'checks and balances in the Russian federal system' (see 'A Letter of 100' in *Johnson's Russia List*, No.8385, 28 September 2004), Johnson repeated that he considers 'the September-October 1993 events ... *the turning point* in post-Soviet Russia' (*Johnson's Russia List*, No.8388, 1 October 2004) (*italics added – A.D.*).

54 *Vedomosti S'ezda narodnykh deputatov RSFSR i Verkhovnogo Soveta RSFSR*, No.44, 1991, items 1455–1456.

55 Stephen F. Cohen, 'Clinton's Yeltsin, Yeltsin's Russia', *The Nation*, 10 October 1994, p.373. Also see Stephen F. Cohen, *Failed Crusade: America and the Tragedy of Post-Communist Russia* (New York – London: W.W. Norton & Company, 2000); published in Russian (Moscow: AIRO-XX, 2001).

56 Deputy Director of the Kennan Institute for Advanced Russian Studies wrote: 'Bolshevist monetarism adapted quite comfortably to the historical terrain of Soviet experience, as the Gaidar team exhibited the same ideological fervor that had motivated its Leninist precursors' (Peter Stavrakis, *State Building in Post-Soviet Russia: The Chicago Boys and the Decline of Administrative Capacity* (Washington, D.C.: Kennan Institute for Advanced Russian Studies, August, October 1993. Occasional Paper No.254), p.56). The term 'Bolshevist monetarism' was later see transformed into a similarly appropriate definition – 'market Bolshevism' (see Peter Reddaway and Dmitri Glinski, *Tragedy of Russia's Reforms: Market Bolshevism against Democracy* (Washington, 2001)).

57 'All the time the two national television news channels, both government-controlled, kept pumping out the line that Parliament was dominated by "Communist hardliners", – the *Guardian* wrote. – The fact that most MPs favoured the market economy, but disagreed with Yeltsin over how to get there, was suppressed' (see Jonathan Steele, 'Inside Story: Chaos Theory', the *Guardian*, 13 November 1993).

58 See decision of the Russian Constitutional Court of 23 March 1993 on OPUS in *Vestnik Konstitutsionnogo suda*, No.1, 1994. For comments on the decision see, e.g. A.A. Belkin, 'Delo o Prezidentskom obraschenii k narodu 20 marta 1993 goda' [The Case of the President's Appeal to People of 20 March 1993], *Pravovedenie*, No.3, 1994, pp.48–63.

176   *Notes*

Vedomosti S'ezda narodnykh deputatov RSFSR i Verkhovnogo Soveta RSFSR,
   No.17, 1991, items 510, 512; No.22, 1991, item 776.
60 An Irish scholar is correct when saying that 'just as an abolition of the Party's
   leading role in society signalled the end of its monopoly on political life, so too
   the centralised Soviet government was undermined by the new parliamentary
   institutions. Their creation inaugurated the final crisis of Soviet power: they
   challenged the legitimacy of central rule from Moscow and heralded the end
   of the Soviet empire ... Indeed, the Spring [of 1990] election campaign ...
   may be seen as the high-point of the democratic debate'. (See Judith Devlin,
   *The Rise of the Russian Democrats: The Causes and Consequences of the Elite
   Revolution* (Aldershot: Edward Elgar, 1995), pp.152–153). March 1990 elec-
   tions were an explosion of democratic sentiments, beliefs and expectations.
   Elections to the Russian parliament of 1990 were 'the freest ever held in
   Russia', concluded the New York-based Lawyers Committee for Human
   Rights. The same conclusion was reached in the *Report of the United States
   Election Delegation Studying the Evolution of the Electoral Process in the
   Soviet Union* prepared by the U.S. Federal Election Commission (March
   1990). (See *Human Rights and Legal Reform in the Russian Federation, supra*
   note 11*, at 45).
61 In his memoirs, the former head of Yeltsin's security service Alexander
   Korzhakov made a stunning revelation: on 28 March 1993, everything was
   ready to gas the Congress deputies with chloropicrin and arrest them if they
   voted to impeach the President. Yeltsin 'approved the plan without any hesitation'. (See Alexander Korzhakov, *Boris El'tsin: ot rassveta do zakata* [Boris
   Yeltsin: From Sunrise to Sunset] (Moscow: Interbook, 1997), pp.158–160.
   Also see a new and more complete version of the book: Alexander
   Korzhakov, *Boris El'tsin: ot rassveta do zakata. Posleslovie* [Boris Yeltsin:
   From Sunrise to Sunset. Epilogue] (Moscow: DetektivPress, 2004)).
62 See Jonathan Hartlyn, *supra* note 13* [Introduction], at 305–306.
63 Cited in Subrata Roy Chowdhury, *Rule of Law in a State of Emergency. The
   Paris Minimum Standards of Human Rights Norms in a State of Emergency*
   (New York: St. Martin's Press, 1989), p.4.
64 Those commentators who believed that the 'gridlock between the president
   and the Supreme Soviet has not been wholly unhealthy', and that 'President
   Yeltsin is forced to accept the Supreme Soviet as a legitimate body; he cannot
   simply sidestep the legislature and govern by decree' (see Bruce L.R. Smith,
   'Constitutionalism in the New Russia', in *Law and Democracy in the New
   Russia* (Washington: The Brookings Institution, 1993. Bruce Smith and
   Gennady Danilenko, eds), p.9), appeared to be naive. 'With a stroke of
   the pen, Yeltsin had wiped out Russia's embryonic and uneasy separation
   of powers. Mao had bested Montesquieu' (Robert Sharlet, 'Russian Constitutional Crisis: Law and Politics Under Yeltsin', 9 *Post-Soviet Politics*,
   No.4, October–December 1993, p.327). 'It was a highly risky decision, since
   it was plainly illegal', wrote the *Guardian* (Jonathan Steele, *supra* note
   58*). 'Rarely in history has there been a coup prepared so ineptly and so
   openly. Yeltsin violated the constitution so flagrantly that there could be no
   talk of his having "made a mistake" or "exceeding his powers"', commented a
   deputy of the Moscow City Council (Boris Kagarlitsky, *Square Wheels. How
   Russian Democracy Got Derailed* (New York: Monthly Review Press, 1994),
   p.197).
65 *Sobranie aktov Prezidenta i Pravitel'stva Rossiyskoy Federatsii,* No.39, 1993,
   item 3597. Texts of the decree and Yeltsin's TV speech *also* see, e.g. *Moscwa,
   osen'–93. Khronika protivostoyania* [Moscow, Autumn of 93. Chronicle of
   Resistance] (Moscow: Respublika, 1995. 2nd rev. edn), pp.i–xiii.

66 *Sobranie aktov Prezidenta n Pravitel'stva Rossiyskoy Federatsii*, No.43, 1993, item 4089; No.44, 1993, item 4188. Moscow City Council was dissolved by a special Decree No.1594 of 7 October 1993 for its resolution (adopted overwhelmingly on the morning of 22 September 1993) condemning Yeltsin's. The irony is that in the 1990 elections (held simultaneously with the Russian parliamentary elections), pro-Yeltsin radical 'democrats' scored a particularly impressive victory in the Moscow city legislature: candidates from 'Democratic Russia' bloc won 292 out of 465 seats.

67 *Vestnik Konstitutsionnogo suda*, No.4, 1994.

68 See, e.g. Alexander Domrin, 'Konstitutsionnaia protsedura impichmenta v SShA' [Constitutional Procedure of Impeachment in the USA], *Zhurnal rossiyskogo prava*, No.7, 2004.

69 *Rossiyskaya gazeta*, 23 September 1993.

70 *Informatsionny Bulleten'* [Informational Bulletin], No.2, 1993, p.26.

71 Next day Yeltsin issued two supplementary decrees: No.1578 *'On Urgent Measures for Ensuring the Regime of a State of Emergency in Moscow'* and No.1580 *'On Additional Measures for Ensuring the Regime of a State of Emergency in Moscow'*, and one more on October 9: No.1615 *'On Extension of a State of Emergency in Moscow'* (See *Sobranie aktov Prezidenta n Pravitel'stva Rossiyskoy Federatsii*, No.40, 1993, items 3748, 3751; No.41, items 3909, 3923).

72 In the opinion of Pavel Felgengauer, defence correspondent for the daily *Segodnya*, the 'use of the army in the attack against the parliament may have made it subsequently easier for the Moscow leaders to send troops to Chechnya ... Once you begin to use force to solve political problems at home, you tend to use it again' (see Stephanie Baker, 'Russia: Today Marks Third Anniversary Of Moscow Rebellion', *RFE/RL Daily Report*, 3 October 1996). 'The first shot on the White House was the first shot of the Chechnya war', an ethnic Chechen and former speaker of the Russian parliament Ruslan Khasbulatov observed (see Brian Killen, 'Russian Democracy Traces Path from Tanks to Polls', *Reuters*, 1 October 1996).

73 *Nezavisimaya gazeta*, 19 October 1993. British magazine *The Spectator* wrote about '1,000 arrested' ('Portrait of the Week', *The Spectator*, 9 October 1993, p.4).

74 'Massovye narushenia prav cheloveka v Rossii' [Mass Violations of Human Rights in Russia], *Nezavisimaya gazeta*, 23, 26 July 1994. One of those who was severely beaten by Moscow OMON (Special Police Unit) was a parliamentarian and Secretary of the Constitutional Commission Oleg Rumyantsev – 'Russian James Madison', as David Remnick called him in *The Washington Post* in 1990.

75 *Sobranie aktov Prezidenta n Pravitel'stva Rossiyskoy Federatsii*, No.43, 1993, item 4080.

76 Ibid, No.41, 1993, item 3921.

77 *Justice Delayed. The Russian Constitutional Court and Human Rights* (New York: Lawyers Committee for Human Rights, 1995), p.6.

78 Eugene Huskey, *Presidential Power in Russia* (Armonk, NY–London; M.E. Sharpe, 1999), p.34.

79 See I.G. Shablinsky, *Predely vlasti. Bor'ba za rossiyskuyu konstitutsionnuyu reformu (1989–1995 gg.)* [Limits of Power. Struggle for the Constitutional Reform in Russia (1989–1995)] (Moscow: Moscow Public Science Foundation, 1997), p.204; Leon Aron, *supra* note 4* [Ch. 1], at 550 (quoting Michael Gordon, 'Yeltsin Attack Strategy: Bursts Followed by Lulls', *The New York Times*, 5 October 1993, p.17).

80 For details see, e.g. Alexander Domrin, 'Burning Bush of October 1993. Russian Liberal Mass Media and New Evidence of the Tragic Events in

Moscow', *Johnson's Russia List*, No.7360, 9 October 2003, quoting new Russian sources.

81 Eugene Huskey, *supra* note 79*, at 34.

82 *Compare:* 'The overwhelming majority of those who were killed at Ostankino were unarmed demonstrators ... There can be no talk in this case of a pre-planned assault carried out by trained groups organised along military lines ... What occurred at Ostankino was the cold-blooded slaughter of people who had no chance to resist, or even to put up passive resistance' (Alexander Buzgalin and Andrei Kolganov, *Bloody October in Moscow: Political Repression in the Name of Reform* (New York: Monthly Review Press, 1994. Renfrey Clarke, trans.), pp.187–188).

83 Summary executions of the White House defenders really happened. Some people who left the White House in the morning of 4 October were found shot dead in the evening. The official figures covered only the period of 21 September–4 October 1993. However, according to some sources, on the night of 4 October 1993, 29 more people were killed (*Nezavisimaya gazeta*, 7 October 1993). The range of an estimated number of victims is quite broad. An early Congressional Research Service Report for U.S. Congress mentioned *'well over one hundred'* killed (Stuart D. Goldman, *Russia's Violent Showdown of October 3–4: Analysis and Implications* (CRS Report for Congress 93-884 F; Washington, D.C.: Congressional Research Service, The Library of Congress, 6 October 1993), p.2). A famous dissident historian wrote about *'hundreds dead, thousands wounded'* (Roy Medvedev, 'Out with the old, and in with what?', the *Guardian*, 9 October 1993. *Reprinted* 'October 1993: The Exploration Begins', *Johnson's Russia List*, 20 August 1996). *The New York Times* wondered if *'1,052'* was the exact number ('Russians Wonder if Revolt's Casualties Were Higher than Reported', *The New York Times*, 11 November 1993). Russian deputy Mikhail Chelnokov estimated the number as *'about one thousand and a half'* (Mikhail Chelnokov, 'Rasputinschina kontsa veka' [Rasputin's Rule at the End of the Century], *Sovetskaya Rossia*, 9 January 1997). French *Le Monde* also reported about *1,500 killed* (see Antonio Rubbi, *supra* note 32*, at 200). When censorship was lifted, *Nezavisimaya gazeta* in a series of eyewitness accounts published a story of an Interior Ministry officer speaking of 'hundreds' of corpses being secretly taken from the White House and burned outside the city. Victor Ilyukhin was quoted in Russian mass media saying that he counted more than 200 corpses at a square at Rochdel'kaya street behind the White House (*Komsomol'skaya pravda*, 15 October 1993).

84 Boris Kagarlitsky, *supra* note 65*, at 218. As an eyewitness Kagarlitsky testified in his book that the official figure of victims (142 killed) 'was a mockery – the real number of dead had to have been several times greater' (*ibid.*).

85 *Information Prepared for the Human Rights Committee on the Periodic Report of the Russian Federation Under Article 40 of the Covenant on Civil and Political Rights by the Lawyers Committee for Human Rights* (New York: Lawyers Committee for Human Rights, 1995), p.4. All in all, 'the rudder of legitimate government and the rule of law – the only principles of statehood most Russians have more or less agreed on since the Soviet empire collapsed in 1991 – was seriously compromised', summed up Peter Reddaway of George Washington University (Peter Reddaway, 'Dictatorial Drift', *The New York Times*, 10 October 1993).

86 Stephen White and Ronald J. Hill, 'Russia, Former Soviet Union, and Eastern Europe', in *The Referendum Experience in Europe* (London: Macmillan Press Ltd, 1996. Michael Gallagher and Pie Vincenzo Uleri, eds), p.163.

87 Calculations made by a group of sociologists headed by Alexander Sobyanin,

and in a separate study by Elena Lukyanova ('Iz istorii bezzakonia. Kak v 1993 godu prinimali Osnovnoy zakon RF' [From History of Lawlessness: How the RF Fundamental Law Was Adopted in 1993], *Nezavisimaya gazeta*, 1 October 1999) indicated massive fraud in the 12 December 1993 vote. According to Sobyanin's report, the constitutional referendum did not really receive a voter turnout of 50 per cent of the electorate, the amount necessary to declare the elections valid. Sobyanin's study showed that *only 46.1 per cent* of the electorate actually went to the polls. (*Izvestia*, 4 May 1994; *also* see Alexander Tarasov, *Provokatsia. Versia sobytiy 3–4 oktyabrya 1993 g. v Moscwe* [Provocation: A Version of Events in Moscow on 3–4 October 1993] (Moscow: 'Phoenix', 1994), pp.58–60). Vyacheslav Kostikov, the former presidential spokesman (1992–1995), wrote in his memoirs (that cost him his job as a Russian Ambassador to the Vatican) that on 13 December 1993 he saw in Yeltsin's office a paper with the results of the referendum. Somebody – loyal Kostikov doesn't say who – with a strike of a pen, added 10 per cent of votes for the Yeltsin's Constitution. (See Vyacheslav Kostikov, *Roman s prezidentom* [An Affair with the President] (Moscow: Vagrius, 1997), pp.266–267). We may never get a definitive answer – the ballots were immediately destroyed.

88 See, e.g. *A Modern Day Czar? Presidential Power and Human Rights in the Russian Federation* (New York: Lawyers Committee for Human Rights, 1995), p.iii. 'Superpresidentialism' of the new Russian constitution became a natural consequence of the coup. 'If you are determined to impose capitalism by any means, to pour the medicine down people's throats against their will, you can't achieve your objective with genuine consent. So you opt for some kind of iron fist, for a czar, even if you choose to call him – as did *Izvestia*'s Washington correspondent, unaware of the contradiction – a "democratic dictator"' (Daniel Singer, 'Putsch in Moscow', *The Nation*, 25 October 1993, p.449). In the same article Singer wrote about 'the blood spilled, not despite but because of Boris Yeltsin' (*ibid.*).

89 N.I. Biryukov & V.M. Sergeev, *Stanovlenie institutov predstavitel'noy vlasti v sovremennoy Rossii* [Formation of Representative Power Institutions in Modern Russia] (Moscow: 'Izdatel'sky servis', 2004), pp.433–434.

90 In an alarming conclusion of another American scholar, Yeltsin 'demonstrates how attempts to copy the American system are likely to end up in dictatorship, as they have so often in Latin America' (Robert V. Daniels, 'Yeltsin's No Jefferson. More Like Pinochet', *The New York Times*, 2 October 1993, p.23).

91 See Amy J. Weisman, 'Separation of Powers in Post Communist Government: A Constitutional Case Study of the Russian Federation', 10 *The American University Journal of International Law & Policy* (Summer 1995), p.1397.

92 See draft constitutions in: *Konstitutsionnoe soveschanie. Stenogrammy. Materialy. Documenty. Tom 1* [Constitutional Assembly. Stenographic Reports. Materials. Documents. Vol.1] (Moscow: Yuridicheskaya literatura, 1995. S.A. Filatov, V.S. Chernomyrdin, etc., eds), pp.11–66, 495–557.

93 Constitutional Commission was formed by the First Congress of People's Deputies of Russia on 16 June 1990 and was headed by Chairman of the Russian Supreme Soviet Boris Yeltsin until he was elected President and immediately got 'dissatisfied' with the results of the work of the Constitutional Commission. In April 1993, Yeltsin convened the Constitutional Assembly, stuffed it with his sympathisers and blocked participation of his parliamentary opponents in the Assembly.

94 On violations of the Constitution by President Yeltsin in the 'trophy art law case' see Alexander Domrin, 'The Trophy Art Law as an Illustration of the Current Status of Separation of Powers and Legislative Process in Russia',

Democracy and the Rule of Law (Washington: Congressional Quarterly Press, 2001. Norman Dorsen & Prosser Gifford, eds), pp.283–288, 419–421.

95 Clinton L. Rossiter, *The American Presidency* (New York & Toronto: The New American Library, 1960. 2nd edn), p.48.

96 Article 93 of the Russian Constitution provides for an extremely complicated five-stage impeachment process that needs to be accomplished in a three-month period. In practical terms, the Constitutions of Russia makes the President technically unimpeachable.

97 'Until the October 1993 events, this was a *civilised* and constructive game compared to other post-World War II transitions, such as the "bullet shows" of Latin America, the military coups in Africa and, nearer to Moscow, the civil wars in the Balkans, the Caucasus and Central Asia', wrote an American scholar. (Robert Sharlet, *supra* note 65*, at 315). 'When Boris Yeltsin abolished Russia's parliamentary system in September 1993, he not only changed the "rules" of the game ... he put an end to the game altogether', concluded another American analyst. (Jeffrey Hahn, 'Analyzing Parliamentary Development in Russia', in *Democratisation in Russia: the Development of Legislative Institutions* (Arnonk, N.Y., London, England: M.E. Sharpe. J.W. Hahn, ed.), p.3). Archie Brown's observation that after October 1993 'neither the state authorities in Russia nor their principal opponents were agreed on the rules of the game'[1] stayed valid until Yeltsin's resignation and Putin's consolidation of political power in Russia during his first presidential term. (Archie Brown, 'The Russian Transition in Comparative and Russian Perspective', 63 *Social Research* 2 (Summer 1996), p.410).

98 See *Johnson's Russia List*, No.8392, 3 October 2004.

99 Probably the most interesting bill on a state of emergency at that early stage was drafted and introduced by Victor Ilyukhin, then Chairman of the State Duma's Committee on Security.

100 *Federal Register*, 18 September 2001 (Vol.66, No.181). Presidential Documents. Page 48199.

101 Bernard H. Siegan, *supra* note 22* [Ch. 2], at 87.

102 Alexander Domrin, *Federal'noe vmeshatel'stvo v dela sub'ektov federatsii. Opyt pravovogo regulirovania i praktika primenenia v zarubezhnikh stranakh* [Federal Interventions Worldwide: Transnational Law and Practice of Its Implementation] (Moscow: Council for Foreign and Defence Policy, [February] 1995). Also see, e.g. Alexander Domrin, 'Chrezvychainie metody pazreshenia conflictnykh situatsiy v zarubezhnykh federativnykh gosudarstvakh' [Emergency Measures of Solution of Conflict Situations in Foreign Federative States], *Vestnik RIA Novosti*, No.8, 1996; Alexander Domrin, 'Federal'naya interventsiya: osobennosti pravovogo regulirovaniya v zarubezhnykh stranakh' [A Federal Intervention: Peculiarities of Legal Regulations in Foreign Countries] in *Ocherki konstitutsionnogo prava inostrannykh gosudarstv* [Essays on Constitutional Law of Foreign Countries] (Moscow: Spark, 1999).

103 Alexander Domrin, 'Federal'noe vmeshatel'stvo v dela sub'ektov federatsii. Opyt pravovogo regulirovania i praktika primenenia v zarubezhnikh stranakh' [Federal Interventions Worldwide: Transnational Law and Practice of Its Implementation], *Nezavisimaya gazeta*, No.36, 28 February 1995.

104 R.G. Abdulatipov, 'Tol'ko zakon mozhet ostanovit' bezzakonie. Ob institute federal'nogo vmeshatel'stva v dela sub'ektov federatsii' [Only Law Can Stop Lawlessness. On the Institution of a Federal Intervention], *Nezavisimaya gazeta*, 16 July 1996.

105 For a more detailed analysis of the new act, see Alexander Domrin, 'Federal'niy konstitutsionniy zakon "O chrezvychainom polozhenii"' [Federal Con-

stitutional Law on a State of Emergency], *Sovet Federatsii i konstitutsionnie protsessy v sovremennoy Rossii* [Federation Council & the Constitutional Process in Contemporary Russia] (Moscow: Institute of Law and Public Policy, No.1, 2002); Alexander Domrin, 'Novy Federal'niy konstitutsionniy zakon "O chrezvychainom polozhenii"' ['A New Federal Constitutional Law "On a State of Emergency"'], *Predstavitel'naia vlast' – XXI vek: zakonodatel'stvo, kommentarii, problemy*, No.3, 2004.

Conclusion

1 A state of emergency in Osh region of Kirghiz Soviet Socialist Republic (of the USSR) was introduced in June 1990 following riots between Uzbeks and Kirghiz that had led to more than 200 victims. It took authorities more than a month to restore order in the region. It was only on 30 September 1995, when Assembly of People's Representatives of Kyrgyzstan voted to lift the state of emergency.
2 Western mass media also reported that Minster of Defence Pavel Grachev repeatedly raised this question (see, e.g. Scott Parrish, 'Debate over Imposing State of Emergency in Chechnya', *Open Media Research Institute (OMRI) Daily Digest*, 14 August 1996). Besides the Minister of Defence, the necessity to impose a state of emergency in Chechnya was recommended by Prime Minister Viktor Chernomyrdin, but was opposed by the Minister of Justice Valentin Kovalev, Security Council Secretary Aleksandr Lebed', and, eventually, President Yeltsin.
3 *Terrorism: Theory and Practice* (Boulder, Colorado: Westview Press, 1979. Jonah Alexander, David Carlton, and Paul Wilkinson, eds Published in cooperation with The Institute for Studies in International Terrorism, State University of New York), p.15.
4 *Ibid*, p.40.
5 See Cmnd., 8803 (1983), para.10.
6 Clinton L. Rossiter, *supra* note 3* [Introduction], at viii.
7 *Minimum Standards of Human Rights Norms in a State of Exception, supra* note 20* [Ch. 2], at 3.
8 Clinton L. Rossiter, *supra* note 3* [Introduction], at 300.
9 *Ibid.*
10 Subrata Roy Chowdhury, *supra* note 63* [Ch. 4], at 55.
11 See Carl J. Friedrich, *supra* note 4* [Ch. 2], at 581.
12 See Gerhard Casper, *supra* note 45* [Ch. 1], at 8.
13 L.A. Okun'kov, 'Nekotorye problemy statusa i polnomochiy prezidenta i praktika Konstitutsionnogo suda' [Some Problems of the Status and Powers of the President and Practice of the Constitutional Court], *Vestnik Konstitutsionnogo suda*, No.2, 1997, p.55.
14 Erica-Irene A. Daes, *supra* note 40* [Ch. 2], para. 390, at 135.
15 Principle 51 says: 'The severity, duration, and geographic scope of any derogation measure shall be such only as are strictly necessary to deal with the threat to the life of the nation and are proportionate to its nature and extent' (see *The Siracusa Principles, supra* note 42* [Ch. 2], at 9).
16 See Subrata Roy Chowdhury, *supra* note 63* [Ch. 4], at 117–118.
17 Carl J. Friedrich, *supra* note 4* [Ch. 2], at 581.

Index

188   *Index*

eBooks – at www.eBookstore.tandf.co.uk

A library at your fingertips!

eBooks are electronic versions of printed books. You can store them on your PC/laptop or browse them online.

They have advantages for anyone needing rapid access to a wide variety of published, copyright information.

eBooks can help your research by enabling you to bookmark chapters, annotate text and use instant searches to find specific words or phrases. Several eBook files would fit on even a small laptop or PDA.

NEW: Save money by eSubscribing: cheap, online access to any eBook for as long as you need it.

Annual subscription packages

We now offer special low-cost bulk subscriptions to packages of eBooks in certain subject areas. These are available to libraries or to individuals.

For more information please contact webmaster.ebooks@tandf.co.uk

We're continually developing the eBook concept, so keep up to date by visiting the website.

www.eBookstore.tandf.co.uk

For Product Safety Concerns and Information please contact our EU
representative GPSR@taylorandfrancis.com
Taylor & Francis Verlag GmbH, Kaufingerstraße 24, 80331 München, Germany